She's *on the* M●ney

Victoria Devine is a multi-award-winning financial adviser who is transforming the way millennials think about money.

With a background in behavioural psychology, her own financial advisory business, Zella, and a chart-topping podcast, Victoria understands what makes her generation tick and she knows how to make hard-to-understand concepts fun, fresh and relatable.

Victoria has been featured in publications such as the *Financial Standard*, *Vogue*, *ABC News*, *Mamamia*, *Elle* and *Yahoo! Finance*, and as a guest speaker at events including Business Chicks 9 to Thrive and RMIT Future of Financial Planning. She has also been named on the *Forbes* 30 Under 30 Asia list for 2021.

If you can't find her, chances are she's at home with an oat latte in one hand and her old English sheepadoodle, Lucy, in the other.

shesonthemoney.com.au

@ @shesonthemoneyaus

f @ShesontheMoneyAUS

She's
on the
M●ney

Take charge of your financial future

Victoria Devine

PENGUIN LIFE

UK | USA | Canada | Ireland | Australia
India | New Zealand | South Africa | China

Penguin Life is part of the Penguin Random House group of companies
whose addresses can be found at global.penguinrandomhouse.com.

Penguin
Random House
Australia

First published by Penguin Life, 2021

Cover design by Alissa Dinallo © Penguin Random House Australia Pty Ltd
Text design by Alissa Dinallo © Penguin Random House Australia Pty Ltd
Illustrations by Louisa Maggio © Penguin Random House Australia Pty Ltd
Author photograph by Miranda Stokke
Internal design by Post Pre-press Group, Australia
Typeset in 10.5/14 pt Mercury Text by Post Pre-press Group, Australia

Printed and bound in Australia by Griffin Press, part of Ovato, an accredited
ISO AS/NZS 14001 Environmental Management Systems printer

A catalogue record for this
book is available from the
National Library of Australia

ISBN 978 1 76104 413 7

penguin.com.au

MIX
Paper from
responsible sources
FSC® C009448

As the author of this book I'd like to acknowledge and pay respect to Australia's Aboriginal and Torres Strait Islander peoples, the traditional custodians of lands, waterways and skies across Australia. I'd like to particularly acknowledge the Wurundjeri people of the Kulin Nation who are the traditional custodians of the land on which I was able to write this book. I pay my respects to Elders past, present and emerging, and I share my friendship and kindness.

*This book is dedicated to my incredibly supportive parents,
Eric and Judi Devine, who brought me up to believe fiercely in
equality, and that I could achieve anything I set my mind to.
And to my beautiful* She's on the Money *community:
because of you I get to do what I love every single day.
Without you this book wouldn't have been possible.*

Contents

Prologue

Hello friend! I'm so glad you've picked up my book.

Is it because you received it as a present? (If so, what great taste your gift-giver has!) Is it because you've been thinking about investing, but don't know where to start? Did you just inherit money? Are you trying to clean up debt? Do you want to get your foot in the door of the property market? Are there issues with money in your relationship? Wondering what you should be doing to get the most out of your super? Are you expecting a baby and don't know where to start? Are you simply trying to be more financially literate, or just trying to 'adult' like a boss?

Regardless of how you answered those questions, and whether or not you're already one of my *She's on the Money* podcast listeners and community members, you are exactly where you are supposed to be. I've created this book to show you how to take control of your financial future, so you can set and achieve goals that will enrich your life while also having a positive impact on the world. My biggest goal is to have financial freedom, which I define as having enough money coming in from investments that I don't have to go to work every day. Perhaps that's your goal too – because who doesn't want to create enough wealth to become free? Free to choose what you'd like to do, where you'd like to go and what kind of life you'd like to lead.

I know that addressing the money side of your life plans can be overwhelming, confusing and uninspiring, and is one of the easiest things to avoid; however, the earlier you get on top of your finances, the greater the long-term benefits will be. Today is the day we start having a significant and positive impact on your financial future. Whether you're trying to pay down debt, start investing, save for your first home or purchase your third investment property, I'm on your team, and this book has all the tools and resources you need to help make your dreams a reality.

Chapter by chapter, I'm going to teach you key money principles that will stick with you for life, no matter what your goals are. This book is designed to help motivate you in the short term, and also set you up for long-term financial success – because finance and money aren't things we just set and forget. They're a journey, and I'm so glad that I'm now a part of yours.

This book goes beyond the basics of financial planning and advice. It's about more than how to save money, or what you need to take into consideration when looking at your super-annuation. It's about mindset, behaviour and how your beliefs, values and past experiences dictate and guide the decisions you make around money every day – consciously or subconsciously.

You will find that I am pretty up-front when putting facts on the table, but if you read something in this book that feels confronting or makes you feel a bit uncomfortable, that's okay – everyone feels a little uncomfortable when presented with change. Remember, I'm on your side, and simply want what's best for you. And while you might not always agree with what I'm saying or suggesting, it's worth remembering that sometimes what's best for us isn't necessarily what we want to hear.

I'm not just someone who's excited about financial literacy and wanted to write a book – I'm a millennial, a financial adviser who started her career working in psychology, and a woman who is empowered by empowering other women. I am driven to provide my fellow millennials with the knowledge and confidence to be the person they want to be, not the person they have to be because they don't know who to ask for financial advice.

When I say I want to empower you, I don't mean I want you to follow my advice to a T. I want to equip you with the knowledge to make your own decisions – those that work best for your personal situation. Not everything in this book is going to resonate with you. At this stage in your life it might not even be the right fit for you, but I want you to read on anyway. You may learn something that could benefit a friend, a family member, someone you work with, or Future You. There's no such thing as being too educated.

Ultimately, I'm here to make it easy for you. I know you, because I am you. I'm not dumbing this information down, because you don't need it dumbed down. You deserve financial security. You deserve prosperity. You deserve to be taken seriously. I want to change your relationship with money for the better and I'm not here to mess around. Finance is a priority and it's time it became yours.

Most importantly – be nice to Past You. She did the best she could with the tools she had at the time. This is a no-judgement zone. I'm not here to make you feel bad, or behind. I'm here to make you feel included. You need to remember that it's not important what happened over the past ten years. It's the NEXT ten that count.

Chapter 1

Everybody's got a story

Money stories are the subconscious and conscious beliefs and values about money and prosperity that we develop early in our lives. Whether we like it or not, they contribute to what we feel is financially possible, and they dictate our behaviour. They form the foundation of how we think and communicate about or react to money. If conflict around money was a central theme in your upbringing, any conversation about money might start with a stomach ache. If money was abundant, conversations about money might allow you to feel invincible, or sometimes even reckless. If money was something your parents took care of and didn't speak about, any conversation about money might make you feel unqualified, lost or uninterested.

In my mind, the most empowering use of money is as a way to transform our lives and the lives of others. Money, after all, is the tool we need to live a comfortable life, both in the present and future. Money is intended for spending, sharing and investing – nothing more.

For something with such a simple and pure purpose, the reality is that money can feel wildly complicated and cause an enormous amount of stress. The term 'money anxiety' has been coined (no pun intended) for a reason. Worrying about where your next meal is coming from, how you're going to pay off your credit card debt, or if you can make a quarter of a tank of fuel last until payday can and will keep you up at night. When it comes to even bigger things, like trying to imagine how you're supposed to survive after retirement, the task can seem so Herculean that you avoid the thought of it altogether, and shove it so far into the back of your mind it doesn't even get acknowledged.

Whatever your money story, positive or negative, dealing with the mysteries of money as an adult can be a struggle. Especially if you're a woman. Today, women are increasingly out-earning men, but in many cases we still don't have the resources and tools available to avoid being disadvantaged. I see it, feel it and hear it all the time: young women feel disempowered around money conversations because finance isn't a topic we've been taught to focus on. We don't learn about it in school, and most of the time, we don't learn about it from our families. Gender stereotypes are still wreaking havoc on our ability to be financially secure and contributing to negative money stories. It's something I'm here to change.

Young women need to know how to be financially free. The impact of this will be felt 30, 40, 50 years down the track. If you start now, creating a secure financial future will involve tiny baby steps instead of unrealistic leaps. If you can set good money habits up front, you can look at your finances holistically and increase your savings as you increase your earnings, instead of experiencing lifestyle creep.

What do I mean by lifestyle creep?

I mean that, more often than not, the more raises and bonuses you earn, the more you will spend. It could be brunching with friends, booking a holiday, buying a luxury car, getting every streaming service under the sun or simply treating yourself to a good coffee each morning. All of these things are fine if they're what you truly value, but they're not going to help you build an investment portfolio that will provide you with financial freedom. The fact of the matter is: you cannot save without sacrifice. Something is going to have to give, and understanding just how beneficial choosing to go without can be is the first step to having a healthy relationship with money.

Have you previously tried setting goals to create more abundance, but didn't make any progress? I strongly believe that your money story can sabotage your plans for prosperity. Now, you can't change your story, but you can reinvent it.

Together, we are going to map out how you can free yourself to create a more balanced, enlightened and positive outlook on money. The truth is, personal finance is just that: personal. And remember, this is a no-judgement zone. I'm here to work with you on your own story and values. We all have a money story, and it's not the product of our own doing. It's important to say, 'This is my starting position, now where can I go from here?'

Understanding exactly where you are right now with your money and knowing where it is that you want to be will give you the clarity and confidence to make wise choices that will set you up for life, both personally and professionally.

Let's get started, shall we?

●●●●●●●●●●●●●●●●●●●●●●●●●●●●●●●●●

CONNECTING WITH YOUR MONEY STORY

- What is the first thing that came to mind when the topic of money stories came up?
- How were finances handled in your family when you were growing up?
- Were financial expectations different for men and women? If so, what were the differences?
- What is your earliest memory about money?
- Was money spoken about as a family? If so, do you think those conversations impacted you in a positive way?
- Did anyone influence your money story in a positive way?

What are your money beliefs?

Beliefs are assumptions we hold to be true. When we use our beliefs to make decisions, we are assuming that the causal relationships of the past, which led to those beliefs being formed, will also apply in the future. In a rapidly changing world where complexity is increasing day by day, using information from the past to make decisions about the future may not be the best approach. Beliefs are contextual: they arise from learned experiences, resulting from the cultural and environmental situations we have faced.

I want you to start thinking about your money beliefs and answer the questions below.

- Do you believe money is good or bad? Or is it just an evil necessity?
- Do you think money should be spent or saved?
- What would you consider a luxury purchase?
- Do you think money is hard or easy to obtain?
- Do you think money should be your responsibility, your partner's, or both?
- Do you think both parties in a relationship should be empowered to make financial decisions?

- Do you think money in a marriage should be separate or shared?
- Where do you think these beliefs came from?

What are your money values?

Your money values are different from your money beliefs. Values are not based on information from the past and they are not contextual. Values are intimately related to our needs. Whatever we need, whatever is important to us or whatever is missing from our lives – that is what we value. A good way to check what your values are is to check your bank statement and highlight what you spend most of your disposable income on. It's basically a bank account audit (which you will do in Chapter 2). While you may think you value paying off your mortgage, your spending habits may reveal that you actually value nights out with friends more, and that's why you have so many pub and wine bar charges. As our life conditions change and as we mature and grow, our values change. When we use our values to make decisions, we focus on what is important to us or what we need in order to feel a sense of wellbeing.

What do you currently think you value? ....

....

Would you be willing to cut back on any of those activities or purchases?

- If yes, why? ....
- If no, why not? ....

Beliefs versus values

Being able to differentiate between your beliefs and your values will help you get your head in the right space to adjust your behaviour with money. Neuroplasticity refers to the ability to retrain your brain and change your habits. As much as your money story is defining your habits right now, you can absolutely change your trajectory.

Reflecting on your beliefs and values, how do they make you feel?

....

Are they aligned with creating the life you want for your future?

....

Are your beliefs getting in the way of your goals?

....

Reframe your thoughts

Most purchases are emotive. Have you ever had a really crappy day and thought, 'I deserve my favourite gelato right now', or, 'If I go and get that facial, I will feel much more confident at my work Christmas party, which will then help me network better and ultimately get me that new account'? This is called retail therapy. It's your mind literally trying to soothe itself through shopping, and while it may hit the spot in the moment, it is detrimental to your bank account in the long run.

Another major cause of money anxiety is the unintentional practice of comparing yourself to others. When you talk to colleagues, friends or family members about salaries, savings, holidays, homes and the latest smart watch or phone, you can often end up feeling like you're not where you're supposed to be in life, which damages your sense of self-worth. It's important to know that the world is not a level playing field, and that we did not all start at the same point. Don't compare your start to someone else's middle.

Our minds constantly give us chatter and feedback, but sometimes these voices in our head can be negative and unhelpful. By learning to tune in to this chatter and reframe the messaging, you can consciously shift the tone to neutral or positive, which can lead to better decision-making in every area of your life.

Over the years, I've learned that people have excuses for everything. When people say, 'I can't', they usually mean, 'I won't make that a priority right now'. It doesn't matter what salary you're on when you say you can't save. You would if it meant a lot to you. You're choosing not to achieve it (even if you don't realise it). Financial independence is about mindset and approach. Since your emotions are guiding your purchasing decisions, you need to be able to reframe your reactions to your thoughts so that they align with your values.

Take one of the money beliefs you came up with earlier that has associated negative emotions for you. It might be a belief that makes you feel mad, sad, frustrated, stressed, trapped or worried.

Write down the thought that created this feeling, and how you usually act upon this belief.

....

....

How can you reframe this event in a way that will bring more positive emotions and less negative ones?

....

....

● ●

I am here to help you build a bigger, better version of yourself. Money is really important, but it's not what matters the most in life. Not making a choice is still a choice. If you're not ready to face your money story, that's fine, but be aware that's also a choice you're making. I know that change is uncomfortable, but your thoughts, behaviours and beliefs are guided by your money story, and it's up to you to change yours.

● ● ● ● ● ●

STEPHANIE, 24 – SA

My parents immigrated to Australia from Poland when I was four. Growing up, my siblings and I could sense that money was tight. We shared a bedroom, ate the same things for dinner every week, didn't go on holidays and always had hand-me-down clothing. My parents often talked about the importance of saving, so even when they wanted to treat us to an ice cream at the pool or offered to take us to the movies, we'd say no because we wanted to be on their savings team.

Fast forward to today, I'm 24 and in my first year of working as a vet nurse. While most of my friends don't have much in their savings accounts, I have $19,000 because I grew up always thinking I needed a safety blanket. Watching my parents struggle made me hyper-aware of not spending money on unnecessary things. While I know this is an amazing position to be in, I feel like my money story is holding me back from investing and making my money really work for me. This year, my goal is to loosen my grip on my savings account balance so that I can allocate more to investments.

CATHIE, 33 – NSW

I struggled through my parents' messy divorce where my mum had terrible money handling skills. I ended up working after school to help support us and was paying bills and rent at 15. In the early years, I followed my mum's lead and went into debt, overspent, and didn't value saving. I have now turned things around with my husband's help – we have bought our own home, done a bit of travelling and saved for our first baby, so I can take maternity leave. Still not as set up as I'd like, but proud of my change.

ERIN, 25 – VIC

Growing up, I had divorced parents. My single mum was never poor, but I remember as a teenager always being conscious of how much things cost. For example, my sister and I knew to try and pick the cheapest things, or opt for the less expensive recreational sport or hobby. It sucked – not for us, but I could sense that Mum almost felt embarrassed about it, which made me sad to see. Years later, she is remarried and earning a higher-end middle-bracket salary; however, she is a spender under stress. Whenever she is stressed *(usually about money), she buys a new plant or the most random things on eBay, which then sit in a cupboard. My mum and stepdad pretty much live pay cheque to pay cheque. They have dipped into their super funds (my stepdad was seriously ill a few years ago and needed/still needs some time off work). They still owe about $400,000 on their mortgage and are both in their mid–late fifties. I honestly worry that they will never be able to retire early or comfortably, which is stressful.*

My dad passed away when I was 17. He lived interstate and we would fly over in the school holidays at his expense. We knew he earned well (we later found out he earned in the six figures); however, we never knew much about the details, except that he could afford to send us to a private school for VCE and we would fly to holiday destinations without much worry. He lived in a nice townhouse and had investment properties. But when he died, we found out he was in a lot of debt. My sister and I ended up inheriting quite a small amount (under $300,000, despite the combined millions tied up in housing and shares – the risky types). Of course, we didn't even care about the money because we were so grief-stricken. Nonetheless, I wonder to this day how he got himself in this situation. Obviously, he was not overly responsible with money.

Finally, my grandad, who also used to earn in the six figures back when he was working in the financial industry (ironically), now lives at home with my mum and stepdad because he became unable to pay his rent after my grandmother passed away. My grandad lost a lot of money on the stock market, multiple times over his lifetime. After my grandmother died, he says he got depressed and so he spent the rest of his money because nothing mattered anymore. This was of course very sad to hear; however, he has more than once told me that even when he earned all that money, he 'never saved' because he didn't really think he needed to. So, here he is approaching 90 years old, having to be so mindful with how he spends his small government pension. My family supports him but I still see how much his life is affected by this. The fact that he feels embarrassed that we pay most of the time when we take him out for lunch is upsetting. We have tried to tell him it doesn't matter, but it has impacted him greatly that he feels he can't leave an inheritance. The worst part is that if he had saved back then, he could have set himself up for such a carefree retirement.

I have been influenced by all these stories. I am also a big stress spender (working on it). I started my first real job (part-time salary) last year, moved out of home into a share house and spent way too much on disposable items, both to celebrate my new-found independence and also to cheer myself up during a very hard graduate year. I remember having about $10 collectively across all my bank accounts as 2020 rolled in and actually having to borrow money from my mum to get me through to my next pay cheque. Since then, I've made it my goal to use this year to get my emergency savings into action, and I have cut back and budgeted so much that I have saved my first $1000 basically EVER in just over a month because I was sick of being broke. I find that my family's money stories have motivated me. I don't want to have to rely on anyone else, especially as I get older. I also know I need to be in a good financial position because it is likely my sister and I will one day need to step in and help my parents financially.

• • • • • •

TAKE NOTE

Money stories are the subconscious and conscious
beliefs and values about money and prosperity
that we develop early in our lives.

....

As much as your money story is defining your habits right now,
you absolutely have the capacity to change your trajectory.

....

When we use our values to make decisions, we focus on what is
important to us or what we need to feel a sense of wellbeing.

....

Chapter 2

Map out your money

While I'd love to call 'ACTION' on a 60-second money-makeover montage that ends with you jumping up and down on a bed covered in cash, we need to be realistic – for two reasons – before we dive into my favourite part of finance: goal-setting.

1. If you don't know what tools and resources you have to get somewhere, you won't know if the destination is even possible. (You can't go to Antarctica in a rowboat and a bikini, can you?!)
2. If you don't create a map, you might get lost or end up needing to detour along the way, which might leave you too tired to complete the trip.

The easiest way to get off-track and disheartened is to set a goal that you can't achieve, and you can't achieve your goals without first understanding what your budget is.

Right now, there's probably no point in saying that your goal is to buy a million-dollar property and go to your friend's wedding in Bali if you're earning $60k a year and have $15k of credit card debt with no clear idea of how you're going to pay it off. I sit down with clients every single week and they say things like, 'I want to save for my first home and purchase it by the end of the year.' More often than not, I have to tell them, 'I'm so sorry – in your current position, that's not going to happen in the next three years. It's going to take you ten years to save the deposit and then on top of that you need to service that loan and you can't currently do that. Instead, you have to use the resources you have to set attainable goals that will then make those unattainable goals attainable.'

The first thing I want you to do can feel invasive and confronting. It might even make you want to shut the book, switch on the TV and bury your head in a glass of pinot noir. Please don't do that! This is your first step to financial freedom, and even though it might feel like ripping off a bandaid, it's worth it. All of your past financial wounds are about to be healed!

● ●

EARN, SPEND, OWN, OWE

What you'll need:

While you may know these figures off the top of your head, it is handy to have access to your bank account, payslips and/or credit card statement.

Write down four monthly numbers: earn, spend, own, owe.

Earn

This is any income that comes into your bank account in a month that you can allocate to something. This may come from a salary, side hustle, investment or allowance.

'But Victoria, what if my earnings vary each month?!'

Great question! In an effort to be conservative, write down the lowest amount you would earn on average. If any extra comes in, this can be considered a surplus and be allocated to savings or investments later on.

Spend

This is any money that goes out of your bank account in a month. From rent to food to fun to bills to bank fees, calculate the total money leaving your possession in a single month. It's okay if this is an average, as this will fluctuate from month to month.

Own

What you own is really important to figure out because that's what's going to create your net wealth. This is what's going to support you through retirement. I'm not talking about whether you have a nice car, because I don't classify that as a wealth investment. I'm asking how much money you have in your superannuation account. Do you own a home yet? What assets do you have? A property? A savings account? I'm talking about anything that could be sold for monetary value or that produces an income.

Owe

Do you have any debt? For instance, a personal loan, HELP (formerly known as HECS), credit card debt or a mortgage? It's important to note that not all debt is created equal. Good debt, like an investment property loan, helps you to build wealth or increases your prospects to build wealth, while bad debt costs you money without improving your financial position. Examples of bad debt include money you borrow through credit cards and personal loans to pay for day-to-day expenses, holidays or an asset – such as a car – that tends to decrease in value. There's also okay debt – we'll talk about that in Chapter 6.

Earn ....

Spend ....

Own ....

Owe ....

Okay, now that you have your four numbers, how do they look? Are you spending more than you earn? Breaking even? Rolling in extra cash?

● ●

The basis of financial freedom comes down to two things: spending less than you're earning, and regularly and continuously saving and investing. Financial freedom looks different for everyone. Once you realise this, you can start working towards your own.

There's a common misconception that making or having an abundance of money automatically provides you with financial freedom. While more money certainly helps, I could give you several examples of people I know who have an abundance of income and/or wealth but still feel like they're sinking in quicksand. They make more than $250,000 per year, but somehow still live pay cheque to pay cheque. With that in mind, you simply cannot say, 'When I make more money, things will be better.' More income will not solve your problems. If you don't change the way you approach money, it will just compound them.

On paper, it's quite simple. If you spend less than you earn and invest regularly and continuously, you will build up a large investment base to cover all your income needs. The investment industry likes to make it seem more complex than it is, because that's how they make money. I'm the opposite – I like to make things as simple as possible.

To find room to grow your savings and investments, you need to go deeper and make sure that your spending is in line with your values. Now here's the fun part I mentioned in Chapter 1.

● ●

BANK ACCOUNT AUDIT

What you'll need:

- three months' worth of bank statements and/or credit card statements
- two different-coloured highlighters
- a strong coffee or glass of wine (optional).

Use one colour to highlight your fixed/necessary expenses and the other for discretionary spending.

Note: A fixed expense is any amount that you have to pay on a monthly basis that does not change. This could be your internet bill or rent. Necessary expenses are monthly bills that may vary depending on usage, such as electricity or water. A discretionary expense is anything you're choosing to buy, such as takeaway food, wine, a new pair of shoes or a streaming service. I've given more examples of each on the following pages.

Where is the majority of your discretionary spending going?

....

Did you think that was where it was going?

....

While we had a general look at what you believe versus what you value in Chapter 1, the above will show you what you actually value in black and white. With this information, this is where you can change your money story.

Are you happy with how you're spending your money?

....

Do you wish your fixed/necessary expenses were lower?

....

Do you regret any of your discretionary purchases?

....

● ●

BUDGET

What you'll need:

- the *She's on the Money* budget template available from our website, or a standard budgeting spreadsheet
- access to your bank account and bills.

Now it's time to make a budget. To make this as accurate as possible, you may need to revisit your bank statements to make sure your numbers represent what you truly spend. To start, plug in all of the numbers you're actually spending. After you've done this, you can reassess your goals and priorities and decide where you can earn more, save more, invest more and spend less.

I like to look at my budget annually, or whenever there are any major changes to my finances. Everyone has their own preference of formats. You're more than welcome to make your own, or alternatively, you can download our pretty *She's on the Money* template from shesonthemoney.com.au. And remember, personal finance is PERSONAL, so your budget may look very different to mine or a friend's.

Depending on your preference, you can work with either monthly or weekly figures. To work out monthly amounts, divide the figure by 12. To work out weekly amounts, divide the figure by 52.

Example: If your car insurance is $900 a year, you can either budget $75 monthly or $17.31 weekly.

What you need to include in your budget

Net income

This is the money coming into your account AFTER tax. If you're an employee, your tax and super will already have been taken out. If you are self-employed or have a side hustle, you'll need to take out your own tax and superannuation payments. Income streams can include salary, bonuses, side hustles, an allowance and sale of an asset.

Fixed/necessary expenses

These can include:

- groceries
- necessary personal care items (toothpaste, shampoo, razors)
- fuel
- public transport
- utility bills
- mobile phone
- internet/cable
- medical costs (monthly appointments, glasses, etc.)
- owner–occupier expenses (rates, taxes, levies, body corporate and strata fees, repairs and maintenance, other household items and utilities)
- home maintenance
- car registration
- car insurance
- health insurance
- life insurance
- income protection insurance

- home and contents insurance
- super contribution (if self-employed)
- side hustle operating costs
- mortgage repayments
- family costs (day care, school, uniforms, extra-curricular activities)
- debt repayment.

Discretionary expenses
These can include:
- takeaway food and alcohol
- events and nights out
- streaming services
- subscription boxes
- buy now, pay later program payments
- clothing
- footwear
- cosmetics
- personal care (lashes, tans, waxing, etc.)
- books and movies
- home and decor
- holidays
- gifts for friends/family.

• •

Budgeting tool

I like to set up a budget using the *She's on the Money* budgeting tool, which shows you at a glance exactly where your finances lie.

budgeting tool

earn	AMOUNT	SELECT FREQUENCY	ANNUAL TOTAL
INCOME			
Emily's income – net after deductions	$8,026.47	Monthly	$96,317.64
Emily's other income (side hustle)	$500.00	Monthly	$6,000.00
Interest income (e.g. term deposit or savings accounts)	$50.00	Monthly	$600.00
		TOTAL OF WHAT I EARN	$102,917.64
spend			
PERSONAL SPENDING			
Groceries/food	$150.00	Weekly	$7,800.00
Takeaway and dining out	$75.00	Weekly	$3,900.00
Clothing	$150.00	Monthly	$1,800.00
Personal care (hair, grooming, lashes, nails, etc.)	$50.00	Monthly	$600.00
Public transport/taxi/Uber	$200.00	Monthly	$2,400.00
Medical/pharmaceutical/make-up	$200.00	Monthly	$2,400.00
		TOTAL OF MY PERSONAL SPENDING	$18,900.00
		TOTAL PERSONAL SPENDING EACH WEEK	$363.46
BILLS + OTHER EXPENSES			
Travel	$250.00	Monthly	$3,000.00
Gym membership	$100.00	Monthly	$1,200.00
Electricity	$150.00	Monthly	$1,800.00
Mobile phone	$35.00	Monthly	$420.00
Internet	$80.00	Monthly	$960.00
Health insurance	$99.00	Monthly	$1,188.00
Emily's work-incurred expenses	$100.00	Monthly	$1,200.00
		TOTAL BILLS + OTHER EXPENSES	$9,768.00
owe			
LOAN REPAYMENTS + SCHEDULED SAVINGS			
Side hustle tax	$150.00	Monthly	$1,800.00
Super	$47.50	Monthly	$570.00
		TOTAL LOAN REPAYMENTS + SAVINGS	$2,370.00
TOTAL INCOME			$102,917.64
TOTAL EXPENSE			$-31,038.00
SURPLUS/SHORTFALL			$71,879.64

She's on the Money budgeting tool

The main thing you want to see is whether you have a surplus or deficit of cash. If you have a deficit, you're going to need to cut back on discretionary spending and/or revisit whether you're getting the best rate for your fixed and necessary bills.

Ultimately, we want to see a surplus because THIS is the money that you are going to save, invest and make work hard for you! #cashflowisqueen

Just in case you need to hear this – stop judging yourself. I will say this over and over again, but please remember that you don't need to feel bad or guilty about where you're starting. Put all of your feelings aside and let's look at your finances pragmatically. You're creating a plan for the future, not beating yourself up about the spending you've done in the past.

Now that you know where your money is coming from and where it is going, let's talk about how each dollar is being allocated. There is a big difference between being on a budget and using a budget to achieve your financial and lifestyle goals. I want you to be a BOSS and give every single dollar a job. While I'm not a fan of micromanagement in the workplace, I'm giving you permission to be hyper-aware of how each dollar you earn is performing.

The best way to stay in control of your money is to set up a fail-proof funnel that will keep your cash going exactly where it needs to go. I've spent hours working on a system that can work for anyone on any income and at any stage of life. Depending on your relationship with money, you may need to put some extra hurdles in place to keep you from getting a dollar to do another dollar's job.

Step #1: Make a cash hub

Your cash hub is where all of your income should be coming in to. (If you have a debit card for this account, cut it up or put it in a drawer!) This can be a checking account, offset account, redraw loan account or savings account. Don't fret if you're silently asking yourself what on earth a redraw loan is. We'll be chatting about all things banking in Chapter 5!

Step #2: Assign job roles

Depending on the type of account your cash hub is, I like to set up weekly automatic bill and BPAY payments to go directly from this account. If you have debt repayments, these can also come from here. You can then set up weekly automatic deposits into cheque and/or savings accounts, so you have money set aside for different purposes. Depending on your current situation and goals, these could include:

Expenses
Weekly groceries, fuel, public transport costs, etc.

Blow card
A weekly allowance that you can spend on takeaway food, nights out, clothing and accessories, cosmetics and personal care, event tickets, etc.

Emergencies account
This figure will look different depending on what stage of life you're in, but this is money set aside for an emergency (such as your hot-water heater failing, an unexpected need to travel or take time off for a family emergency, etc.). Notice I didn't mention unexpected job loss. That's because you should have insurance for this – more on that in Chapter 14. I'll come back to emergency funds again in Chapter 6.

Invest
We are going to talk about investing in detail in Chapters 9, 10 and 11, but it's important to consistently allocate funds that can be invested into either shares, property or a side hustle.

House deposit
If you're someone who would like to be an owner-occupier, saving for a deposit can be one of the biggest hurdles. Allocating money weekly from as early an age as possible can help you reach this goal much more quickly.

Holiday
Do you have the travel bug? Does your family live overseas? If travel is important to you, then you should 100 per cent be saving for this year-round.

Taxes
If you're a business owner or have a side hustle, please don't forget to put money away for taxes! This could majorly bite you in the bum if you forget! (For more on taxes, head to Chapter 11.)

Superannuation
Just like taxes, if you're self-employed, you'll need to remember to make a payment to your superannuation fund, which we will discuss in detail in Chapter 8.

● ● ● ● ● ●

'But Victoria, aren't you going to tell me a percentage that I'm supposed to allocate to each of these?'

While this is a good idea in theory, it's ridiculous to hold someone to a percentage because of how different everyone's income is. For example, someone who is earning over $400,000 should be saving or investing more than 20 per cent of their income. Someone on a $45,000 salary may start missing meals if they aim for 20 per cent. Like I said, personal finance is personal. Simply look at your capacity, make sure you're staying true to your goals and values and then decide what you can actually maintain.

• •

Example: Lauren, 20

Lauren is in her last year of uni and works part-time. She has a credit card with a $3000 balance, as well as some book fees for uni. Her goal is to get out of debt so she can find a surplus to start investing.

budgeting tool	AMOUNT	SELECT FREQUENCY	ANNUAL TOTAL
earn			
INCOME			
Lauren's income – net after deductions	$1,500.00	Monthly	$18,000.00
Interest income (e.g. term deposit or savings accounts)	$0.00	Monthly	$0.00
Other investment income	$0.00	Monthly	$0.00
TOTAL OF WHAT I EARN			$18,000.00
spend			
PERSONAL SPENDING			
Groceries/food	$80.00	Weekly	$4,160.00
Takeaway and dining out	$150.00	Weekly	$7,800.00
Personal care (hair, grooming, lashes, nails, etc.)	$50.00	Monthly	$600.00
Clothing	$50.00	Monthly	$600.00
Public transport/taxi/Uber	$200.00	Monthly	$2,400.00
TOTAL OF MY PERSONAL SPENDING			$15,560.00
TOTAL PERSONAL SPENDING EACH WEEK			$299.23
BILLS + OTHER EXPENSES			
Mobile phone	$50.00	Monthly	$600.00
Internet	$80.00	Monthly	$960.00
TOTAL BILLS + OTHER EXPENSES			$1,560.00
owe			
LOAN REPAYMENTS + SCHEDULED SAVINGS			
School fees	$1,200.00	Monthly	$14,400.00
Credit card	$250.00	Monthly	$3,000.00
Savings account	$50.00	Weekly	$2,600.00
TOTAL LOAN REPAYMENTS + SAVINGS			$20,000.00
TOTAL INCOME			$18,000.00
TOTAL EXPENSE			$-37,120.00
SURPLUS/SHORTFALL			$-19,120.00

Lauren's budget

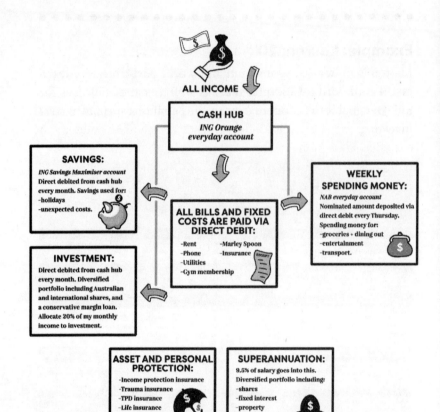

ALL INCOME

CASH HUB
ING Orange everyday account

SAVINGS:
ING Savings Maximiser account
Direct debited from cash hub every month. Savings used for:
-holidays
-unexpected costs.

ALL BILLS AND FIXED COSTS ARE PAID VIA DIRECT DEBIT:
-Rent   -Marley Spoon
-Phone   -Insurance
-Utilities
-Gym membership

WEEKLY SPENDING MONEY:
NAB everyday account
Nominated amount deposited via direct debit every Thursday. Spending money for:
-groceries + dining out
-entertainment
-transport.

INVESTMENT:
Direct debited from cash hub every month. Diversified portfolio including Australian and international shares, and a conservative margin loan. Allocate 20% of my monthly income to investment.

ASSET AND PERSONAL PROTECTION:
-Income protection insurance
-Trauma insurance
-TPD insurance
-Life insurance
-Private health
-Car insurance

SUPERANNUATION:
9.5% of salary goes into this. Diversified portfolio including:
-shares
-fixed interest
-property
-cash.

Lauren's cash allocation

●●●●●●●●●●●●●●●●●●●●●●●●●●●●●●●

Example: Abby and Shane, 34 and 37

Abby and Shane are married with two kids. Collectively, they earn just over $161,000 a year after tax. Their total expenses are around $155,000 a year. This leaves them with a surplus of roughly $6000 for wealth creation. Here's how they've set up their budget and cash flow allocation.

budgeting tool	AMOUNT	SELECT FREQUENCY	ANNUAL TOTAL
earn			
INCOME			
Abby's income – self employed	$4,580.00	Monthly	$54,960.00
Shane's income – net after deductions	$8,026.47	Monthly	$96,317.64
Shane's other income	$200.00	Weekly	$10,400.00
		TOTAL OF WHAT I EARN	$161,677.64
spend			
PERSONAL SPENDING			
Groceries/food	$300.00	Weekly	$15,600.00
Takeaway/dining out/entertainment	$75.00	Weekly	$3,900.00
Personal care (haircuts, grooming etc.)	$30.00	Weekly	$1,560.00
Clothing	$200.00	Monthly	$2,400.00
Public transport/taxi/Uber	$100.00	Monthly	$1,200.00
Medical/pharmaceutical/make-up	$200.00	Monthly	$2,400.00
Petrol	$300.00	Fortnightly	$7,800.00
		TOTAL OF MY PERSONAL SPENDING	$34,860.00
		TOTAL PERSONAL SPENDING EACH WEEK	$670.38
BILLS + OTHER EXPENSES			
Travel	$500.00	Monthly	$6,000.00
Gym membership	$145.00	Monthly	$1,740.00
Water	$250.00	Monthly	$3,000.00
Electricity	$333.00	Monthly	$3,996.00
Rates	$250.00	Monthly	$3,000.00
Housing/building repairs	$400.00	Monthly	$4,800.00
Mobile phone	$70.00	Monthly	$840.00
Internet	$80.00	Monthly	$960.00
Home and contents insurance	$220.90	Monthly	$2,650.80
Car insurance	$183.00	Monthly	$2,196.00
Pet Expenses – vet & food	$84.00	Monthly	$1,008.00
Professional services and memberships	$250.00	Monthly	$3,000.00
Abby's work-incurred expenses	$480.00	Monthly	$5,760.00
Education expenses – daughter	$400.00	Monthly	$4,800.00
Education expenses – son	$417.00	Monthly	$5,004.00
Daughter's dance	$134.00	Monthly	$1,608.00
Son – activities	$30.00	Monthly	$360.00
Annual gifts – Christmas/birthdays/parties	$435.00	Monthly	$5,220.00
Mortgage repayments	$4,082.00	Monthly	$48,984.00
		TOTAL BILLS + OTHER EXPENSES	$104,926.80
owe			
LOAN REPAYMENTS + SCHEDULED SAVINGS			
Tax – Abby	$875.00	Monthly	$10,500.00
Super – Abby	$435.00	Monthly	$5,220.00
		TOTAL LOAN REPAYMENTS + SAVINGS	$15,720.00
TOTAL INCOME			$161,677.64
TOTAL EXPENSE			$-155,506.80
SURPLUS/SHORTFALL			$6,170.84

Abby and Shane's budget

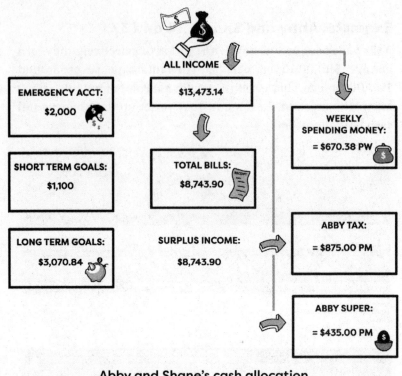

ALL INCOME

$13,473.14

EMERGENCY ACCT:
$2,000

SHORT TERM GOALS:
$1,100

LONG TERM GOALS:
$3,070.84

TOTAL BILLS:
$8,743.90

SURPLUS INCOME:
$8,743.90

WEEKLY SPENDING MONEY:
= $670.38 PW

ABBY TAX:
= $875.00 PM

ABBY SUPER:
= $435.00 PM

Abby and Shane's cash allocation

● ●

Example: Emily, 29

Emily is single and currently earning around $96,000 after tax for her full-time role, and approximately $500 additional per month from her side hustle. She has $50,000 in savings, which was partially funded by an inheritance. Emily is interested in purchasing a property soon. Here's how she set up her budget and cash allocation to make that dream a reality.

budgeting tool

earn

INCOME	AMOUNT	SELECT FREQUENCY	ANNUAL TOTAL
Emily's income – net after deductions	$8,026.47	Monthly	$96,317.64
Emily's other income (side hustle)	$500.00	Monthly	$6,000.00
Interest income (e.g. term deposit or savings accounts)	$50.00	Monthly	$600.00
		TOTAL OF WHAT I EARN	$102,917.64

spend

PERSONAL SPENDING	AMOUNT	SELECT FREQUENCY	ANNUAL TOTAL
Groceries/food	$150.00	Weekly	$7,800.00
Takeaway and dining out	$75.00	Weekly	$3,900.00
Clothing	$150.00	Monthly	$1,800.00
Personal care (hair, grooming, lashes, nails, etc.)	$50.00	Monthly	$600.00
Public transport/taxi/Uber	$200.00	Monthly	$2,400.00
Medical/pharmaceutical/make-up	$200.00	Monthly	$2,400.00
		TOTAL OF MY PERSONAL SPENDING	$18,900.00
		TOTAL PERSONAL SPENDING EACH WEEK	$363.46

BILLS + OTHER EXPENSES			
Travel	$250.00	Monthly	$3,000.00
Gym membership	$100.00	Monthly	$1,200.00
Electricity	$150.00	Monthly	$1,800.00
Mobile phone	$35.00	Monthly	$420.00
Internet	$80.00	Monthly	$960.00
Health insurance	$99.00	Monthly	$1,188.00
Emily's work-incurred expenses	$100.00	Monthly	$1,200.00
		TOTAL BILLS + OTHER EXPENSES	$9,768.00

owe

LOAN REPAYMENTS + SCHEDULED SAVINGS			
Side hustle tax	$150.00	Monthly	$1,800.00
Super	$47.50	Monthly	$570.00
		TOTAL LOAN REPAYMENTS + SAVINGS	$2,370.00
TOTAL INCOME			$102,917.64
TOTAL EXPENSE			$-31,038.00
SURPLUS/SHORTFALL			$71,879.64

Emily's budget

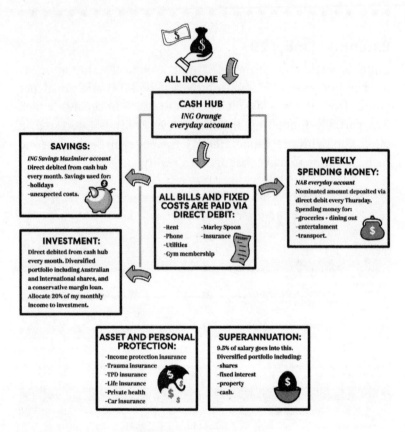

ALL INCOME

CASH HUB
*ING Orange
everyday account*

SAVINGS:
ING Savings Maximiser account
Direct debited from cash hub
every month. Savings used for:
-holidays
-unexpected costs.

**ALL BILLS AND FIXED
COSTS ARE PAID VIA
DIRECT DEBIT:**
-Rent   -Marley Spoon
-Phone   -Insurance
-Utilities
-Gym membership

**WEEKLY
SPENDING MONEY:**
NAB everyday account
Nominated amount deposited via
direct debit every Thursday.
Spending money for:
-groceries + dining out
-entertainment
-transport.

INVESTMENT:
Direct debited from cash hub
every month. Diversified
portfolio including Australian
and International shares, and
a conservative margin loan.
Allocate 20% of my monthly
income to investment.

**ASSET AND PERSONAL
PROTECTION:**
-Income protection insurance
-Trauma insurance
-TPD insurance
-Life insurance
-Private health
-Car insurance

SUPERANNUATION:
9.5% of salary goes into this.
Diversified portfolio including:
-shares
-fixed interest
-property
-cash.

Emily's cash allocation

It's important to stress how different cash flow will look for everyone. Depending on your stage of life, values, goals, current assets and past spending habits, what works for one person may not work for another. I'm here to help you make the best decisions for you, which brings me to my favourite part: GOAL SETTING.

TAKE NOTE

The basis of financial freedom comes down to
two things: spending less than you're earning, and
regularly and continuously saving and investing.

....

Mapping out your money gives you more control and the
ability to automate everything. It means that money doesn't
disappear or dissolve into thin air, because you've accounted
for every single dollar and given each one a specific job.

....

Look at your budget before setting goals.

....

Chapter 3

Cash flow is queen

Okay, so you would have heard the saying 'cash is king' before – and while I get the premise, I can't agree. Cash FLOW is actually king – but let's call it queen! I'll explain why in this chapter. But before that, I think it's important to define exactly what cash flow is, and why it's so important.

Simply put, cash flow is the difference between how much money you have coming in to your bank account each month, and how much you have going out. You want to be in a position of POSITIVE cash flow, which means you spend less than you earn, so you can direct that cash flow towards your savings or investment goals. In order to increase your cash flow, you can do one of two things: increase your income, or decrease your spending. To be on top of your cash flow, you need to make sure you aren't allowing the cost of your lifestyle to creep too much beyond what you can afford, and that you have a plan in place so that incoming funds seamlessly flow between accounts and expenses. If you don't have a plan in place, you are likely to lose funds to small expenses that add up significantly over time, and that until now you haven't given much thought to.

Whether you're earning $50,000 a year or $500,000 a year, managing your cash flow is the single most important thing you can do for Future You. Mastering your cash flow is going to be the key to your future financial wellbeing and success. It all sounds pretty dramatic, but this is why cash flow, not cash, is queen. I am lucky that I get to work with a broad range of clients across all demographics. From start-up investors to retirees, university students to ultra-high-net-worth business owners – I've worked with them all at some point or another, and what I can tell you right now is that the key to their success is not how much money they earn but the way they manage their money.

What does this look like, though? I'll give you an example. I have two clients, a couple, who have recently retired. They've consistently earned approximately $90,000 a year between them, and have invested regular monthly deposits of $1000 over 40 years, with an initial deposit of $20,000 and an annual interest rate of 7.5 per cent. They have two children who are now adults, they now own their family home outright, and they've retired with an investment portfolio worth approximately $3.4 million dollars. This means that each year their investment portfolio – even if it only ever returned 5 per cent per year return – provides them with approximately $170,000 in income! They have more money coming in now than they ever have before, and they literally don't know what to do with it all.

Conversely, I have two other clients who are in their fifties and would like to retire in the next ten years. They've had a very high combined income of approximately $500,000 a year for the last decade or so, and have a fancy lifestyle to match. The husband has a number of expensive cars, their children have gone to one of the best private schools money can pay for and they've been on two international family holidays every single year since they got married – flying business class, of course.

Right now they're in a position where to retire would mean making *significant* sacrifices to their current lifestyle, because saving and investing haven't been a priority to them until now. While they have afforded some incredible experiences and really enjoyed life, they only have about $20,000 currently invested. Now, if they want to have the same size investment portfolio as my other clients, it is going to cost them *$20,000 a month* to reach the same outcome. Obviously this is insane. To achieve this they are going to need to change their lifestyle drastically, sell some of their cars to free up cash flow, not go on the holidays they usually take, and make a number of other significant lifestyle sacrifices.

Why are these client stories useful when trying to understand the importance of good cash flow? Because the reason my retired clients are comfortable now is because they've always prioritised their cash flow. It wasn't their income that made them wealthy, it was their solid budgeting and cash-flow plans. They invested approximately $1000 conservatively each and every single month – and didn't compromise that goal – and now, 40 years later, they've got the portfolio to show for it. That's why cash flow is important. Because when you have a plan in place for the long term, you can achieve anything. Just imagine what you could be capable of if you set your mind to it.

The first step to creating a solid cash-flow plan is to have the right banking structure in place.

The only six bank accounts you'll ever need

I get asked all the time who I bank with, what accounts I have set up and how I manage my cash flow. I'll be sharing ALL that with you. But first of all I want to explore banking as a whole. The first *She's on the Money* rule of banking is that you do not need to be loyal to your current bank. I know many Dollarmites kids who had their bright yellow chequebooks in the playground and who now, as adults, have a Commonwealth Bank account because it was the first one they got, and changing banks feels hard and hasn't been a priority. Until now.

Nine times out of ten a bank will give a better deal to a new customer than one who has been banking with them for 30 years – so sometimes we need to make use of that.

Here in Australia the most important thing a bank needs is to have a banking licence and be an authorised deposit-taking institution, or ADI for short. All banks in Australia have the same level of security, and the Australian Government actually guarantees up to $250,000 per bank account if something goes wrong with a bank, which is pretty cool.

If you did your bank account audit earlier and found that you're paying banking fees, now is the time to cut that right out. It's 2021 – you shouldn't be paying fees for standard transaction accounts. You can do one of two things here: you can call your bank and have a chat with them and ask them to remove your banking fees OR you can move to a new bank that won't charge you. There are so many options when it comes to banks in Australia, and there's actually no right or wrong as long as each account meets your needs.

I actually have three different banks I bank with, because that's what works for me. (And I have been using them since before starting the podcast.) You might prefer to have all your accounts with the same bank because you want to manage them all on one app. It actually doesn't matter who you bank with, or how many banks you have, as long as you've got your six accounts set up and ready to go.

First account

Okay, so the first bank account you're going to set up or rename is your **Cash Hub** account. This is the bank account that will have your income coming into it every week, fortnight or month. Ideally, this bank account shouldn't have a debit card associated with it – and if it does, don't keep it in your wallet. This account is going to have all your direct debits attached to it, and will house the money that you need to cover your bills and other expenses. Personally, this account for me is with NAB. I have literally no reason for this other than this is the bank that I've been with since I got my first job as a teenager and I've had no reason to change it yet as it doesn't charge any fees.

Those who have a mortgage might like to consider structuring their Cash Hub as an offset account for their mortgage. This is where we start making your money work even harder. For more on offset accounts, see Chapter 5 on Banking 101.

Second account

The second account I recommend you have is called your **Personal Spending** or your 'Food, Fuel and Fun' account. This account has a debit card associated with it, since this is the account that funds your weekly spending. Each week on the same day you transfer your total Weekly Personal Spending amount calculated in your budget to this account. This is literally how I manage my money. I have mine direct debited and transferred into my account on a Thursday, because this is what works best for me. Maybe you want your 'pay day' to be Mondays or Fridays. Whatever works – it actually doesn't matter. This is the only account you will have moving forward that has a debit card associated with it, in order to minimise 'money leakage' and always be on top of your spending.

Personally, this account for me is with UP Bank. I really like their push notifications that let me know what I'm spending so I always know how much money is sitting in that account, and when I transfer money from NAB it's instant because I use BPAY's Osko.

Third account

Your third account is your **Emergency Fund**. This fund is SO empowering and is the start of your journey to financial freedom and security. Yes, it's an emergency fund – and we've all heard of those before. It exists because we can't predict when we will get a flat tyre, or need to pay an insurance excess or take unpaid leave from work. But this fund is so much more than that – it is going to end up giving you the power to say 'no' to any situation, place, relationship or job you don't want to be in anymore. Sadly, more often than not, finance is a big reason why people don't change their situations when they really want to. This fund is going to become your back-up plan. How much you have in here really depends on your life stage, your values and what makes you feel secure. I know people who have $2000 in their emergency fund, I know people who have three months' worth of expenses in their emergency fund – and I even know someone who has THREE YEARS' worth of expenses in their emergency fund. This is completely up to you. But if you'd like a bit more guidance than that, personally I like the idea of three months' worth of your bare basics expenses in an emergency fund, because if something serious happens, you can cover yourself until you're either back on your feet or your income protection insurance policy kicks in (more on that in Chapter 14).

If you don't yet have an emergency fund, building this is your first priority before you start contributing to your short- and long-term savings goals.

If you're currently in debt, smashing down your debt absolutely needs to be your priority. But consider allocating a small amount of funds to this account each month to help you sleep easier at night, and increase your contribution when your debt is under control.

Personally, I have this fund with NAB like I do my Cash Hub. I want to be able to access this money easily if I ever need it.

Fourth account

Your fourth account is labelled **Short-Term Savings**. This is going to be for goals you're planning to achieve in the short term, like going on a holiday, purchasing something big or planning to get married in 12 months. This account should also be a fee-free high-interest savings account.

If you're currently in personal debt or have a credit card, you won't be contributing to this fund just yet – because your main goal is to get out of debt before achieving other financial goals. Personally, this fund is an ING Saver for me.

Fifth account

This is your **Medium- to Long-Term Savings** account. This is where your funds for any medium- or long-term savings goals will live. This could be anything from saving for a home, working towards financial freedom or saving money towards the cost of having a family one day. This money is going to be there for the long term, so having it in a high-interest savings account is a good idea; or you could talk to a financial adviser about some ways to invest your money if you wanted to.

Sixth account

Six accounts sounds like a lot, but I promise you there's a reason for each one! This account is your **Not an Emergency But it Still Feels Like an Emergency** account. If you can think of a better, shorter and sassier name, go for it. You'll notice that I don't have a 'treat yourself' fund – and I don't for a reason. We're here for the long haul, and I want any changes to your budgeting to be sustainable for you – which is why personal care, entertainment, dining out and clothing is included in your personal spending. To me, budgeting is a bit like a diet. If it's really strict, pretty bland and takes a lot of energy it's not going to last, and at some point you're going to binge eat to make up for what you feel like you've been denied.

This 'Not an Emergency But it Still Feels Like an Emergency' account has been really useful to me.

This fund exists because sometimes you want to go to a friend's birthday dinner organised last minute, or you got invited to join in on an experience next weekend – but you don't have the money in your everyday account to do so. I strongly discourage dipping into your savings, and this is how I mitigate having to do that. In my mind, once your money is in your savings account it shouldn't come out again until you're achieving that savings goal. If you create the habit of pulling money out of your savings when you want something, you're not putting Future You first.

This account exists so you don't have to miss out on the things that are important to you – not so you can blow it all because you deserve to 'treat yourself' following a bad week at work. That mentality is negative, and actually puts us in a worse financial position. After a bad week at work you're going to sacrifice Future You? I don't think so!

So, before taking money out of this account I do want you to think about it, because it does have to be replenished at some point, but it's my way of making sure you're not missing out. Savings and good money habits unfortunately don't come without any sacrifice. While you won't be able to rely on this fund every weekend, having it ticking over will mean you can still treat yourself without sacrificing your savings and investment goals. After all, we're millennials and we want to have our smashed avocado and eat it too!

Personally, at the end of every week (my money week being Thursday mornings) I transfer any additional cash I have left in my Personal Spending account into this fund to top it up. That way I can top it up without sacrificing my savings goals, and each week I get to start my personal spending on a clean slate.

For me, this account is again with NAB. I'm pretty consistent like that.

Your cash-flow plan in action

So, those are my six bank accounts, my Cash Hub, my Personal Spending account, my Emergency Fund, my Short-Term Savings my Medium- to Long-Term Savings, and my Not an Emergency But it Still Feels Like an Emergency Fund. After spending literally years working out what works best for me, this is where I've landed. And so far, my clients seem to be thriving with this structure too. So I know this structure will work well for you.

Once you've got your six bank accounts set up and ready to go, or you're really excited to get those established soon, it's time to talk in a bit more depth about how they all work together to make sure every dollar that comes into your Cash Hub is given a job, and that it works as hard for you as you do for it.

'But Victoria, aren't you going to give me a list of percentages that I'm supposed to use for each of the accounts in my cash-flow system?'

The answer is no. While in theory this is a great idea, it's not practical to hold someone to a specific percentage because of how different everyone's income is. For example, if I were to say in theory that you need to be saving a minimum of 20 per cent of your income, I would probably expect someone earning $150,000 to be able to save far more than only 20 per cent, whereas saving 20 per cent for someone earning $45,000 is a serious stretch that would mean they are potentially missing out on a lot of other things. Sometimes our incomes don't allow us to save as much as we would like, or achieve things as quickly as we would hope to – and I'm not here to put unrealistic pressure or standards on you if you're in that boat. We're all doing the best we can with the resources we have. You need to work out what works best for you and your personal situation, and your budget will help you work out what is possible.

Hopefully, the following sample cash-flow system will resonate with you, and you can use it as a guide to how your own cash flow could work.

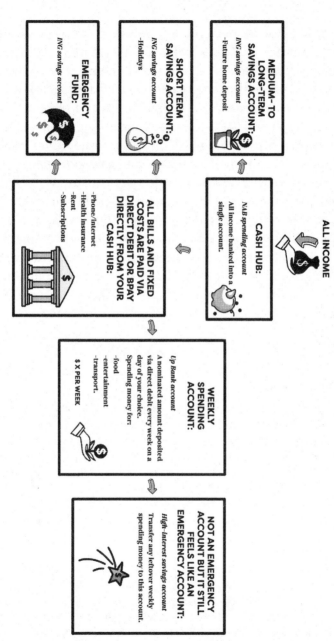

Victoria's 'not-so-secret' cash-flow plan

Setting up your cash-flow system this way will ensure there is no transferring of money back and forth from one account to another, that you don't find yourself dipping into savings when you forget to budget for an expense, and that you know where all the money you've earned is going – because a small money leak over a long period of time can become a big problem.

Your cash-flow system can be as automated or as manual as you like. Personally, I prefer to automate everything because I like to know everything is ticking away in the background and I don't have to worry about logging online to make a BPAY transfer for a bill I forgot. I completely understand that some of you will want to take a more hands-on approach to this as well. We're all different – and this system is structured in a way that works, whether you take an automated or manual approach. In the short term, it's your first step to reclaiming control over your finances; in the long term, it will put you on the money!

● ● ● ● ● ●

LEE, 24 – SA

I've been working multiple casual jobs while I figure out what I want to do with my life, and having money coming from different places at different times meant I wasn't able to easily track where it was coming or going from, which meant I was always stressed and always short for something. I also used to feel overwhelmed when comparing myself to my friends, because even though I was working my butt off I was earning less than them despite putting in more hours and energy – it was really disheartening. For my birthday my mum gifted me Victoria's cash flow and budgeting masterclass (in a not-so-subtle hint to get my act together – thanks, Mum!) and since working out how to track my income, and actually see the life I am creating for myself, I'm so much more confident and happy. It sounds silly, but I've come to the realisation that it's not about what I earn but what I do with it (I really should have listened to Victoria when she said it on the podcast, but it took a while to really sink in). I'm now earning about

$64,000 each year, and even though my friends are earning far more than me I'm on a better path to saving and investing for my future – and I'm so excited for the life I'm creating.

● ● ● ● ● ●

TAKE NOTE

Cash flow is the difference between how much money you have coming into your bank account each month and how much you have going out.

....

Managing your cash flow is the single most important thing you can do for Future You.

....

Wealth isn't created by how much you earn, but rather, how much you're able to save and invest.

....

Chapter 4

Be a goal getter

As I say repeatedly on the podcast, I believe that we can achieve everything. Just not all at once.

The easiest way to make a change or get to where you want to go is to break it down into digestible parts, set your goals and strive to make the changes you need to. BUT, it's also important to celebrate your successes, taking note of your fabulous achievements and acknowledging what you've excelled at. I've got an inkling you're a pretty brilliant being, so instead of always focusing on what you need to change, take a moment to revel in the magical bits of YOU that we wouldn't change for the world.

Goal setting for me is a little bit like a process of elimination. It's nice to be open and optimistic about it at the beginning and to see how big you can dream. You may as well write down ALL of your dreams – no matter how wild. That way, you can keep coming back to them and choose which ones you can tackle at any given time.

YOUR GOALS WISH LIST

Write down every personal goal you can think of that can be achieved with money. Share them. Vocalise them. Creating accountability for these will increase your chances of achieving them. Note: these should be your personal goals. We'll talk about goal setting as a couple in Chapter 15!

You might like to break these down by dividing your life into categories. This will help you assess where you feel you're sitting in each area so you can easily define what you'd like to improve and why. Categories could include family, relationship, friendship, health, community, travel and, of course, finance. As clichéd as it sounds, listing your goals in a doc on your computer or in a diary by your bedside will help you to cement them and then bring them to life – so hop to it!

....

....

....

Now choose the goals that you want to accomplish (like, yesterday). Have a look at the list you've just created and highlight the ones you most want to achieve. Alternatively, some people find it easier to rank them, so do what works for you. For me, I like to pick the ones I feel are most achievable so I can kickstart my motivation, and hopefully I'll be more likely to commit to them in the long term because I feel like I've already got momentum behind me.

....

Do these seem achievable with the budget you currently have?

....

For me, the magic number of goals I like to focus on at a time is five. I like to have one long-term goal, two medium-sized goals and two short-term goals. A long-term goal is something you want to achieve over the next ten or more years, a medium-sized goal is something you'd like to achieve in the next three to five years, and a short-term goal could be something you want to achieve this month or over the next 18. These are flexible based on your personal situation, so use this as a general guide to categorising your goals – as always, there is no right or wrong. If you tick one off, you can replace it with a new one! This stops things from feeling overwhelming and allows me to reassess what's really a priority.

- 1 × long-term goal could be saving for a house deposit.
- 2 × medium-sized goals could be going to Europe with a partner, and buying a car.
- 2 × short-term goals could be going to a friend's wedding down the coast, and getting rid of $250 worth of buy now, pay later debt.

I'm also a huge believer in working backwards. I want to know what the final outcome is, when that will be achieved by and what that will cost me per month or week.

Achieving goals is actually a real challenge – especially if the goals aren't set in the correct way or if the timeframe isn't realistic. This is why I use the *She's on the Money* goal-setting framework.

Being clear on the goals you set and how you're going to achieve them is the start line of your journey. If I gave you a map with no directions, where would you be going? (Nowhere!) So let's work out what your start line looks like, set out a clear path, and get you a starting gun, and a ribbon to run through at the end when you've achieved your goal.

Your goals should follow the *She's on the Money* framework – they should be Specific, Optimistic, Time-bound and Measurable.

Specific | The more specific the goal, the better. Knowing an exact amount needed and a deadline for completion will keep you focused, motivated and on track. For example: 'I will save $5000 to put towards stock investments by 1 December' or 'I will double my credit card's minimum repayment every month until it is paid off'.

Optimistic | If your goals don't match your values, it'll be mighty hard to stick to them. And while I want you to be realistic, I also want you to be optimistic. You might think you can't break old spending habits or ever earn enough to invest in shares or property, but I'm here to tell you that you can. If you need someone to give you permission to be financially independent, I will be that person!

Time-bound | Put a date on it and work backwards. Let's say it's 1 April and you want to go to New Zealand for a ten-day trip in exactly six months. You also know that the accommodation will cost $2000, flights are $500, and you'll need $250 a day for food and fun. All up, the trip will cost you $5000. In this scenario, you'll need two goals: 'I will save $125 every month so that I can purchase my plane tickets by 1 August. I will save another $750 per month so that I have $4500 in my holiday account by the time I go on my trip on 1 October.'

Measurable | Creating goals that you can quantify will keep you accountable. For example: You want to save $40,000 for a house deposit and have given yourself 36 months to achieve this. Break down the numbers. If you want to have $40,000 in a savings account in three years, you will need to save roughly $1112 a month OR you can break it down weekly. Give yourself numbers you can actively measure and work with. That way, if you don't meet your savings goal at an intended milestone, you can identify that. Take pause to look at your bank statements or your budgeting/spending spreadsheet. Notice where you fell down and continue with that goal but adjust your behaviour. Alternatively, you can readjust the goal to something more realistic and achievable – this is fine too, so long as you are still making progress and feeling positive about your goal(s)!

Understanding that you need to have a plan is crucial. The easiest way to fail is by spreading yourself too thin. That said, don't forget that you're human and your journey is not a straight line. If you fall off, jump back on. You're not going to achieve anything by beating yourself up because of it, so let's see it as a lesson rather than a failure. Next time, you'll have experience and will be able to implement what you've learnt – how great is that! It's not about always being perfect; it's about what you can do today to achieve this goal. While this is your financial journey, I'd really like a constant goal of yours to be financial freedom (which will be achieved by achieving your other financial goals!). I want you to get to the point in your life where you don't have to work anymore. I want you to have investments that produce an income for you so that you have the CHOICE to either show up for work or not.

● ●

YOUR FIRST FIVE GOALS

Goal 1

My specific goal is: ....

....

I will measure this goal by: ....

....

My milestones for this goal are: ....

....

I will know I have achieved my goal when: ....

....

When I achieve my goal I am going to: ....

....

Think: ....

Feel: ....

Do: ....

Goal 2

My specific goal is: ....

....

I will measure this goal by: ....

....

My milestones for this goal are: ....

....

I will know I have achieved my goal when: ....

....

When I achieve my goal I am going to: ....

....

Think: ....

Feel: ....

Do: ....

Goal 3

My specific goal is: ....

....

I will measure this goal by: ....

....

My milestones for this goal are: ....

....

I will know I have achieved my goal when: ....

....

When I achieve my goal I am going to: ....

....

Think: ....

Feel: ....

Do: ....

Goal 4

My specific goal is: ....

....

I will measure this goal by: ....

....

My milestones for this goal are: ....

....

I will know I have achieved my goal when: ....

....

When I achieve my goal I am going to: ....

....

Think: ....

Feel: ....

Do: ....

Goal 5

My specific goal is: ....

....

I will measure this goal by: ....

....

My milestones for this goal are: ....

....

I will know I have achieved my goal when: ....

....

When I achieve my goal I am going to: ....

....

Think: ....

Feel: ....

Do: ....

● ●

PARIS, 23 – NSW

Growing up, my family seemed to live quite comfortably. We lived in a nice house, in a good area and I never believed money was a problem. I remember my mum taking me shopping every weekend as a child and buying a lot of clothes. Our grocery shopping came to around $600 a week. I didn't think we had any issues, however my mum often made comments about using the credit card or would make remarks about hiding purchases from my father, coaching me into saying that brand-new purchases were old.

When it came to taking responsibility for myself, I had no sense that spending or using credit cards was a problem. I went overseas and did big trips once or twice a year for about four years after leaving school. I had no idea of the problem I was creating for myself until my only option was to move five hours from home to move into a role where I could work lots of overtime, away from friends and family, and focus on reducing the debt I had accumulated. I was able to clear that debt; however, I fell back into old spending habits of 'treat yourself, you only get to go on this holiday with these friends once'.

I then met my boyfriend and realised that having goals and things to look forward to meant that I needed to save and take responsibility. I now have zero credit card debt, just my HELP debt and my car repayments, which I am working on. We are slowly saving for a house, but we needed to move out into a rental due to my boyfriend's work requirements (a backyard that could have a working dog), so it is a very slow process. We have had to learn to say no to dinners out and holidays to Bali to be able to achieve our goals. We have a collective debt of $7000, which we owe to my brother, who gave us the money to pay off my boyfriend's credit card debt.

ADINA, 27 – VIC

My mum is the thriftiest person I know. From using the old 'he is under 12 years old' trick on my 16-year-old brother to snag free kids' entry to an event to buying fabulous outfits from the op shop to single-handedly running the accounting side of things for my dad's business, she is my money hero. I learnt so much respect for money by watching the way my mum handled it, but all of that changed when I moved out of home and interstate. When I first moved from Tassie to Melbourne, my first full-time job was working in a fashion boutique in High Street, Armadale, which just so happens to be one of the fanciest places I've ever been in my life.

At the boutique we sold clothing brands such as Alexander Wang, Alexander McQueen, Balmain, etc. We even stocked coats that were well over $5000 – AND THEY SOLD! Just like that, I wanted to have all the expensive clothing I couldn't afford. I started spending money I didn't have to keep up with fast-changing fashion, so that people would see my $600 leather jacket and think that I had quite a few dollars, when really that was all I had. It even got to the stage where my partner was lending me money for bills. I was so ashamed of my spending I had started hiding my shopping from him and making up excuses as to why I needed another pair of shoes. Eventually, after leaving this job, I realised that the clothes I wore and the shoes on my feet didn't define who I was as a person, and that wearing a $500 designer dress was no different than fronting up in a $50 dress I'd snagged from Facebook Marketplace. Finally, after speaking to a friend who recommended She's on the Money, I started listening to the podcasts and joined the Facebook group. I'm happy to say I finally have money goals and have started saving for a house, something that back then felt so impossible.

I've learnt so much from the She's on the Money community and I love hearing everyone's stories and knowing that I'm not alone on my money journey. Thank you so much for changing my money story from drab back to fab! Moral of the story: Mum knows best.

● ● ● ● ● ●

TAKE NOTE

You can achieve everything, just not all at once.

....

Set SOTM goals: Specific, Optimistic, Time-bound and Measurable!

....

Read and say your goals daily!

....

Chapter 5

Banking 101

Raise your hand if you were a Dollarmites kid. Now raise your hand if you got a credit card in the mail on your eighteenth birthday.

Now, hold my drink while I take a moment to rant. Most of us did not learn enough about financial literacy at school. So, as we venture into the adult world, we need to skill up and get informed on banking and how to make it work best for us.

The first thing to know is that banks are not going to be loyal to you. As I've mentioned, nine times out of ten, they will give a better deal to a new customer than one who has been banking with them for 30 years. Second, depending on what stage of life you're in, you are going to require different things from a bank. For example, at 16 you might just need a savings account. As you get older and are ready to purchase property or invest, you might need a bank with a caveat-free redraw loan facility or access to a wider range of financial products. While the big four banks (Commonwealth, Westpac, ANZ and NAB) may meet your needs at some point in time, it's important that you explore all your options.

I'm particularly into digital banks like Up, UBank and ING.

Because they have lower overheads, they're able to offer zero account fees, zero foreign transaction fees, zero overseas ATM fees and really competitive interest rates on their savings accounts. Personally, I use Up and I love how progressive their banking app is. Designed to support your savings goals and help keep you accountable, they offer features like push notifications for when a direct debit is taken, and will notify you of your balance. They also have Osko, which means your pay-anyone transactions are immediate, as well as a relationship with TransferWise, which allows them to offer better currency rates than the big banks. (This isn't sponsored, and they haven't asked me to say this – I'm just a fan and feel you deserve my honest opinion!)

I know people are wary of banks they can't see or touch – and don't get me wrong, it's good to be wary. But at the end of the day, a bank is a bank. To reiterate, as long as they have a banking licence and are an authorised deposit-taking institution (ADI), all banks have the same level of security and the Australian Government guarantee of deposits being reimbursed up to $250,000 per account if something were to happen to the bank.

Regardless of where you are on your journey right now, it's important for both Current You and Future You to know the A to Z of banking.

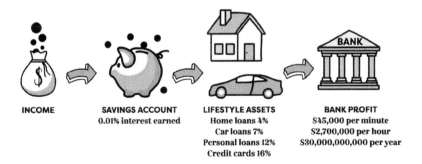

INCOME	SAVINGS ACCOUNT	LIFESTYLE ASSETS	BANK PROFIT
	0.01% interest earned	Home loans 4%	$45,000 per minute
		Car loans 7%	$2,700,000 per hour
		Personal loans 12%	$30,000,000,000 per year
		Credit cards 16%	

How banks make money

Types of accounts and banking products

Normal transaction account

This is your typical everyday account. It usually comes with a debit card and lets you do your day-to-day spending. It's what you're tapping in-store and using for online purchases. Banks love these types of accounts because they encourage people to spend, and the bank pays little to no interest on the balance of the account.

Hot tip: You shouldn't have the bulk of your money sitting in this type of account, because it's too easy to spend. If you do have your income coming into a transaction account, I suggest putting the bank card in a drawer or cutting it up. Plus, depending on your situation, your money is better off in a savings account, because it's earning interest, or something like an offset account, where it's offsetting the interest of a home loan. (You can read up on home loans in detail in Chapter 10.)

Things to consider when opening a normal transaction account:

- You want this type of account to have zero fees. If your account has transaction, transfer or ATM fees, you need to review it.
- Is there a minimum balance or deposit amount needed? And if so, can you actually meet these requirements?
- Can the debit card be used as credit? (This isn't a bad thing – in fact, it'll mean you're able to use your debit card to check into hotels, or use in situations where a credit card is requested while negating the need to actually have one!)
- If you're a traveller, are there any overseas fees? Ideally, we avoid these completely.

Savings account

While a savings account sounds like something you'd just put savings into for safekeeping, they can actually do a bit more! Even though this type of account is not intended for daily spending transactions, it's a great way to have the bulk of your dollars earn some money before they go to BPAY and direct debits.

Hot tip: SHOP AROUND. Just because you have your everyday account with one bank, doesn't mean their savings account option is the best one for you.

Things to consider when opening a savings account:

- Ideally, you'd like a savings account with zero fees, an interest rate of 2 per cent or higher and the ability to use BPAY and direct debiting.
- Is there a minimum balance or deposit amount needed for interest to start being paid?
- You may need more than one. As discussed in our cash allocation section, money can and should flow from your cash hub into multiple savings accounts.
- Ask what the bonus interest rate is.

Term deposit

A term deposit is a savings account that locks your money away for a specified period of time. While it's important to discuss this here, I will cover it more in depth in Chapter 9, as it's also a type of investment. This is a great type of account for short(ish)-term, large sums of money, such as house deposits.

Hot tip: This is a great account if you can't trust yourself and need to put your money where you can't touch it!

Things to consider when opening a term deposit:

- Is there a fee for early withdrawal?
- Are you sure you won't need access to these funds?
- What is the interest rate?

Offset account

An offset account is linked to a mortgage and can be used as a normal transaction account, making it a convenient way to access money while saving interest on your home loan. Whatever balance you have in your offset account offsets the interest you pay on your loan. Let's say your mortgage is $400,000. If you have $10,000 sitting in your offset account, then you are essentially only paying interest on $390,000. (More on this in Chapter 10.)

Spoiler: Depending on your financial goals and cash flow, an offset account is not as magical as people think. Realistically, you have to have a large sum of money in that account that you never touch for there to be a significant impact.

Things to consider when opting for an offset account:

- Are there any fees or restrictions?
- Could your money be working harder somewhere else?
- Does this type of account make it too easy for you to access your funds?

Redraw facility

A redraw facility is an added feature that some home and personal loans offer. Again, we will expand on this option in Chapter 10, but a redraw facility essentially enables you to make extra repayments on your home loan, while allowing you access to any funds that you're in credit for over the minimum repayment. From here you can set up BPAY and automatic transfers, making this a great cash hub option.

Hot tip: It's important to note that not all redraws are created equally. Some banks (cough: the big four) will charge you to take money out, or will have a minimum amount you can access.

What to consider when choosing a redraw facility:

- Does it fit your lifestyle? Are you in a position to make extra repayments?
- Is this the best option for the type of property you're buying?

And last but not least:

Credit card

A credit card is a card with a unique number that allows you to purchase goods and services on credit. Credit cards come with different limits, interest rates and terms for repayment.

Spoiler: They do more harm than good – UNLESS you're a business owner and need to maintain a steady cash flow. More on side hustles in Chapter 13.

Reasons why people THINK they need a credit card:

- because their parents told them they do
- to earn a credit score
- to earn points
- for health and travel insurance
- for emergencies
- to book a hotel or hire car
- because it came with their home loan
- to spend money they don't have.

Let's unpack this for a second.

The parents excuse

Your parents also may have signed you up to be a Dollarmites kid. As good as their intentions are, our generation is living in a different economic climate. What may have been true in the 70s, 80s and 90s is simply not the case anymore.

Credit score myth

A credit score is a number between zero and 1200 that 'shows' banks how good you are at paying back your debts. To be honest, they don't really matter, and they can be improved through loan repayments or a rental history.

To earn points

Gone are the glorious days when the points you earn were actually worthwhile. Do you have any idea how much you have to spend to earn points these days? The risk of overspending and having to pay a hefty amount of interest far outweighs any reward you might think you'll receive.

'But Victoria, I get heaps of points, I always pay the balance off every month and I love my credit card!'

That's all well and good, but I guarantee that you are the exception. Statistics say that the average person spends 14 per cent more when shopping with a credit card than with cash or debit. That means the points are obliterated, because they're ultimately spending more money.

Needing health and travel insurance

Please, please, please don't get a credit card simply because you think this is the best way to get travel and health insurance. For starters, you should compare coverage and policies with other providers and get feedback from friends or family on their experiences with making claims. To date, banks who unfairly denied their clients coverage have been ordered to pay back millions of dollars. More on insurance in Chapter 14!

For emergencies

If you're over the age of 18, you should be futureproofing yourself in every way possible, and that means having an emergency savings fund, as well as every kind of insurance for any kind of emergency! You shouldn't rely on a credit card for emergencies. Way more on this in Chapter 14.

To book a hotel or hire car

The myth that you need a credit card to book a hotel or hire car is just that: a myth. If you have a debit card with a Visa or Mastercard logo on it, you should be able to run the transaction through as credit, negating the need for a credit card!

It came with your home loan

You just took out a home loan – why on earth would you want any extra debt that needs servicing? Just because something is on offer doesn't mean you have to put it on your plate.

To spend money you don't have

I get it. You want things. You want food. You want to travel. You want to pay your rent. As mentioned previously, I'm a firm believer that you can have everything. You just can't have it all at once. And I promise that credit cards don't help clean up messes – they make them.

● ● ● ● ● ●

Look, credit cards aren't bad. It's just that people are bad with credit cards. And it's okay that we aren't super amazing in every aspect of our lives. I just think we need to be realistic about which financial products are enabling us. What things are making us stray from our values and goals?

Statistics say that credit cards encourage you to unconsciously spend more, because it's not your money and there isn't really any pain when parting with it. Let's say you walk into a grocery store with $200 in cash. You're going to spend it differently because you can see what your limit is. You're going to buy what you need, not what you want. Your mind knows that the crisp yellow notes will be broken and returned in small purple notes or gold coins. It's like when you were a kid and had $1 to spend at the canteen or lolly shop. Do you remember figuring out the best way to end up with the most amount of lollies? For me, it was always, 'Do I want the fancy push pop or ten Pythons?' (Or was it more of a Milkos and Ghost Drops kind of day?)

Kids inherently understand the value of money. Unfortunately, due to electronic transactions, the tangible value gets lost as we grow because we don't get to see or feel that connection anymore.

When you go shopping with credit, you literally just tap your card, phone or watch and *poof*! You have what you wanted, and can deal with paying for it later. The pain of the transaction has been eliminated.

Let's go back to the days of bartering. Bartering is exchanging goods or services for other goods or services without using money. When someone needed a warm blanket, they might literally give up their cow to make that happen. If someone needed fresh milk and bread for their family, they might swap their only mattress. Getting what you need used to mean detaching from a physical object or a chunk of your time. Spending money is simply becoming far too painless.

If there are three things you're going to take away from my credit card rant, let them be:

● No-one is getting into credit card debt with the intention of getting into debt. The system just makes it too easy to happen.
● Banks are spending millions of dollars on behavioural psychology to get you to spend more money without you realising it.
● This is not the place to judge yourself. If you're in debt, that doesn't define you. It doesn't make you a bad person. We are going to get out of it together.

Where do you sit?

In order for you to find the right types of bank accounts and financial products, it's important to figure out what type of person you are when it comes to willpower. While there are plenty of 'exceptions' out there – aka women who wouldn't dare dip into their savings, nor fail to pay off the balance of their credit card every month – that's not usually the case. This is totally fine, it just means we need a foolproof structure and hurdles in place to save you from yourself.

● ●

WHO AM I?

- Do you frequently take money out of your savings to cover daily expenses?
- Are your money goals constantly changing due to poor cash flow?
- Do you find yourself dipping into savings or blowing food and fuel money on things like clothing or an event?
- Are you currently dependent on credit cards?

If you answered yes to any of these, I want you to go back to your money map and cash-flow structure. If you haven't picked a bank yet, focus on putting hurdles in place when setting up your accounts. This might mean automatic transfers into accounts that don't have cards and are difficult to transfer from. If you've already set up your accounts but can already see how easy it is to slide money over, find a different way.

You absolutely have the capacity to set up a banking structure that is going to make every dollar work for you and save you from yourself. It's okay if it takes you a couple of tries to get it right. It might need to change depending on where you are in your life. As long as it's getting you one step closer to financial freedom, you're heading in the right direction.

● ●

PAIGE, 33 – NSW

I've been with the same bank since I got my first job. My mum took me down to the bank she used and we opened an account in my name. Since then, I've collected a couple of other accounts at other banks for no real reason, just because I got motivated and thought it would help me get my money together. However, they never worked, and I was paying fees on accounts I wasn't even using.

Since joining the She's on the Money *community and learning about Up from the Facebook group and all of their posts about the Up Money Wins, I've since shut all my other accounts and just bank with Up. I can't begin to tell you how liberating it is to always know exactly what's in my account after making a purchase, and I've even set up their round-ups feature to help me save. While all of that is amazing, what I most love is how flexible the Up Savers account is because I'm one of those people whose goals are always changing, and it was silly to set up bank account after bank account each time I had a new goal in mind. I know a bank isn't the most important thing that's going to help me achieve my goals, but it sure does help to feel like they're a part of my own money team.*

● ● ● ● ● ●

TAKE NOTE

You do not need to be loyal to a bank. The little
guys have a lot to bring to the table!

....

Credit cards aren't bad. People are bad with credit cards.

....

It's okay if it takes a couple of tries to get
your cash-flow structure right!

....

Chapter 6

Dealing with debt

One thing I love to tell my clients is that looking after your finances is the ultimate form of self-care. The sooner you take care of your money, the faster it will be able to start taking care of you. Essentially, the goal is to create assets that help you feel safe and secure, and give you the freedom to say no to any place, situation or relationship you don't want to be in. While I fully understand that this can seem daunting, particularly for those currently in bad debt or those afraid to take on good debt, it's completely necessary to change the way you think about budgeting and financial planning. This is particularly important when dealing with the three types of debt: good debt, okay debt and bad debt.

The scary thing about debt, and specifically bad debt, is that it's invisible. You can't see it hanging on your wall, it's not branded across your chest and it's not mentioned in your online dating profile. When you can't see something, it's easy to push it to the back of your mind, to be dealt with another day. Funnily enough, true wealth is also usually invisible. Often confused with its ostentatious cousin, richness, wealth is the culmination of years of sacrificing, saving, investing and setting up Future You. More often than not, rich people just have stuff, and bad debt. Wealthy people have assets (and possibly good debt).

'Rich'   ## Wealthy

$450

$800

$7,960

$900

$90

$45

$65

$50

Net worth: **$15,000**   Net worth: **$1.2 million**

The finance twins

Mistaking material items for wealth is a common reason people find themselves in bad debt. This is a result of us constantly comparing what we have to others. People buy cars and homes they can't afford, larger homes they don't need and designer clothing, thinking this is a reflection of their wealth. In reality, their frivolous spending is costing them more than just the figures on the price tags. This brings me to a very important question: what is the true price of comparison?

At the end of the 2017 financial year, Australians collectively had $45 billion worth of credit card debt. A review by the Australian Securities and Investments Commission (ASIC) of more than 21.4 million credit card accounts opened between July 2012 and June 2017 found that as of June 2017, there were 14 million open credit card accounts in Australia, with outstanding balances totalling nearly $45 billion (check out the ASIC website for further details). Of that amount, approximately $31.7 billion was incurring interest charges. Between 2016 and 2017, credit card holders were charged roughly $1.5 billion in fees for simply having a credit card, overdrafting, or being late with a payment.

Even though we are one of the most financially literate countries in the world, it's clear that we are still getting ourselves into trouble, which is why we must continue to talk about it. I recently read that Australians are more scared of a credit card than death. This makes me wonder WHY on earth we are still applying for them. My guess? A classic case of trying to keep up with the Joneses.

In a time when influencer marketing has never been more prevalent, young women are trying to keep up with lifestyles that social media makes us feel like we should have. As I write this, numerous articles are circulating online exposing the fact that many influencers are going into debt themselves in order to buy the clothing, accessories, holidays, meals and cars they need to portray the life they want you to think they have. While I'll be the first to admit that it's fun to look at beautiful photos of exotic places, museum-worthy gowns and the type of food that warrants a flatlay photo shoot, there is a huge lack of transparency when it comes to an influencer's sponsored posts and/or invisible debt, and it's harming our mental health and bank accounts.

When speaking to your friends about the latest property they just bought, the pool they put in, the holiday they booked or car they just leased, you need to remember that they're probably not detailing the amount of debt they racked up in pursuit of these things. Just because they're wearing a Gucci belt or sipping a glass of Veuve Clicquot doesn't mean that their invisible debt isn't looming in the background. On the flip side, many people have the privilege of affording these things, and that's okay. As long as it aligns with their values and isn't preventing them from achieving financial freedom, I don't care how someone decides to spend their money. The trick is working out how to take other people's privilege on board without letting it affect your own journey or ego.

Even before social media was a thing, I remember kids my age in high school being given BMWs for their birthdays and feeling like I needed to keep up. I was experiencing money envy, which is a very real thing. While I didn't miraculously find a way to get myself an expensive car, I did take out a personal loan so that I could study overseas. I'd like to say it was a necessary investment in my education, but the reality is, I wanted to go because my friends were going. I didn't want to miss out. The debt from that trip massively set me back from achieving my future goals – it was extremely difficult to pay back. It's something I regret to this day, and it's why I advocate against bad debt so passionately. I'm a firm believer that the average Australian cannot have financial freedom with a credit card, personal loan, car loan or mortgage they aren't in a position to service.

One of my all-time favourite sayings is, 'If you live fake rich now, you'll live real poor later.' If the people surrounding you seem better off, remember that they may have debt, privilege or both. When it comes to spending more than we earn, it's easy for people to assume their situation will improve in the near future. I'm constantly peppered with excuses or reasons like: *I'll make more money next month. I'm getting a bonus. This will be the last holiday I take for years. I deserve to treat myself.*

I'd like to take a moment to redefine what 'treating ourselves' means, so that we are *actually* treating ourselves well. Let's say you just did 30 hours of overtime in a week. Your eyes are burning. You have RSI in your wrist from typing away furiously. An extra $1000 just landed in your bank account. What do you do? You treat yourself to that handbag you've been dying for. You tell yourself that you've earned it, that this is what hard work looks like. Question: how are you treating yourself if you're buying something that doesn't impact Future You? How did that handbag get you closer to financial freedom? If you treat yourself to that handbag, you are putting yourself in a position where you have to work hard to earn money again. It's like shooting yourself in the foot. Why would you want to do that to yourself? Why work hard to get ahead, only to end up in exactly the same financial position you were in before? No thanks! Instead, why not treat yourself to a $1000 investment, an extra mortgage repayment or the security of knowing you have the money in your emergency fund? The global economy is fragile, so treat yourself to the opportunity to make hay while the sun is shining.

Look, people overestimate what they can do in a year and underestimate what they can do over a long period of time. Like I said in the last chapter: you can have everything you want, just not all at once. You need to be realistic about how long it will take you to achieve your goals. If having a European car is a value to you, map out a way to get it so that when you drive it home, you park it in a spot you own. If you desperately need that handbag, put assets in place that generate enough wealth that you don't have to work 30 extra hours a week to get it.

Remember:

- The world is not a level playing field.
- We did not all start at the same point.
- Do not compare your start to someone else's middle.

Now it's time for another lesson: Debt 101.

Types of debt

Good debt

Good debt helps you create your future wealth. It's an asset that appreciates in value and/or provides an income. Examples include an investment property or investing in a side hustle.

Notice that I did not say your family home. I don't consider this good debt or an investment for Future You because you would have to be willing to sell it to get capital growth. We'll chat more about estate planning in Chapter 17.

Okay debt

Okay debt doesn't necessarily return a monetary income you can see, but doesn't terribly affect cash flow either. Things like solar panels, the mortgage on your primary place of residence, VET and HELP (Higher Education Loan Program) debt can fall into this category.

The reason why I consider your family home okay debt instead of good debt is because, even though it's technically creating an asset for you, it's going to cost you a lot of money to maintain. It comes with taxes, repairs, and the need for furnishings and fixtures. And like I said, you'd also have to be willing to sell it to reap the benefits of capital growth.

HELP debt, formerly known as HECS (Higher Education Contribution Scheme), is an indexed government loan that people can take out for study. Indexation is not interest. Interest is paying for the privilege to borrow money. Indexation is just the amount that the debt is going to increase each year to be in line with the cost of living. Currently, 2.9 million Australians have outstanding HELP debt. Of that number, 200,000 have an outstanding balance of more than $50,000. This both is and isn't concerning. While as a country we may be in more HELP debt than we've ever been, it also means we are more educated than we've ever been. However, okay debt is still debt, and not something people should take on lightly. Statistics from Studiosity indicate that one in three Australians regret their choice of degree. It's really common for people to jump straight into university from high school. They may feel pressure from parents or friends to maintain the momentum of their education. But picking a degree is such a big decision. If you're uncertain about what you want to do, it's worth taking a gap year to think about which career path you want to take. University will still be a choice for you in 12 months, 18 months or even five years. You can take time to work, travel or meet with a career counsellor so that you can find clarity before committing to a choice.

If you have a HELP debt, you should be aware that as of the 2019/2020 financial year, repayments happen automatically (they're deducted from your pay cheque) when you're working and earning $45,881 or more a year. If you're self-employed, it's compulsory that you make these payments through the ATO online portal.

If you earn less than this, you don't pay any HELP debt. Essentially, your tax component will be slightly higher to pay off HELP.

Note that this repayment goes up in percentages based on what you earn.

$0 – $45,880	NIL
$45,881 – $52,973	1%
$52,974 – $56,151	2%
$56,152 – $59,521	2.5%
$59,522 – $63,092	3%
$63,093 – $66,877	3.5%
$66,878 – $70,890	4%
$70,891 – $75,144	4.5%

$75,145 – $79,652	5%
$79,653 – $84,432	5.5%
$84,433 – $89,498	6%
$89,499 – $94,868	6.5%
$94,869 – $100,560	7%
$100,561 – $106,593	7.5%
$106,594 – $112,989	8%
$112,990 – $119,769	8.5%
$119,770 – $126,955	9%
$126,956 – $134,572	9.5%
$134,573 and above	10%

Repayment of HELP by salary
(Source: ATO)

When it comes to paying off debt, HELP is something you shouldn't make extra repayments on. This is for two reasons:

1. You're better off using your money to pay off your other debt and build your wealth.
2. HELP debt dies with you. Unlike credit cards and personal loans, which your family members inherit, HELP debt is absorbed by the government scheme.

Bad debt

Bad debt is any debt that decreases your future wealth and impacts your cash flow. Examples of bad debt include, but are not limited to:

- personal loans
- quick, same-day and payday loans
- family and friend loans
- car loans and leases

- credit card
- buy now, pay later programs
- tax debt.

Too often people confuse bad debt with an investment and end up damming their cash flow, which stops Future You from flourishing. Instead of having $500 coming into your account each month that you can use to create financial freedom, you're spending that $500 paying off something like a car that was out of your price range, or a trip you couldn't truly afford. Couple that with enormous interest and this set-up simply isn't helping you get anywhere financially. When you have bad debt, you're living in the past, because you're paying for decisions that Past You made. I want you to try and make decisions today that mean Future You doesn't get stuck paying for things that aren't creating the future that you want or deserve. Every time you get paid, you want that income to cover your lifestyle expenses, protect you from an emergency and create wealth.

If you have 80 per cent of your income going out to cover bad debts, you're going to be treading water because you can't actually move forward with your wealth creation. I've said this before and I will say it again: cash flow is queen! Now, let's take a closer look at all the ways people find themselves in bad debt.

Personal loans

A personal loan allows you to borrow money for a particular purpose or need. It might be used to purchase a car, go on a holiday or to consolidate debt. The amount lent varies, but you are always charged interest and given between five and 12 years to repay it. Between 2018 and 2019, 619,000 personal loans were processed in Australia, advancing a total of $476 million. Personal loans are highly popular among millennials, with cars and holidays being the main reason behind the splurging. Over the last ten to 15 years, personal loans have become increasingly easy to get hold of. Because people love instant gratification and usually lack financial literacy, personal loans are becoming a bigger issue.

Types of personal loans

Unsecured loan: An unsecured loan means that the amount lent is not secured against any of the borrower's assets. These usually have a higher interest rate of around 15–22 per cent.

Secured loan: A secured loan is secured against an asset that the borrower already owns. If the borrower fails to make payments, the lender can take the asset and sell it on their behalf to repay the debt.

Quick, same-day and payday loans

These are all high-cost, short-term loans, usually of around $2000 to $3000. These loans are usually sought out of desperation. Unlike a personal loan, which is generally the result of someone weighing up their options when deciding how to fund their holiday or car, quick loans tend to be taken out to cover urgent payments such as rent or bills. We will learn more about compound interest in Chapter 9, but when it comes to quick loans, most people end up having to pay four to six times the amount that they borrowed. This is obviously an abhorrent structure; the 2017–2019 banking royal commission looked into this and reprimanded many banks and lenders for offering these types of loans.

Another way

In Australia, the number one quick-loan customers are single mums, which is completely understandable. If you are a single mum or someone who is falling behind on rent, google 'financial counselling' and your area. There are organisations out there that can direct you to companies like Good Shepherd Microfinance, who have no interest loan schemes, aka NILS loans, or Centrelink for a pay advancement. You can also try calling your landlord or energy provider and explaining your situation. Many offer payment programs for those experiencing hardship.

Family and friend loans

While some may argue this could be considered okay debt, especially if it's interest free and with long payment terms, my stance is that you either get the money back or the relationship back, but rarely both.

Food for thought: if you're someone who is fortunate enough to be in the position where a family member or friend is willing to lend you money, this needs to be done in a professional and well-documented manner. But always ask yourself: is this the best decision for all parties involved? Parents always want to do the best for their children, but that doesn't mean you're doing the best for them.

Car loans and leases

From the bottom of my heart, I'm pleading with you: don't buy a car you can't afford. While I understand you may need a car to get to work, overextending yourself on something that will cost you money to own and that depreciates in value the minute you drive it home is a recipe for disaster.

Let's say you're purchasing a $35,000 car and getting a seven-year loan. The interest is 12 per cent pa, which makes your monthly repayment $617.85. This means that over the seven years, you will have paid $51,899.03 instead of $35,000. And let me remind you: that car is worth $35,000 the day you buy it. It loses value every single day after that. You've invested in a depreciating asset that is not creating wealth for you, and that is costing you money to maintain it.

As for 0 per cent and 1 per cent finance offers, these rates are only usually applicable at the start of the loan, or come with massive monthly repayments. Always check when and by how much they increase. And remember, however you finance it, you're still going to be paying off a depreciating asset that is costing you money.

Buy now, pay later programs

These are programs offered by companies like Afterpay, Zip Pay, BrightePay, Payright, Openpay, Humm and Make It Mine.

I'm not saying buy now, pay later programs and similar services are right or wrong, but the minute I hear someone mention them, I think of bad credit and debt. I think of people wanting instant gratification, and not giving any long-term thought to their purchasing decisions. I'm not sure if this is because I'm a financial adviser or not. On one hand, I have girlfriends that use them all the time and love it. One friend in particular likes that she can order multiple dresses online at once, try them on and send back the ones that don't fit without having the actual cost come out of her account all at once. She's a really good saver and is fabulous with her money. For her, I don't think these programs are negative. They're a tool for her to budget. (Spoiler: she's the exception.)

Unfortunately, on the other hand, there is a greater pool of people using these services as a way to avoid taking responsibility for their spending. They're not looking at the cost of an item as $200. They're rationalising that it's just $50 now. They're spending money they don't currently have, thinking that they will magically make that amount the next month.

That said, buy now, pay later programs are revolutionising the way purchasing happens, both online and in-store. One company has already been rolled out to over 1100 dental and optometrists' offices nationally, and is actually about to expand into GP clinics, radiology centres and pharmacies. This is great news for people who don't have access to the $300 they need for a medical procedure, scan or specialist appointment. When used appropriately, buy now, pay later programs can be a tool that enables people to get access to medical procedures that they need right away.

However, this could potentially leave more vulnerable patients in a position where they're paying for services they might not need, or choosing elective services that are not within their budget. While buying now and paying later for your root canal may be deemed necessary, using it to pay for veneers that aren't in your budget will simply contribute to bad debt.

My vote: if you're not already using buy now, pay later as a budgeting tool to make your dollars work harder for you, steer clear!

Credit cards

I feel like you probably picked up what I was putting down about credit cards in Chapter 5, but since so many people find themselves in a credit card pickle, I'm going to keep talking about them. Finder.com.au says the average credit card purchase is $108.04, whereas if you were purchasing on a debit card, you'd only spend $46.75. While people think they're getting security when they get a credit card, they're actually being enabled to do more unconscious spending.

Here's the thing: no-one gets a credit card so that they can spiral into unmanageable debt. People get credit cards because they're a solution to an immediate problem, and they make our lives easier at that point in time.

For example:

● I'm going on a holiday and want to feel secure.
● I have a heap of uni fees coming up and want a credit card just in case.
● My hot-water heater broke and buying a new one means I will struggle to pay my other bills.

Getting a credit card comes from a really wholesome place. But more often than not, it takes us somewhere we don't want to be.

Why are we struggling to pay off our credit cards?

As a whole, people are too optimistic about their future financial behaviour. When getting a credit card, they often don't factor in life events, unexpected expenses or what their actual cash surplus is every month. They naively believe that they'll magically earn more money when they're older, or get a pay rise, and can deal with the debt then. After all, a $2000 limit is nothing, right?

Wrong. A $2000 credit card could potentially take you 17 (yes, 17!!!) years to pay off if you only make the minimum repayments.

If you take that $2000 debt and apply the average credit card interest rate, which is 17 per cent according to Canstar, and then only make the standard bank's 2 per cent repayment ($40 a month), it would take you 17 years to pay that $2000 back, and you'd end up paying more than $5000 in total.

However, if you managed to double the repayment amount to $80, you'd pay it off in seven years AND save yourself $2000.

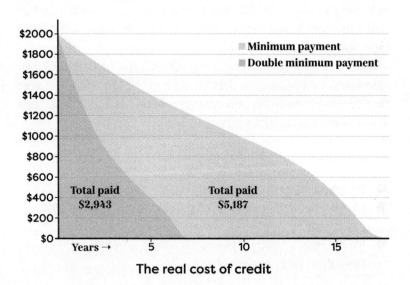

The real cost of credit

For you to be able to pay off your credit card in full every month (or 45 or 60 days, depending on the terms) so that you don't accrue any interest, you have to be able to make that payment from your surplus cash. That's the money left after you've paid your other bills, put food on the table and saved. If you don't have enough money to pay off the entire balance, and can only make the minimum repayments, the amount of interest you'll have to pay can drastically slow down your journey to financial freedom.

The truth about your credit rating

A credit rating, also known as a credit score, is an estimate of a person or company's ability to fulfil financial commitments based on previous dealings. This is a number between zero and 1200, and is included in a detailed personal report.

Excellent	801 – 1000
Very good	701 – 800
Good	626 – 700
Average	551 – 625
Below average	0 – 550

● ● ● ● ● ●

Myth: I need a credit card to establish a credit score so that I can get a home loan.

This is a very American idea. In Australia, you just need to be making good financial decisions, paying your bills on time and not going into unnecessary debt. Every time you pay rent, a mobile phone bill, car payment or electricity bill, you are contributing to a positive credit rating. If you default on your loans, this information can stay on your credit rating for five to seven years. To improve your credit score, you just need to clean up your act and consistently pay your bills on time and in the right amount.

Wondering what your credit rating is? In Australia, people should know what's on their credit report because sometimes in dramatic cases where identity fraud has happened, it's a good way of checking what debts you have and what's going on in your financial world. Mine talks about the business I have, the phone plan I'm on, and previous finance dealings. However, I want to flag that checking your score actually gets reported on your credit report, and this can sometimes have a negative impact. I recommend checking once every five years. You can do this by using online services like Equifax, illion Credit Check or Experian, which have options to let you check your credit score for free.

Bankruptcy

Sometimes people get in too deep. A business venture fails, something catastrophic happens to an investment, or a family loses their ability to earn an income. While bankruptcy is not something I like to recommend because of the negative impacts on a person's life, it's important to know that it's available when you well and truly cannot cover your debt repayments and this is significantly affecting your mental health.

Offered through the Australian Government, bankruptcy is a legal process that usually spans three years and is designed to release you from debt so you can make a fresh start. This is not something to be entered into lightly. I suggest speaking to a financial adviser before exploring this option.

So long, bad debt!

As much as I love goal setting, I love helping people get rid of debt even more. If I could magically Marie Kondo your bank account for you, you'd better believe I would. Until I can make that dream a reality, let's get you set up with the tools you need to do this for yourself!

● ●

IDENTIFY YOUR DEBT

What you'll need:

- While you may know these sums off the top of your head, it is handy to have access to bank statements so that you can work with exact figures.

Write down all of the debt you currently have in the table below, starting with the smallest balances.

Bad debt	Total:
....	
Okay debt	Total:
....	
Good debt	Total:
....	

● ●

To begin, we are going to focus on getting you out of bad debt. This is the type of debt that stays with you. If you die, your parents or a family member may inherit it. This is the beast we need to slay!

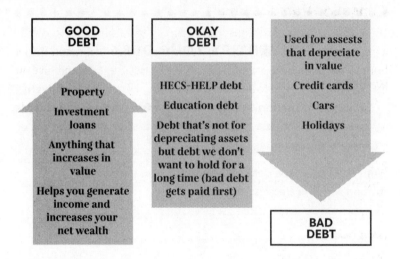

Knowing the difference between good, okay and bad debt

But first: how's your emergency fund looking?

Before you start making extra payments on your loan or credit cards, ensure that you have enough money in your emergency fund. Safety nets are incredibly important, and will prevent you from ever feeling desperate enough to take out a quick loan if an unexpected cost arises. That figure is going to look different for everyone depending on their income and size of their family.

When thinking about how much to have in an emergency fund it's really important to remember that this figure will be different for everyone. I've got clients who only have $1000 in their emergency fund, and I also have a client who has THREE YEARS' worth of her expenses built up. An emergency fund needs to cover emergency costs, so if you're single, having $1000 might be more than sufficient; however, if you're a young family you might want to aim for a number closer to $5000 to make sure you feel extra secure and you're covered for anything unexpected.

Consolidation options

If you have credit card debt that's eligible to be consolidated into a personal loan, or a personal loan that can be consolidated into a home loan, this can be a way to simplify your repayments and save on interest. But you need to be incredibly careful when considering this.

While you might think it makes sense to transfer three credit cards with 15 per cent interest each onto an interest-free credit card, have you checked to see how long the interest-free period is? Often it's only six months, and then the interest rate skyrockets to 21 per cent. Unless you have a plan to pay off your debt within that six-month period, consolidating may not be beneficial.

The same goes for transferring your debt onto your mortgage. While yes, your home loan interest rate is much lower, the time you've now added to paying off your pre-existing debt has been dramatically extended.

Speak to a financial adviser or bank about which debt consolidation options make sense for you.

● ●

MAKE A PLAN

The one thing that will give you the highest chance of getting out of debt is staying motivated. Depending on the amount you owe, this journey can feel arduous and soul-destroying. However, it can also be incredibly empowering. A lot of people lose steam because they set unrealistic timelines for paying off loans and credit cards. Patience is going to make this possible. Just like in Chapter 4, I want you to set goals and identify milestones along the way so that you can celebrate your accomplishments.

While you may want to focus on the card or loan with the biggest balance, I want you to order your bad debt from smallest to largest. Focus on the small amounts first, because these will give you quick(er) wins.

Example:

Credit card 1 balance: $745

Credit card 2 balance: $3800

Personal loan: $17,000

Look at your budget and identify any surplus money that can be allocated to extra debt repayments. Pay the minimum repayment on your personal loan and credit card 2. Throw the absolute maximum amount you can afford at an extra repayment on credit card 1.

● ●

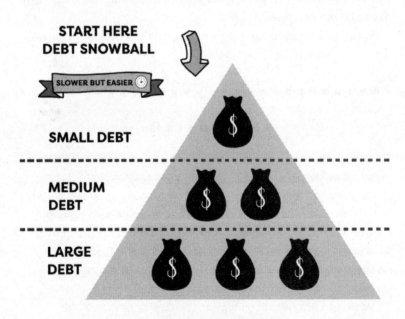

The debt snowball effect

● ● ● ● ● ●

JAMEY, 25 – UK

As the youngest in my family, I was the first to go to university and the first to leave the small seaside town I'm from to seek work in a big city. I've had to recreate my money story to survive and THRIVE. I grew up with two brothers and a single mum. Like so many other people, money didn't come easily, and I learnt from a young age that comparison is the thief of all joy.

I now work in the charity sector. When I decided I wanted to work in this industry, I left uni believing I simply would never be wealthy. There were no stories about women working for charities and being in well-paid leadership positions, no advice for those who want to be successful and do good. All I saw were stories about women from the corporate world earning lots of money, so I told myself I would have to compromise my personal goals if I wanted to achieve financial freedom and I quickly made peace with this. Naturally, as I thought I would never have lots of money, I made poor money decisions after leaving university and starting my first job. I used to say, 'I don't earn enough to save' or 'Well, I have hardly any money now, so I may as well spend what I've got.' Of course, these decisions kept me on trajectory for financial instability.

Then one day, my student loans company rang me and told me I had wrongly paid my loan in my final year of university and had to pay back £3000 [around AU$5500] immediately. It broke me. I felt defeated and buried my head in the sand. I ignored letters and calls from debt collectors and kept spending.

However, I soon realised this wasn't going to go away and I had to do something. I gained some advice and put together a plan suitable for my circumstances to start paying off the debt. This inspired me to take back control and in one year I paid off my student overdraft of nearly £2000 [AU$3500] as well. I realised the more energy I spent feeling financially 'poor', the longer it was going to stay that way.

Fast forward two years, I'm now invested in my personal growth and feel confident and passionate about challenging society's stereotypes of women who work in the charity sector being unable to create wealth. I recently secured a new senior role at a social enterprise, which will be my best-paying job to date! So, the moral of my story is never give up, never compare and ALWAYS look forward.

AMY, 25 – VIC

Well, I emotionally spent my money and got myself into $3500 of credit card debt at the age of 18. I paid it off, but then I didn't cancel the card so it crept up again and at the age of 24 I have $5500 in credit card debt and a personal loan of $13,000 for a car. Both the credit card and the personal loan have insane interest rates (21 per cent and 19 per cent respectively). Since January 2019 I have been focusing on paying off my credit card. I was doing really well, but then I hit some life curve balls and I spent my money on things that made me feel better in the short term. Long story short, here I am in February 2020 with $2900 of credit card debt, $7000 of personal loan debt, a $700 loan to my parents, and a $800 GO Mastercard balance.

Where I fell short is that I did not have a cash reserve when I was paying off my debt, so every time I had an issue or wanted to go out with friends, I had to use credit. I was doing it so aggressively that I did not leave money for me or my emotions.

I have had wins – I no longer use buy now, pay later programs, I paid off $1000 of Zip Pay debt and closed both accounts. I have addressed my emotional clothes spending (but have some work to do on my emotional snack buying).

If I had stuck to my original plan, I would be almost completely debt free, but life isn't that simple, and I let it get in the way of my goals. I have just had to readjust my priorities for health reasons, which is a tough pill to swallow, but I think this new direction and less pressured approach (more cash in bank account) will allow me to achieve my goals. This is a very truncated version of my story, but you get the idea. I have been in the shit for almost eight years and I really want to get myself out successfully this time. I feel guilty that I am earning pretty well but have no cash associated with me, and that my decisions have affected me poorly, but I know I will get there no matter how shocking the past eight years have been. The thought of having no debt-based emotional stress is euphoric to me.

VALENTINA, 25 – NZ

I grew up in a middle-class family with three brothers and my mum and dad.

Growing up, Dad had his own business and Mum was a stay-at-home parent raising four kids under five years of age (Wonder

Woman). Money was not a subject ever discussed openly with us as kids, but we did have our own bank accounts for our pocket money.

When we were in high school, Dad declared bankruptcy and Mum had to go back to work full time, which was a massive adjustment. The severity of my parents' situation was never discussed with us, so we couldn't understand what it all meant.

I started my first job when I was 14 and nine months. Every penny I earned was spent at the shops with friends, or on items I didn't need.

I was so fiercely independent that I thought I didn't need my parents' help managing money.

Fast forward to 18, I'd graduated high school and was determined to become a travelling Insta-blogger. This was an expensive lifestyle to have while working three retail jobs. So, without my parents knowing, I took out my first $5000 personal loan and went overseas for a month. I also got an 'emergency' credit card to fund the trip. When I got back I took out a car loan worth $15,000 and I pledged to myself to pay back the loan and credit card within a certain time. However, the travel bug had hit, and a month later I was off to Hawaii with an increased credit card limit.

By then my total debt was up to $24,000.

I knew this was out of control and so I consolidated my debts to make them 'manageable'.

Fast forward to April 2019. My partner and I finally discussed my financial situation (which I had kept a secret and my family still didn't know about). He was horrified and I was mortified.

He told his parents and they EXTREMELY GENEROUSLY offered to pay off my debt, a total of $22,000. I knew I had to pay this back ASAP. I set up a payment plan with them and paid back $1000 a fortnight for nine months. I paid everything back by December 2019. Through those nine months I came across the She's on the Money podcast, which kept me motivated, and I educated myself on budgeting and learnt tricks to manage my income. I am still learning, and now that I am debt free, I feel empowered and proud of what I can achieve when I put my mind to something!

● ● ● ● ● ●

TAKE NOTE

If you live fake rich now, you'll live real poor later.

....

People overestimate what they can do in a year and
underestimate what they can do over a long period of time.

....

I'm gonna sound like a broken record, but here it is again:
you can have everything you want, just not all at once.

....

Chapter 7

Save, sister, save!

'But Victoria, I'm a student. I will start saving when I graduate and earn $80,000.'

I hear a lot of excuses for why people can't save, but the notion that they don't earn a high enough wage is the one I want to debunk first. Saying that you'll start saving when you earn more money is like saying you'll start going to the gym once you're skinny and fit. When it comes to your financial future, you must start creating healthy habits with whatever salary you have. This is not an easy thing to do, but saving is the key to achieving your goals, and it's what will ultimately give you the choice to work or not later in life.

When people come to me for financial advice, they often speak to me like I'm the elusive Oracle of Saving. It's like they truly believe I hold a coveted secret to frugality, and if deemed worthy of my wisdom, they'll finally be able to stop running out of money three days before every pay cheque and bask in the glory of a stacked savings account. While I'm not the Oracle of Saving, I do have good news for you: if you simply spend less than you earn, you will, by default, save.

But let's be honest – it's not that simple, is it? Saving does not come without sacrifice, and it's the sacrificial element that people seem to struggle with. I said it in the last chapter, and I will say it again: *you can have everything you want, just not all at once.* Saving is essentially delaying gratification. As a loud and proud millennial, I will be the first to admit that our generation's need for instant gratification is affecting our ability to save. Hungry? There's a delivery app for that. Need a new race day outfit? Try buy now, pay later. Want to live closer to work and have a guest room? Look, there's an apartment we can't afford with our name on the lease! We're so conditioned to instant gratification that we're ignoring the needs of our future selves. I don't know about you, but 50-year-old Victoria is counting on me to make sure she is well fed, dressed and has a safe place to live. She'd be super pissed if I spent all her money on a side of halloumi at brunch every weekend.

In order to be a successful saver, you need to get your mindset in the right place. Making money work for you is a mental state, so before we dive into why, where and how to save, I want you to work on believing that no matter who you are, what you earn, or what you owe, there's a capacity to save. I want you to actively shift the dialogue in your mind from, 'I don't get to go to brunch with my friends anymore' to 'If I'm strategic about how often I go to brunch and what I order, I will have money to look after Future Me.'

Statistics from the Grattan Institute say that the median Australian salary is $57,918 a year before tax. On average, Aussie men are saving $507 a month, while for Aussie women that figure is $346. In a way, these numbers make sense because women still earn less than men, but that doesn't get us off the hook. When

it comes to saving, people are really good at not taking ownership of their shortcomings. They like to blame things like their
upbringing, salary, gender, partner or the lifestyle they think
they deserve. But the truth is, some women are finding it tough
because they haven't been tough enough on themselves. Our
attitude towards saving sometimes needs work – it's a harsh, but
true, reality of life.

One roadblock we seem to face when trying to save (or budget,
invest in the stock market, or buy a house) is learnt helplessness.
This is a state of mind that causes people to believe that there's
nothing they can do to escape their negative situation, when in
fact the opposite is true. Historically, that might have been the
case for you, but it doesn't have to be now. Learnt helplessness
is tied in with your money story because experiences from your
childhood can influence your current state of mind. However,
it can come from adult experiences as well. The more often you
experience failed attempts at saving, the more likely you are to
believe that you're simply not capable of it. In other words, you
start to believe that your inability to save money is a part of who
you are. But (and now this is the Oracle of Saving speaking) learnt
helplessness is something you can absolutely overcome.

But you need to accept that it might not always be smooth sailing.
Hiccups occur. Tragedies happen. Momentum can suddenly halt.
There's no shame if you feel like you're in a position where you
can't save money right now. Perhaps all of your money is going to
childcare and you cannot possibly spare a cent. Perhaps you are
currently out of work and are doing everything you can to cover
your bills. This is an okay place to be right now. However, right
now cannot last forever. Eventually, you will need to find a way to
spend less than you earn, or begin to earn more than you spend.
The most important thing you can do to ensure success is to never
give up. Every moment is a new opportunity to begin again.

Let's revisit what the goal of budgeting is: to create a surplus
of income that can be saved or invested for Future You! If you've

made it this far into the book, then you know what else I'm going to say. If you're having issues saving:

- Re-examine your values.
- Map out your money.
- Identify whether your purchases are in line with your values. If they're not – go back and adjust your budget so your dollars can do the jobs you want them to do.
- Identify your 'why'.

Aside from having an emergency fund and being able to pay bills on time, it's important to identify WHY else you're saving. Having clear financial goals with milestones is going to make 'sacrificing' so much easier.

Common reasons why people want to save money

- To invest in shares.
- For a holiday.
- To pay for a university degree.
- To furnish an apartment.
- To buy a car.
- To pay off debt.
- To start their own business.
- For a house deposit.
- For a wedding.
- For an investment property deposit.
- To feed their fashion addiction.
- To donate to charity.
- To have more available dollars to work for them.

● ●

SET YOUR SAVINGS GOAL(S)

What are you saving for?

....

How much money do you need for this?

....

When do you want to meet this goal by?

....

What surplus of cash can you allocate to this?

....

How will you feel when you've reached this goal?

....

● ●

Whatever your reason (or reasons) may be right now, it's important to note that they will probably change over time. While a trip overseas might be what's driving you today, the idea of taking extended maternity leave in the future might fuel your savings fire! (More on family planning in Chapter 16.) With every new savings goal, be sure to ask yourself those five questions so that you can track your progress and celebrate your wins. Just like in Chapter 4, be sure to set goals that are realistic. The last thing you want to do is set yourself up for failure by creating a goal that is unachievable. If setting micro goals is all that your current budget allows, start there.

Savings tips, tricks and hacks

It only takes $27.40 a day to spend $10,000 in a year.

Make your money less accessible

Depending on your relationship with money, you might be able to save more money if you have hurdles in place that prevent you from making impulse purchases. If that means banking with two different banks, do it. If it means cutting up a debit card, do it. If you need to take your digital wallet off your phone or watch, do it. If saving is an issue for you, go back to your budget and cash flow allocation to create a system that won't let you fail.

Hustle, and hustle hard

Just because your internet provider sends you a new modem and slides an extra charge onto your bill doesn't mean you have to accept it. Same goes for your insurance renewal. Do an annual review of all your services and insurance to make sure you're getting the best rate possible. This should be done for your banking products as well. Are you being treated as well as their new customers? Have they changed their ATM fee policy? Is a competitor offering a better rate? Call them and ask them to match or beat their price. Every year is a new year to check in and make sure you are in control of where your money goes.

Things to review:

- Mobile phone plan – Did you know that once you're done paying off your phone plan, it might make more sense for you to take advantage of a bring-your-own phone plan with the same carrier? Also, don't be afraid to consider off-brand carriers. Chances are they use the same towers as the two main providers.
- Internet package – Are you constantly going over your data allowance? Not using anywhere near it? Make sure you're on a plan that actually suits your needs.

- Energy provider – This includes both gas and electricity. Have you been comparing your bill with friends and family? Find out if yours is on par.
- Health insurance – How much is your premium? Are you even using the extras? Head to Chapter 14 to find out what other questions you should be asking.
- Mortgage – Do you have the optimal structure in place? Have you explored the idea of an offset account or redraw facility? We'll break down the benefits of both in Chapter 11.
- Streaming services – Do you really need Netflix AND Stan AND Disney+ AND Amazon Prime?

Reduce your living expenses

If you're renting, stay up to date with real estate prices and don't be afraid to renegotiate your lease. One of the questions I get asked a lot is: What percentage of my income should be going towards my rent? This definitely depends on where you live and the lifestyle costs of the city, state or town, but I never want to see someone spend more than 30 or 40 per cent of their income on rent. If you want to live in an apartment that costs you 70 per cent of your income, saving is going to be really hard for you. Ultimately, it comes down to your goals. Revisit what you want for Future You. Perhaps it makes more sense to move into an apartment or share house that's more in line with your goals now, and live in a nice house later.

If you're a home owner, this could be not running your air conditioning as much, turning off power points, setting your irrigation system on a timer to run during off-peak times and investing in things like solar panels or a bore. Really want to save some money? Consider getting a roommate or renting out your home as short-stay accommodation when you're out of town.

Think twice before adopting that insanely cute puppy

My friend's mum recently totalled that over 13 years, she spent more than $40,000 on her two dogs. And no, they weren't show dogs! This amount simply covered vaccines, desexing, check-ups, flea and tick meds, worming meds, collars, leads, food, surgeries and boarding fees. Adopting a pet is a huge financial commitment and one that needs to be budgeted for. You may even want to consider pet insurance.

Embrace and ask for a student discount

From movie tickets to public transport fares, chances are you can get a lower rate with a student concession card.

Look for government rebates and health care schemes

Depending on which state you live in, you may be eligible for government rebates and vouchers. For example, in New South Wales, each child over the age of five is eligible for a $100 Active Kids and Creative Kids voucher every year. The Victorian Government offers a rebate for home owners who install solar panels. Visit your state or territory's government website to find out what you and/or your family might be eligible for.

If you've been thinking about seeing a psychologist but are worried about the massive hourly rate, ask your doctor about a mental health care plan. You could be eligible for ten reduced-price sessions via Medicare.

Meal plan

Have you ever gone to the supermarket hungry? Did you walk out $300 later with bags full of items you were craving, but that don't really work together at all? Do you often end up buying lunch out every day because you didn't do any meal prep for the week? Meal planning is one of the quickest ways you can reduce your food spend (and cut down on your food waste). If you're notorious for getting food delivered, delete any and all apps that enable you! There are many great websites and books out there that offer suggestions for low-cost recipes and meal planning – do a bit of research and you will find something that suits your lifestyle.

Put time between you and your purchase

With instant gratification being the main cause of a person's inability to save, try putting 24 hours between you and your spending. Delaying your purchase for a month will put you in an even better position. This allows you to really think about what you want to buy, how it will affect your life and if it's something you're willing to wait for.

Ditch takeaway coffees

At $4.50 and rising, this is a quick and effective way to save money every day! As a latte lover myself, I would never ask you to quit caffeine, but it's worth investing in a way of making it at home. Consider using instant coffee, a French press, or getting an espresso machine! For a double whammy money win, perhaps check online to find a secondhand one!

Tackle your transport

Whether you drive a car, partake in ride-sharing, take the train or hop on the bus, think about what this is costing you on a weekly basis.

Car ownership

- Registration
- Insurance
- Fuel
- Services
- Licence renewal (Did you know if you don't get any demerit

points on your licence, you're eligible for a discounted licence renewal in some states?)

- Toll roads (Confession: I recently saw a bunch of charges on my card and thought they were fraudulent activity. Turns out it was just me using toll roads. As long as you're not burning more petrol by avoiding toll roads, it's worth leaving slightly earlier to avoid having to use them. This could save you quite a bit of money.)

Ride-sharing companies
Ask yourself:

- Does this make sense financially?
- Am I choosing the cheapest option they have available?

Train, tram and bus fares

- Check your city's schedule to see if there are off-peak ticket prices.

Create a capsule wardrobe
I'm a huge advocate of capsule wardrobes. As someone who works in an office nearly every day, it makes sense to have a closet full of neutral and timeless pieces that never go out of style. When considering purchasing something like a sweater or jacket, I always make sure it works with at least five items in my wardrobe. The whole cost-per-wear argument is a moot point if the piece doesn't work with anything!

Make outfit-repeating sexy
Do you have any idea how often I hear people justify the purchase of a new outfit because they already had photos taken in another dress (that they wore once)?! Why on earth would you buy a dress that you feel amazing in only to wear it once and then go

buy another one? Social media makes us think we need a new outfit for every weekend or that we can't wear the same dress to multiple events – but that's crazy! Let's be loud and proud about wearing the pieces in our wardrobes over and over again!

Sell your used clothing or organise a wardrobe swap with friends

While I want you to have a capsule wardrobe, I'm not saying you have to wear the same item of clothing for the rest of your life. Be thrifty – have a one in, one out policy. You can sell old pieces at markets, on eBay, in Facebook groups and even through Instagram pages. This has even become a side hustle for some people! The other fun low-cost activity I love is having a 'Friday night in' clothes swap with friends.

Change the way you socialise

I know firsthand how difficult it is to find things to do with friends that don't cost money. Whether we're brunching, meeting up for a movie, getting festival tickets or going out for dinner and drinks, every meaningful catch-up seems to result in spending money. Don't be afraid to have discussions about money with your friends. This doesn't mean you need to divulge how much you earn, spend and owe. Try using dialogue like, 'Brunch is pretty expensive and I'm saving for a holiday. Why don't we just grab a coffee and go for a walk?' I bet your friend will be relieved and grateful for the suggestion as it means extra savings in their pocket, too.

Pretend like the money didn't exist

I'm not going to lie – this tip came from my dad. From the time I earned my first pay cheque (when I was around 15), my dad told me to save a small percentage of every pay and pretend it never existed. As your salary increases, increase the amount. Obviously, this is easier earlier in life – before kids, mortgages and other expenses.

Understand your partner's money story

As you begin to live life with your partner, it's important to under-stand their money story, values and goals. It's scary to think about, but if they have a negative money story or bad spending habits, this could potentially become part of your money story. We'll chat more about relationships and money in Chapter 15, but make sure you factor in your partner's influence and attitude.

Go above and beyond

One of my favourite digital assets to share with my followers are the *She's on the Money* savings grids. Available in $1000, $5000 and $10,000 amounts, these are available to download from shesonthemoney.com.au and are intended to help you go above and beyond what you're already saving in your budget. Simply pick an amount from the grid each week, move it into your savings and check it off like on a bingo card. You might be able to find these sums from your personal spending account, from a small side hustle, from selling something online or at a yard sale, or from finally cashing in those coins that have been collecting under your bed!

$20	$7	$33	$51	$9	$17	$22
$3	$25	$19	$11	$34	$12	$40
$15	$21	$8	$0	$23	$5	$27
$22	$18	$31	$60	$21	$9	$19
$11	$17	$5	$29	$15	$19	$26
$8	$20	$4	$22	$18	$17	$20
$28	$6	$15	$35	$19	$22	$28
$19	$9	$6	= $1000!!!			

She's on the Money savings grid

If you want to create a structure for sustainable saving, start by tweaking small things instead of taking an all-or-nothing approach. Be reasonable and be aware. Before you go out to dinner or take a tour through a city or head off on a road trip think about what you're going to spend. The power has always been and still is in your hands. It's up to you to make good decisions.

Saving for a wedding?

A few years ago, ASIC revealed that in Australia, people spend an average of $35,000 on their wedding. *Bride To Be* magazine says that figure is $65,482, while the wedding company Wedded Wonderland says it's $53,168. While these amounts vary dramatically – probably because of where they collected their data from – it's safe to say that no matter how you look at it, weddings are expensive!

What blows my mind is how many couples are willing to take out loans and rack up credit card debt in order to pay for their wedding. I can't think of anything worse than starting married life in a whole heap of debt. Even if you didn't borrow money to cover the cost, it's important to remember what the true cost of a large wedding budget is.

Let's say you and your partner decide to spend $35,000 on a wedding. That's $35,000 you didn't invest in superannuation or shares, which means realistically the true cost of your wedding is closer to $200,000 over the long term.

I'm not saying that you shouldn't spend money on a wedding, but I am saying that you and your partner need to make sure the amount you budget is in line with your values, and that it doesn't negatively impact your capacity to achieve financial freedom.

I don't know if it's Instagram culture or simply the pressure millennials feel from their family to invite every Tom, Dick and Sally, but it's okay to find your own financially friendly way to say your vows. Also be aware that companies spend a lot of money to normalise the notion that weddings are expensive, and that they're just something we as happy and active members of society should be paying for. They've been selling us the idea of 'happily ever after' since we were three and playing with Bridal Barbie.

A lot of couples think that a big wedding is a healthy way to start a marriage, but – let me put my financial adviser hat on for a second – one in two marriages end in divorce. Why are we spending so much money on something that could be a bad investment? What do you think a client would say if I said, 'You can spend $65,000, but there's a one in two chance of you losing the whole amount. (Oh, and PS, it's money that you could have invested to achieve financial freedom down the track.)' Chances are they wouldn't be that confident. On the flip side, if they did come back and say, 'Look, Victoria, this is absolutely my number one goal in life. It 100 per cent aligns with my values and I can actively save for it!' then I would support them!

I'm going to leave you with one more interesting fact: according to a 2015 study in *The Economist*, those who have a wedding above their means are more likely to get divorced – citing 'money problems' as one of the key reasons for splitting. #notsurprised

● ● ● ● ● ●

MIA, 23 – QLD

I am 23, fiercely independent and financially savvy. I'm a country gal who had to move out at 18 to attend uni in the big smoke. From that day forward I have been independent and have always had a strong work ethic to support my lifestyle. At uni I received no support at all (from either my parents or the government), which meant I had to work my butt off in hospo jobs whenever I wasn't studying. I graduated at 21 and got myself a full-time job. The only debt I have is HECS-HELP, which is about $80,000. I have never had Afterpay, a credit card or a loan of any description. I earn a $65,000 salary a year and roughly $20,000 in commission. I am great at budgeting and I always pay my savings accounts first.

This is what my savings currently looks like:

- *Miscellaneous savings (for rent, bills, splurge, etc.)*
  ($1500 current balance)
- *House deposit ($60,000 current balance)*
- *Travel fund ($11,500 current balance)*
- *Investment fund ($7500 current balance)**
- *Emergency fund ($9,500 current balance)*

*My plan is to build this to $8,000 while I research and learn more, about investing and decide how I want to go about it (goal is to get this sorted in 2021). I've had to use way more than I would've liked!

I'm proud of how well I have been able to set myself up financially. All the money I have saved I have earnt myself, absolutely no handouts! I really want to use my story to help others understand that it is possible with a bit of work ethic and determination to set yourself up right.

GEORGIA, 25 – TAS

I'm 25 and newly committed . . . to saving. I've been working full time since July 2017 and when I started I would say I had close to zero in personal savings. For the last 12 months and counting my goal has been to save for a house. I currently earn $55,000 a year before tax and have no personal debt except for a $35,000 HELP loan. This means that I'm bringing in approximately $1660 a fortnight. I have no lines of credit, including personal loans, credit cards or buy now, pay later programs (purely because I know it would be a temptation to me if I had one). I've been quite an avid traveller over the years and that has meant that instead of saving for a long-term goal, I normally save some money and then spend it on a holiday from anywhere between four to 16 weeks.

Since starting to actively save about 18 months ago, I have managed to save $18,000 to date. I'm looking to buy a first home to the value of $350,000 or less, which means I essentially need another $20,000 to cover the deposit and costs. My main expenses are groceries and subscriptions. I'm lucky enough to have a work car which I can use for personal use, so I don't pay any vehicle-related expenses. I also just swapped over fully to my work phone and cancelled my phone plan (which I was notoriously bad at paying), which is saving me $100–300 a month (I used to cop A LOT of late charges . . . I know!). I will also start paying health insurance soon but am shopping around for a good deal. My worst money habit is spending too much on online shopping and nights out with the girls at dinner and drinks.

My best money habit is that I automatically deposit $300 from every pay into a progress saver account and have quite a systematic way of saving (three accounts that I move money across each pay cycle).

KAITLIN, 23 – WA

At 20 I relocated from a small country town in Western Australia to Perth to undertake university studies. I had about $10,000 in savings and moved into a share house. I worked 20 hours per week for the first six months, which gave me about $450 per week in wages. My savings were depleting faster than I was replacing them. I ended up sending my savings to my mum, because I was dipping into them so frequently just to survive. Back then I didn't really understand that I had to tweak my lifestyle – I was still shopping and eating out a lot.

In 2019 I opted not to house-share and my living expenses increased like crazy. I got into tax debt and credit card debt, totalling about $5000. I realised this cycle wasn't working, so I got a second job to double my income. At this point I was working full time and studying full time, and within a few months I became exhausted and stressed. I realised this wasn't sustainable, so I poured every dollar I could into paying down my debts.

Fast forward to now and I'm debt free, with about $3000 saved and growing – and I have dropped back to one job to retain a healthy work–life balance. I think the hardest thing for me was that my new friends at uni got to live at home, so any wage they made was 'fun' money. I spent a lot of money trying to keep up with them when it just wasn't possible in my situation. It took me two years, but I am now a budget and spreadsheet queen and I don't stress as much about how I'm going to make ends meet. Financial education saved me!

● ● ● ● ● ●

TAKE NOTE

Saving does not come without sacrifice.

....

Hustle, and hustle hard.

....

It only takes $27.40 a day to spend $10,000 in a year.

....

Chapter 8

What makes superannuation so super?

What's all the fuss about superannuation? Well, for starters, superannuation is going to help look after Future You. While it may feel too far off to be worth your full attention now, the sooner you start taking your superannuation seriously, the sooner you'll start creating some of the wealth you'll rely on when you retire. (Basically, you need to treat that girl right.)

'But Victoria, what even is superannuation?'

Superannuation, commonly referred to as super, is a tax structure designed to ensure that we as individuals save enough money throughout the course of our working life to generate an income after we stop working. Sounds a lot like an investment, doesn't it?

While it's not an asset class itself, the money in your superannuation fund does get invested on your behalf. The purpose of this is to grow your wealth over time so that when you get to the age of retirement, you have more money available than what you originally contributed. In a nutshell, it's the Australian Government's way of making us act like responsible adults.

Depending on your age and employment status, having a superannuation fund is usually compulsory. As of 2019, it applies to everyone over the age of 18 who earns more than $450 before tax as an employee in a calendar month. It also applies to everyone under the age of 18 who earns more than $450 before tax as an employee in a calendar month AND works more than 30 hours in a week. If you are employed by a business, you most likely qualify for super guarantee (SG) contributions, which means your employer is required by law to contribute 9.5 per cent of your salary into your super fund. Often, they will deduct this sum from your salary, but some employers pay this on top of your salary. If you are self-employed or a freelancer, you're not required to contribute to your own super – you probably should – but more on that soon.

Hot tip: When speaking with your employer about a job offer and salary package, be sure to ask if it's including or excluding superannuation. For example, they might say the job is $50,000 including super or $50,000 PLUS super. This is an incredibly important question to ask, and a key negotiating tool, because it could mean gaining or losing 9.5 per cent of your earnings.

After you start working or leave a job, it's also wise to check that your employer is/was actually paying into your super. If you feel that you have unpaid super, you can visit the Australian Taxation Office (ATO) website to find out:

● what amount you were/are entitled to
● advice on how to speak to your employer about unpaid super
● how to use the online portal to lodge a formal report with the ATO, who will then investigate if your employer is at fault.

While employers arrange contributions from your pay to go into your superannuation account, if you are self-employed, you will need to set this up yourself. Make sure that you take 9.5 per cent of the before-tax amount that you earned and deposit it. You have no idea how many times freelancers and side hustlers confess to me that they haven't been contributing to super. While this is not illegal, it is detrimental to their future selves. Here's why: the interest you're earning on the balance of your fund compounds over time, which means the sooner you can start contributing, the better.

For example, if you are 21 and start saving $500 a month until the age of retirement, you will have $240,000. If you had taken that same $500 a month and contributed it to your super or invested it instead, you could potentially have an investment portfolio of $1.2 million. It's really important that we consider where we're putting our money. If you're starting small and starting early, that interest will have the luxury of time to perform for you.

Now class, it's time to move on to Super 101

You should now have a general understanding of what super-annuation is and why it's important to treat it like the superstar that it is. Now let's break it down even further, so you have a firm understanding of the different types of funds, contributions, caps, taxes, insurances and fees. Broadly, there are two types of super funds – accumulation funds, and defined benefit funds.

Accumulation funds

In an accumulation fund, your money grows or 'accumulates' over time. The value of your super depends on the money that you and your employers put in (known as super contributions), and on the investment return generated by the fund.

Defined benefit funds

In a defined benefit fund, your retirement benefit is determined by a formula instead of being based on investment return. Most defined benefit funds are corporate or public sector funds. Many are now closed to new members.

Typically, your benefit is calculated using:

- the money put in by you and your employer
- your average salary over the last few years before you retire
- the number of years you worked for your employer.

Currently, there are roughly 500 different super funds in Australia to choose from. (Talk about keeping your options open!) There are also six specific types: corporate, retail, industry, self-managed, public sector and MySuper.

Corporate fund

Corporate funds are exclusive funds that an employer sets up with a financial institution on behalf of their employees. The incentive here is group discounts and associated added benefits.

Personal fund

Personal funds are standard retail funds that are available to everyone.

Industry fund

Industry funds are also available to everyone, but if you work in a particular industry or under a particular industry award, they can be particularly beneficial. These funds are not for profit, so all of the money they make is reinvested for the benefit of the members. For example, some employers might contribute up to 17 per cent versus 9.5 per cent. However, just because you're in that fund doesn't mean you're going to get the 17 per cent. Be sure to check the defined member benefit.

Self-managed super fund (SMSF)

The DIY version of super funds. In an SMSF, each individual is responsible for the investment strategy, operation and administration, and accounting of their compulsory contributions. An SMSF is an enormous amount of responsibility and shouldn't be entered into lightly. I personally feel that if you have less than $300,000 in your current super fund, the accounting fees on the flip side would not be worth it. Many people have fallen into the trap of using an SMSF because you can buy property in it. The issue here is that it's not diversified enough. If this is something you've been considering, consult a financial adviser because more often than not, it's not a good idea.

Public sector super fund

A public sector super fund is specifically designed for employees of federal and state government offices. While they offer lower fees, they tend to have less investment options. Also: from 1 July 2005, no new members are allowed to join. There may be exceptions if you are a preserved member or an invalidity pensioner.

Contributions

When it comes to actually depositing money into a super fund, there are two types of contributions: concessional and non-concessional.

Concessional

A concessional contribution is money that goes into your account from your pre-tax income, meaning you're not paying income tax on this money. These include compulsory employer contributions (usually 9.5 per cent), as well as any salary sacrificing or extra contributions that don't exceed $25,000. Concessional contributions can also include amounts paid by your employer from your before-tax income to cover administration fees or insurance premiums. Note: while you're not paying income tax, this money will be taxed at 15 per cent once it's in your super fund.

Non-concessional contribution

Non-concessional contributions come from your after-tax income. These include extra contributions your employer may make, voluntary contributions, sums deposited by a family member, retirement benefits you withdraw from your super fund and re-contribute to super, and contributions over your capital gains tax (CGT) cap amount. The annual cap for these types of contributions is currently $100,000. However, if you're under the age of 65, you may be able to use something called the 'bring forward rule' to make a larger non-concessional contribution in the present moment. However, you won't be able to make further contributions for the next two years if you go over your cap. For example, let's say you got a huge bonus or sold a company and wanted to make an extra $300,000 contribution to your super fund. With the bring forward rule, you can contribute $300,000 at one time, but then not make any extra non-concessional contributions for the next two years.

Warning: If you exceed the non-concessional contribution cap, that money will be taxed at 47 per cent – which, yes, that's a lot!

You also need to take into account that if your total super balance goes over $1.6 million, you can't make any further non-concessional contributions. A lot of people try to achieve this cap quickly to reap the compound interest benefits. Note: you can continue to receive concessional contributions from your employer.

Total super balance (as of 30 June 2017)	Non-concessional contributions cap for the year	Bring-forward period
Less than $1.4M	$300,000	Three years
$1.4M to less than $1.5M	$200,000	Two years
$1.5M to less than $1.6M	$100,000	No bring-forward period and the general non-concessional contributions cap applies (meaning the amount you deposit can't push your balance over $1.6M.)
$1.6M or more	Nil	N/A

Limitations on non-concessional super contributions
(Source: ATO)

Non-concessional contributions and tax

Good news: If you are making non-concessional contributions into your superannuation, you may be able to claim them as a tax deduction. This usually applies to any non-concessional contribution made from your after-tax money or if you contributed as a business owner or freelancer. Essentially, any contribution made directly from your bank account into your super account can be claimed.

Hot tip: BEFORE claiming, make sure you've filled out and given your fund a **notice of intent to claim or vary a deduction for personal contributions** form. (This is available from the ATO website.)

Do you already have a super fund?

When you started your first job, chances are your employer signed you up with their corporate fund or an industry fund. If you started a second job and didn't give them your super details, that employer might have signed you up with the fund of their choice. Having multiple funds is more common than you think, but it's not ideal – the various fees add up fast. On average, the total fees on a super fund over a lifetime are $14,000. If you have five funds, they could end up costing you $70,000 in fees!

According to the ASIC Money Smart superannuation calculator

1 SUPER ACCOUNT

$100 annually in fees

$250 annually in insurance

$14,000 IN FEES*

AFTER 40 YEARS

5 SUPER ACCOUNTS

$100 annually in fees

$250 annually in insurance

$70,000 IN FEES*

AFTER 40 YEARS

* IN TODAY'S DOLLARS

Consolidating your super accounts

IDENTIFYING YOUR CURRENT SUPER(S)

If you're not sure which super fund you're with, how many you have or what they stand for, take a moment to find out by contacting the ATO. This can be done through your myGov account.

List your current super fund(s) and balances:

....

....

....

....

Are there any insurances held within these super funds? If yes, what are they?

....

Who is the nominated beneficiary?

....

● ●

Hot tip: Under superannuation law, you are limited to who you can nominate as your beneficiary. A beneficiary is the person or persons who receive the payout from your super fund when you die. Currently, you must choose either someone who is dependent on you or the 'estate'. For these purposes, a dependent includes your spouse or de facto partner, a child, stepchild or adopted child (if they're under 18, they will receive the money tax-free), anyone who is financially dependent on you at the time of your death and anyone you have an interdependent relationship with at the time of your death. If you wish to have your parents or a sibling be the beneficiary, you will need to nominate the estate and then update your will to instruct that once the super money is received by the estate, it is paid to those specified beneficiaries.

How to choose the right super fund for you

When you pick your super fund, you actually pick a risk profile. A risk profile is essentially how your money is going to be invested. The default for most funds is a balanced or conservative profile. This means a large percentage of your contributions will stay sitting in cash. While this is low risk, that money is not exposed to the share market and will not get the returns you might expect. Whether you already have a super fund (or funds) or are still deciding on which fund to go with, it's definitely worth checking what risk profile you're invested in and if it's aligned with your values. Each super fund website makes it easy to log in and check which profile is ticked and what other profiles they offer. It's super easy to change – but of course, talk to a financial adviser first, because if they put you in the right fund from the beginning, you will be far better off.

Things to consider when choosing a super fund:

- What type of risk profiles do they offer?
- Are their investments in line with your values? If you're someone who doesn't want to see your money invested in certain commodities, it's important to ask what they're investing in.
- What are their ACTUAL fees compared to other funds? When visiting a fund's website, don't take their own fund comparisons as gospel. Companies put fees in different ways. Some mask their management fees with performance fees, while others charge the bulk in admin.
- How are they currently performing? This information will be presented as a percentage.
- How do their fees compare to their performance? If you're mostly worried about the fees you're paying in your super you're on the wrong path, because performance is just as important. You could have a no/low-fee super fund with

terrible performance versus a higher-fee fund with brilliant performance. Often, you might be better off paying the fees. Sometimes if you pay peanuts, you get monkeys.

● What type of insurance do they offer? We are going to dive much deeper into insurance in Chapter 14, but many super funds can provide life insurance and income protection. Known for being slightly more lenient than independent insurers when it comes to medical exams, this is something to consider when deciding to leave a super fund if you already have coverage.

Now that you know what fund(s) you have and what types of questions you should be asking, take a moment to consider consolidating your super or finding a completely new fund. Whichever one you choose to go with will make the changeover process as painless as possible, because let's be honest – they want your business!

Warning: I will say this a million times – especially in Chapter 14 – but make sure you're not letting go of a valuable life insurance policy that came with your super fund. These can be difficult to get as you get older, depending on your health and age, so it might be worth holding on to a fund that can provide coverage you would struggle to get elsewhere.

Your superannuation values will change throughout your life as you do. Just like your insurances and banking products, your superannuation needs may evolve as you change jobs, get a partner, have children or start a business. In short: don't be afraid to switch. A 16-year-old with a retail fund with low-level fees is perfect. As you get older, you may look at a more complex strategy with more options for diversification of investments. When you're close to $1 million in super, I'd say sit down with your financial adviser and decide what you should do.

How much should you have in your super by the time you retire?

The Association of Superannuation Funds of Australia (ASFA) suggests that the balance of a combined couple's fund should be $640,000 at the time of retirement and $540,000 for singles. I don't necessarily agree with this, and here's why: if you have $640,000 invested at a 5 per cent return, that's only $32,000 a year. To me, that doesn't feel like enough for two people to live on in a year. Perhaps if you owned your home outright, had other investments or extremely low lifestyle costs it would suffice, but I'm confident a large portion of the population would agree that this is not enough. Most of the couples I speak to say they'd like to have $100,000 coming in a year. If that's the case for you, your goal would need to be $2 million.

Currently, you can't access your super funds until you reach your preservation age, which is either 55 or 60 depending on the year you were born. We will discuss this further in Chapter 18, but with the age of retirement inevitably stretching out, I think it's important to think about your values, and whether putting all your eggs in a not-so-easy-to-access basket is right for you. While I 100 per cent think it's a fantastic savings plan and tax-savings initiative and something you should prioritise at 9.5 per cent, sacrificing large sums of your salary or making non-concessional contributions may not be the best choice. Personally, I don't want my money locked away for that period of time. I don't want to wait until I'm 60 to have financial freedom. I'd rather invest those savings elsewhere, knowing that I could access them tomorrow or in ten years.

Taking money out of super early

While this is something I don't usually recommend because it takes away from Future You, you can access your super early under very limited circumstances. These can include:

- having a medical condition that prevents you from working or means you need to scale back on hours
- needing to access funds to modify your home or car due to an injury or illness
- suffering severe financial hardship (for example, COVID-19 has caused an enormous amount of financial hardship for those across Australia)
- needing to make a mortgage payment in an effort to not risk losing your home
- needing to use the funds for IVF treatment.

When considering accessing your superannuation early, it's best to speak to a financial adviser about the pros and cons based on your personal situation. More information can be found through the ATO and Services Australia.

● ● ● ● ● ●

SOFIA, 24 – ACT

I used money from my super to pay for IVF. My private health insurance covered my hospital fees, but I paid an extra $8000 using my super and $2000 cash I'd saved. In order to access my super, my surgeon/gynaecologist and my doctor both had to sign paperwork, which then I uploaded through the ATO.

The ATO contacted my super fund, and within ten days the money had been released into my bank account. I also took money out of my super for gastric sleeve surgery, which cost $10,000. I was taxed 22 per cent on the money I took out.

Drawing on my super was a hard decision, and so stressful, because you're losing a lot of money in the long run, but at the end of the day, I'd rather live my life now. I'll be dead if I continue down the obesity track (I have a hormone condition for obesity), and I don't feel like my life will be worth living if I cannot have children, so by using this money I'm investing in my future.

Being 24, I'm still very young. I have time to build my super back up. Overall, it was super simple and quick to do. But it wasn't an easy decision.

● ● ● ● ● ●

TAKE NOTE

Performance is more important than fees; don't be afraid to pay for a bigger return.

....

Check which insurance policies come with your super fund before consolidating and closing an account.

....

Just because you're self-employed doesn't mean you don't need to make contributions!

....

Chapter 9

Investing 101

As confusing as words like 'dividends', 'indexation' and 'compound' may seem, the mechanics of wealth creation are actually quite simple. You have to spend less than you earn and invest consistently over a long period of time. While you may have images of Gordon Gekko screaming into a phone to 'sell, sell, sell!', the reality is that investing can come in many different shapes and sizes and isn't just for men with slicked back hair. It's something everyone should be doing, especially women, because it gives you the power to achieve and maintain your financial independence by making your money work for you.

As of 2019, 6.48 million Australians currently own investments listed on the share market. Of that figure, only 31 per cent are women. While there is a whole slew of reasons for this imbalance, a key factor is that, typically, women are more conservative than men. Men are often willing to go into a risky investment, while women usually feel the need to be across the entire situation before dipping a toe in. This chapter is designed to get you comfortable with cannonballing into the stock market, because it's more important than ever for women to achieve financial freedom. For starters, women live longer than men, which means we'll need more money. Women also tend to have less money in superannuation than men. There are two reasons for this. One: we still often get paid less than men, and two: we may take time off when having children.

Consistency, time and diversification

When you strip back all the financial jargon, an investment is essentially something that you purchase with money and that you expect to produce an income or profit for you. Ideally, you'll achieve both an income and growth in an investment, because this is what's going to take care of both Current You and Future You. Before we get deep into the four types of investments, also commonly referred to as asset classes, I want to highlight three very important things: consistency, time and diversification.

In order to set yourself up for the best possible result, you need to be in a position where you can consistently invest money for more than seven years. I'm talking 20, 30 or 40 years. I know that sounds like forrrrreeeeeevvvvverrrrrr (any *The Sandlot* fans here?!), but it's time and consistency that's going to make your money grow, and it's diversification that will minimise risk. On average, money doubles every ten years. Australia has had an 8.9 per cent return over the last 30 years, so if we look at that, your money will potentially double in seven to ten years. Couple that with consistently reinvesting your dividends (the money earned from the investment) and your interest is on track to compound. Unlike simple interest, which is calculated daily on the balance of a loan or deposit, compound interest is calculated on the balance PLUS the interest that's been accumulating. In a nutshell, the longer you leave the interest earned on top of the principal of the deposit or investment, the more exponential the growth becomes.

Since 1990 (30 years)

Asset classes	Value at 29 Feb 2020	Return since 1 Jan 1990
Australian shares	$131,270	8.9% pa
International shares	$78,689	7.1% pa
US shares	$194,147	10.3% pa
Australian property	$135,192	9.0% pa
Australian bonds	$98,911	7.9% pa
Intl. shares (A$ hedged)	$103,664	8.1% pa
Cash	$47,768	5.3% pa

Since 1970 (50 years)

Asset classes	Value at 29 Feb 2020	Return since 1 Jan 1970
Australian shares	$1,016,849	9.7% pa
International shares	$1,100,260	9.8% pa
US shares	$2,450,874	11.6% pa
Australian bonds	$508,327	8.1% pa
Cash	$430,376	7.8% pa

Return on investments over time
(Source: Vanguard. See p. 303 for disclosure.)

For example:

Let's say you purchase $10,000 worth of shares with a return of 9 per cent pa. The interest earned after one year would be $900. This is called a dividend. If you withdraw that money, then the next year you will also only earn $900. But let's say you consistently reinvest those dividends. Suddenly, your investment changes because you're recalculating the interest on a balance that's accumulating interest.

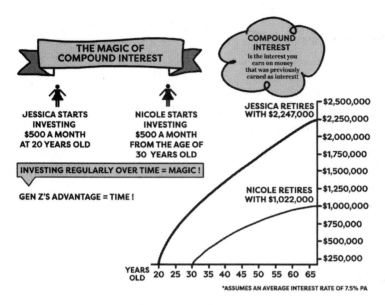

THE MAGIC OF COMPOUND INTEREST

COMPOUND INTEREST is the interest you earn on money that was previously earned as interest!

JESSICA STARTS INVESTING $500 A MONTH AT 20 YEARS OLD

NICOLE STARTS INVESTING $500 A MONTH FROM THE AGE OF 30 YEARS OLD

JESSICA RETIRES WITH $2,247,000

NICOLE RETIRES WITH $1,022,000

INVESTING REGULARLY OVER TIME = MAGIC!

GEN Z'S ADVANTAGE = TIME!

$2,500,000
$2,250,000
$2,000,000
$1,750,000
$1,500,000
$1,250,000
$1,000,000
$750,000
$500,000
$250,000

YEARS OLD   20 25 30 35 40 45 50 55 60 65

*ASSUMES AN AVERAGE INTEREST RATE OF 7.5% PA

Compound interest

9 per cent compound interest projection – initial investment: $10,000

Year	Investment	Interest	Balance
2020	$10,000.00	$900.01	$10,900.00
2021	$0.00	$981.02	$11,881.00
2022	$0.00	$1,069.30	$12,950.29
2023	$0.00	$1,165.55	$14,115.82
2024	$0.00	$1,270.42	$15,386.24
2025	$0.00	$1,384.77	$16,771.00
2026	$0.00	$1,509.39	$18,280.39
2027	$0.00	$1,645.22	$19,925.63
2028	$0.00	$1,793.31	$21,718.93
2029	$0.00	$1,954.71	$23,673.64
Totals	$10,000.00	$13,673.64	$23,673.64

Compound interest projection at 9 per cent

If you had a simple interest investment or constantly took out the dividend, aka interest earned, this is what your growth would look like over ten years:

**9 per cent simple interest projection –
initial investment: $10,000**

Year	Investment	Interest	Balance
2020	$10,000.00	$900.00	$10,900.00
2021	$0.00	$900.00	$11,800.00
2022	$0.00	$900.00	$12,700.00
2023	$0.00	$900.00	$13,600.00
2024	$0.00	$900.00	$14,500.00
2025	$0.00	$900.00	$15,500.00
2026	$0.00	$900.00	$16,300.00
2027	$0.00	$900.00	$17,200.00
2028	$0.00	$900.00	$18,100.00
2029	$0.00	$900.00	$19,000.00
Totals	**$10,000.00**	**$9,000.00**	**$19,000.00**

Simple interest projection at 9 per cent

Time is also going to help mitigate risk. Unfortunately, risk is in the nature of investment. You can win and you can lose. If you're only thinking in the short term, it's easy to get caught up in the volatility of the market and pull out before you give it time to recover, which makes you much more prone to loss. Sorry for the cliché, but investing is a marathon, not a sprint.

The other thing that is going to mitigate risk is diversification. We've all heard the saying that you shouldn't put all your eggs in one basket and this is especially true of investing. When choosing which companies, property markets and banks to invest in, you need to find ways to lower your overall risk, because regardless of what the economy does, you want to ensure that you still have assets that will benefit and neutralise any potential losses.

There are many different ways to approach investing, and it's important to find a strategy that you feel comfortable with. To help with this, I've included an investment personality quiz at the end of the share market section. But first, let's have a look at investing for beginners.

When considering where to invest, you essentially have four options. These are referred to as asset classes. The four asset classes are:

- cash
- fixed interest
- share market
- property.

These asset classes are often described as either a defensive or growth asset.

What's a defensive asset?

A defensive asset is a lower-risk, lower-reward asset like cash and fixed interest investments. They usually aim to provide income rather than capital growth and offer more stable returns in the short term. People who are about to retire or don't have a long period of time to invest usually invest in defensive assets.

What's a growth asset?

A growth asset is a return-seeking asset that aims for capital growth. These assets often have the potential for higher returns over a long period of time, but come with more risk and volatility. Examples include both domestic and international shares.

Cash – low risk and low return

Yes, all the money sitting in your bank account is technically an investment because it is earning interest from the bank. You or someone you know has probably talked about seeking out a high-interest savings account as a safe place to put your money. This is a contentious point, because if you break down what the actual rate of return on a 'high-interest bank account' is – the interest rate, minus the rate of inflation and income tax – it's actually quite low and possibly even counterproductive.

People often forget that the interest earned on their bank account balances counts as income, and therefore tax will need to be paid on it. They also forget that inflation (which is an increase of prices due to the decrease of monetary value over time) factors into what your money is worth.

Let's say you have $100 in a savings account that pays a 1 per cent interest rate. After a year, you will have $101 in your account. But if the rate of inflation is running at 2 per cent, you would need $102 to have the same buying power that you started with. You've gained a dollar, but you've lost buying power. Any time your savings don't grow at the same rate as inflation, you will effectively lose money.

While this is an incredibly low-risk place for your money, you need to ask yourself if this option is actually going to create wealth for you because, in reality, it might cost you money.

Fixed interest – low risk and low return

Fixed interest investments are things like Australian Government bonds, corporate bonds and term deposits. These are essentially loans that you provide to a bank. In return you receive interest, as well as the promise of the full amount loaned being returned upon maturity.

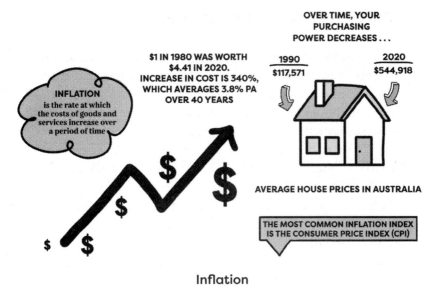

OVER TIME, YOUR
PURCHASING
POWER DECREASES . . .

$1 IN 1980 WAS WORTH
$4.41 IN 2020.
INCREASE IN COST IS 340%,
WHICH AVERAGES 3.8% PA
OVER 40 YEARS

1990
$117,571

2020
$544,918

INFLATION
is the rate at which
the costs of goods and
services increase over
a period of time

AVERAGE HOUSE PRICES IN AUSTRALIA

THE MOST COMMON INFLATION INDEX
IS THE CONSUMER PRICE INDEX (CPI)

Inflation

When looking for a bond or term deposit, you'll see them advertised with a 'yield'. A yield is the term for earnings that have been generated and realised on an investment over a specific period of time. This figure is always expressed as a percentage. The Australian Securities Exchange (ASX) long-term investing report averaged a 6.2 per cent yield pa on Australian bonds and term deposits over the last ten years.

The benefits of bonds and term deposits is that they maintain consistency and are a great way to diversify your portfolio. In Australia, we have AAA-rated bonds that have a history of always returning. While there is technically a risk, there has never been one default. They're also protected by the Australian Government's financial claims scheme, which guarantees that the government will pay you up to $250,000 for deposits in the unlikely event that your bank, credit union or building society fails.

How to invest in bonds

Investing in bonds basically means you're lending money to a company or government, and receive interest in return. Investing in bonds through the Australian Securities Exchange (ASX) can be done through a broker or online trading platform. With a minimum investment of usually around just $100, this can be a great way to get started.

- Bond ETFs – ETF stands for exchange traded fund. By purchasing bonds in this manner, you're essentially investing in a collection of bonds. Caution: some hybrid bond ETFs could contain other asset classes that are riskier.
- Exchange Traded Bond Unit (XTB) – Unlike bond ETFs, which track a collection of bonds, XTBs represent a single ASX-listed corporate bond. These offer more predictable income amounts and a fixed maturity date before you invest. The minimum investment here is $500.
- Exchange Traded Treasury Bonds (ETB) and Exchange Traded Treasury Indexed Bonds (ETIB) – These funds track government bonds, and both provide fixed-interest returns for the life of the security. However, the value of an ETIB is adjusted with the consumer price index, which means the interest rate can become variable.

How to invest in a term deposit

If you'd like to set up a term deposit, there are a few things you need to consider:

- What amount of money would you like to deposit? On average, banks have a minimum deposit amount of $1000.
- Would you like it to be short term or long term? Short term is defined as one to 12 months, while long term is 12 months to ten years. The longer you leave the money, the higher the rate of return you'll receive.

- Do you have enough money in your emergency fund? When considering investing, you need to think carefully about putting your money in places where it's difficult to retrieve. There are fees for withdrawing funds early from term deposits, and some banks may require at least 31 days' notice.
- Would you like to receive interest while the money is deposited, or in a lump sum at the end? Depending on your values and financial situation, some people use term deposits to help reach savings goals, while others may use them later in life as a safe investment during retirement. While this isn't true for all banks, term deposits that pay monthly interest usually have lower return rates.

Share market – high risk, high return

The share market is how people buy and sell shares that represent ownership of a company. This is often referred to as the stock market. If you think of a company as a pie with a million pieces, a share is a piece of the pie and you as the owner are entitled to a share of the income that the company produces and the growth that the business achieves. Investing in shares can yield high returns, but also comes with high risk. Depending on your goals and values, there are two ways to approach investing in the share market: trading and long-term investing.

Trading

This type of investing is not something the majority of the population is comfortable with, nor good at. When trading stocks, you're essentially speculating when the market will go up and down. If you're not equipped with a team of analysts, the odds are not in your favour.

Long-term investing

When it comes to creating an investment portfolio that will give you financial freedom – the choice of whether to work once you reach the age of retirement – the best way to achieve this goal is to stay in the share market long enough that you've created an asset that is providing you with a substantial passive income.

How to invest in the share market

The investment personality quiz at the end of this section will help you determine your risk profile. Essentially, this is going to show how aggressive you're willing to be (or not be) with your investments. It will help you discover how long you're willing to part with large sums of money for, and how you'd react to volatility in the market. While I don't want you to jump ahead to the quiz, I do want you to keep in mind that there are different ways to structure your portfolio to suit your goals and values.

Types of investment funds

There are a number of ways to begin investing in the share market.

Exchange Traded Fund (ETF)

Similar to a bond ETF, this is a managed investment product that comes in many different shapes and forms. Essentially, it's a big bucket that you (and many other people) put money into to be managed by a funds investor (not to be confused with a stockbroker). When you invest in an ETF, you're putting your money in that fund manager's hands and trusting them to make good investment decisions, so you don't get a choice of what that fund buys or sells.

Pros:

- Gives you exposure to international markets with less risk.
- Provides quarterly performance statements.

Cons:

- The shares are not in your name.
- There is not a lot of transparency. The funds manager can sell a share at any point without consulting you, which means you have less control.
- Depending on the amount of money you have invested and how it's performing, the cost of exiting the fund could be prohibitive because of capital gains tax. Basically, you have less flexibility when it comes to diversifying your portfolio.

Index Exchange Traded Fund

The difference between an ETF and an index ETF is that the fund manager of an index ETF is literally just trying to achieve an average return.

Pros:

- Involves less risk.
- Provides performance statements.

Cons:

- Yields benchmark returns.

When considering an ETF, it's important to do your research. Check the returns, make sure you understand the fees and determine how you'd feel being in the fund given its performance. If you're unsure of how the fund is being managed, speak to a financial adviser for further clarification.

Separately managed account (SMA)

Just as easy to buy as an ETF or index ETF, an SMA allows you to own your bucket yourself. This gives you the ability to customise it and have a certificate for every share that you own. If you're conscious of choosing investments that align with your values, SMAs will enable you to actively screen for certain product areas so you can avoid them, such as coal or tobacco. SMAs are a great option for many as they often carry less risk, give you direct ownership of the underlying asset (unlike an ETF) and are more flexible when it comes to moving your shares around from platform to platform. It's worth noting that SMAs generally have higher fees than ETFs because they take more energy to manage from the fund manager's side of things – but more often than not, that directly translates to a higher return.

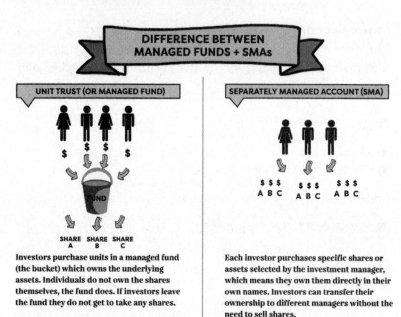

DIFFERENCE BETWEEN MANAGED FUNDS + SMAs

UNIT TRUST (OR MANAGED FUND)

Investors purchase units in a managed fund (the bucket) which owns the underlying assets. Individuals do not own the shares themselves, the fund does. If investors leave the fund they do not get to take any shares.

SEPARATELY MANAGED ACCOUNT (SMA)

Each investor purchases specific shares or assets selected by the investment manager, which means they own them directly in their own names. Investors can transfer their ownership to different managers without the need to sell shares.

Unit trust v. separately managed account

Hedge fund

Hedge funds use more than one investment strategy and often invest in private businesses. Hedge funds (which are less cute than hedgehogs) are considered an alternative investment using 'pooled funds' that employ different strategies to earn a return for their investors. More often than not, these funds are more aggressively managed than most other assets, and it's important to note that hedge funds are often only accessible to accredited investors as they're subjected to less regulation than other investments like ETFs, managed funds and SMAs. In the media, hedge funds are often portrayed as a 'sexier' option. They are often more expensive, have high levels of risk and have low levels of transparency for their investors.

When and where to invest

A lot of people ask me how much money they should have saved up to invest. This is going to vary from person to person, but if you're going the traditional route, I feel that the bare minimum is $500. Once you factor in the brokerage fees on the share, it's just not cost effective to invest any less than that. For example, let's say you buy a $1 share, but the brokerage fee is $12. That share has cost you $13. It would have to perform to be more than $13 for it to be worth it. Try looking at bulk-buying shares, because a $12 fee on $1000 worth of shares feels quite reasonable. In terms of frequency, some people buy shares once a year while others may purchase shares five times a month. Depending on your own personal financial situation, you can factor an investment fund into your budget and then work out a sustainable frequency.

When it comes to the actual act of purchasing shares, there are a lot of different ways to go about it. The most common way to purchase is online through banks or companies like Vanguard, BlackRock, CommSec and IG.

I get questions on a regular basis about what the difference between a financial adviser and a stockbroker is, so let's quickly clarify what they are and when you might need one. There are many similarities between the two, so I completely understand the confusion! It's not impossible for someone to be both a financial adviser and a stockbroker, or for professionals in the field to switch from one career to another. A financial adviser exists to give you very specific tailored financial advice based on your personal situation. They'll usually charge a fee and may manage your whole portfolio, including your superannuation, insurances and all forms of investments. A stockbroker's role is to buy and sell shares and make trades on behalf of a client – and while they might have some great tips or advice when it comes to specific shares, they certainly won't be taking your holistic situation into consideration.

The ASX website has a fantastic share-market game that lets you play with fake money. It's essentially like Monopoly, and means you get to understand how it all works before actually putting your money on the line. Think of it as an investment in your financial education, which will pay off over the long term. That said, if you want to be managing investments yourself, this by no means teaches you what is a 'good' portfolio or helps you to research the stocks. It simply allows you to play with performance and see how the share market works.

What is micro-investing?

Micro-investing is when you intermittently or consistently invest small amounts of money. Examples include rounding up on your transactions or committing to small weekly investments. Micro-investing is often one of the first steps that members of the *She's on the Money* community take to dip their toes in the investing waters. Micro-investing can be a great option for beginner investors and, well, anyone who wants to do something with their money but lacks the resources to start investing in a more traditional way. We've seen the *She's on the Money* community really embrace micro-investing, as it suits those who don't have a lot of capital to start with or invest over the long term, but ensures you're getting exposure to the share market and making use of dollar-cost averaging. Micro-investing works in a number of different ways – micro-investing platforms generally utilise

ETFs and managed funds, but some build their own investment products from scratch.

There are a lot of great companies out there like Spaceship Voyager, CommSec Pocket and Raiz.

Reinvesting

If you decide to invest in a product like an ETF fund, they will provide you with performance statements. Depending on whether they've made a profit, they may either reinvest themselves or share a portion with you as a cash amount. (This is called a dividend, remember?) Depending on your investment goals (make an income or facilitate high growth), in order for your interest to compound, you'll want to reinvest those dividends!

'But Victoria, my parents lost heaps of money in the GFC! I don't want to invest!'

One of the major excuses I hear for why people don't want to invest in shares is that someone knows someone who lost everything in the global financial crisis (GFC). I am confident that if you looked deeper, you'd find it's because they cut their losses and pulled out. In order to be successful in the share market, you must be willing to ride the waves and not panic at the volatility in the market. I have many clients who watched what was once $1000 become $100 in 2008. You know what they did? They bought even more stocks when prices plummeted, which has put them in a better financial position today. If we look at the Australian share market from 1985 (including the GFC), the average rate of return is 10 per cent.

How to track your investment performance

You have probably seen the ASX share market ticker. This is a constantly moving feed showing a company's symbol, a green up arrow or a red down arrow, and a corresponding percentage.

These fluctuations in price represent the value of a share increasing or decreasing. If you look at past performance reviews of an individual company, you may not see much movement over, say, a six-month period. However, when you look at three or five years, you'll be able to see more fluctuations. These are indicative of how the share is performing. If you notice a huge dip in price, it's worth looking into the company further. Is there any issue with their leadership? Was the market disrupted by a new company?

What's the deal with bitcoin?

Bitcoin is a cryptocurrency that is inherently flawed because it relies on perceived value, and it can be easily stolen. What makes something valuable is the scarcity around it. While people want you to think bitcoin is finite, it's not. Compare it to gold – there's only so much in the ground and in circulation. With a digital currency like bitcoin, you can literally just make more and more of it. This is one I'd be wary of!

Cryptocurrency is a form of digital currency, based on blockchain technology. A blockchain is essentially like a chequebook that's shared across an enormous number of computers around the world. It's so named because all transactions are recorded in blocks, which are then added to a chain of all previous transactions. It's a distributed ledger that records all of the transactions made. Unlike regular types of currency like dollars or yen, cryptocurrencies are 'decentralised', which means they are unregulated by a financial authority and exist independently from governments or central banks.

This decentralisation has a few perks, like cryptocurrency being a global currency with the same value everywhere in the world; however, the flip side of that is that cryptocurrency is extremely risky . . .

You're not wrong to think cryptocurrency is taking off – Tesla has even bought it. But be aware of its volatility. Cryptocurrency has so many unexpected changes in market sentiment that can lead to very large increases and decreases in price. It's not uncommon for the price of cryptocurrencies to quickly drop by thousands of dollars in a day, which makes it a very risky asset. Of course, investing in anything carries a risk. However, you should always avoid unnecessary risk – especially when it comes to the money you've worked so incredibly hard to save. Don't take unnecessary risks; Future You is far too important for that.

As of December 2020 the total value of all cryptocurrencies was in excess of US$645.7 billion. Of this, the total value of all bitcoins came in at around US$421.7 billion, so bitcoin is the key player here. However, it's not the only type of cryptocurrency. There are more than 6,700 different cryptocurrencies out there according to CoinMarketCap.com.

Property – low risk, moderate returns

Property investments are when you purchase a piece of land, unit(s) or home that you can rent out for an income or sell for a profit. Depending on the market, this type of investment usually increases in value while providing an income.

There's an enormous amount of pressure for millennials to purchase homes. This comes from our parents and grandparents, who were living the Great Australian Dream of working hard, buying a home, paying it off and then saving for retirement. Unfortunately, that's not going to be the case for many people because their income isn't ever going to support what they'd like to purchase. Over the last 30 to 40 years, people have made a lot of money from the way property has increased in value. But our generation won't be able to achieve this type of growth because our income isn't going up at the same rate as house prices. For example, a home used to cost three or four times our parents' yearly salary. Today, it's more like ten.

Personally, I do not consider your owner-occupier property an investment (unless you are renting out various rooms while living there). As I mentioned in Chapter 6, even though your primary place of residence may be increasing in value, it's constantly costing you money and can't be claimed at tax time. You're also going to need to sell it to reap the benefits at retirement, and I don't think you should have to sell your family home for financial security.

Let's talk about what I do deem worthy property investment strategies.

Rentvesting

Rentvesting allows you to buy a property in a location that has good capital growth, a good rental yield and the ability to create wealth, while enabling you to live in an area that gives you the lifestyle that you want. For example, you might pay to rent an apartment in Manly, while collecting rent from an apartment you own in Sutherland.

Rentvesting changes a property that you purchase from an owner-occupier asset to an investment asset, which means you can now claim costs associated with it at tax time. While there are a whole heap of different rules and regulations around this, it can be extremely beneficial for multiple reasons.

Benefits of rentvesting:

- It allows you to pay off a mortgage faster and gain access to equity.
- It provides tax benefits.
- It provides lifestyle benefits.

Negative, neutral and positive gearing

Depending on the rent being returned and the amount of your mortgage repayments, a property investment can be negatively, neutrally or positively geared.

Negatively geared

This means that the income coming from rent is less than the amount of your mortgage repayment and maintenance costs.

Neutrally geared

This means that the income from rent is roughly the same as the amount of your mortgage repayment and maintenance costs.

Positively geared

This means that the income from rent is more than the amount of your mortgage repayment and maintenance costs.

Myth: You want your investment to be negatively geared for tax purposes (because this means you'll be able to claim property expenses on tax, thus getting cash back).

This is a myth I can't wait to debunk! The ideal situation is for your investment property to be positively geared. This is because it means you're making money. In regard to tax, for every 30 cents you pay, you're still making 70 cents! Plus, this means you're able to pay off the debt faster, which will save you interest.

When your property is negatively geared, you may be saving 30 cents in tax, but the property itself is still costing you 70 cents.

Off the plan

In this edition of Victoria Rants About ... I'm going to let fly about buying apartments off the plan.

Just like clear bra straps, buying an apartment off the plan is never a good idea! They're simply too risky – they're rarely finished to the standard you'd expect, and there's also an over-supply. They're usually priced with huge builder commissions and offer little room for growth (like the opportunity to add an additional room or renovate an existing bathroom). The value you pay up-front is not reflected in the purchase price.

Here's a thought: try looking for something older or smaller. Maybe a unit with six to ten apartments, versus 150. Chances are, something older will offer larger room sizes, and/or the potential for you to update. At the end of the day, you need to look at WHY you're purchasing. Are you going to live in it for the rest of your life? Okay then, maybe. But if it's an entry into the market and a future investment – think again.

Flipping houses

With every other TV show portraying a cute couple in lightly distressed jeans and plaid shirts flipping houses, I think it's important that we touch on this type of investment. While flipping houses can be both profitable and gratifying, it's crucial that you do a cost-benefit analysis and factor in any potential unforeseen costs. I have many friends who have embarked on renovations or subdivisions only to run into a soil quality issue, delays with council, or issues with tradies not showing up, (because they always give preference to builders, who give them way more consistent work than you can). If you're living in the property while doing the construction, you must also factor in your mental health and safety! Basically, if you don't have the technical skills or access to *affordable* people with those skills, as well as access to affordable materials, this type of investment can simply be too risky.

Shares versus real estate

Real estate pays rental income. Shares pay dividends. And over time they both grow your wealth – so how do you pick? Some things to consider when deciding between shares versus real estate:

- You need a greater sum of cash to begin investing in real estate than in shares.
- Investing in real estate also requires the ability to secure finance (in the form of a mortgage).
- If you own your home, a large portion of your net worth is already exposed to real estate, so you might want to diversify into shares.
- If you don't have the stomach for ups and downs in your portfolio, the slow pace of real estate might be a better fit for you. Real estate is very illiquid (it takes a long time to buy and sell, and thus prices move slowly), whereas shares are very liquid (you can buy and sell quickly with just a few taps on your iPhone). Hence stock prices are much more volatile. This can be a mixed blessing: it's easy to buy and sell impulsively, but it also means prices can reach irrational levels, creating opportunities for the discerning investor.
- If you're busy or you travel a lot, hold off on real estate until you're ready to settle down a bit. Generating positive cash flow from rental properties doesn't just happen magically – you have to find GOOD property managers and vendors, and create systems, and all this takes work to set up.
- On the other hand, shares require zero work on your part, since the company you've invested in is run by the CEO.
- If you're not a numbers person, real estate financials are MUCH simpler to understand than company financials. There's rent, vacancy, expenses, improvements, mortgage – not much else to it! Researching shares involves a lot of reading and

parsing financial statements. I'm an introvert, I'm analytical, and I'm a big nerd, so personally I love this kind of thing, but it might not be for you.

● It's possible to achieve financial security with either, so it really comes down to what you are more comfortable with. Most importantly, whichever path you choose, you have to get STARTED!

● ●

QUIZ - WHAT TYPE OF INVESTOR ARE YOU?

I want you to think about investing like you do your favourite pair of jeans – it's all about getting the right fit. As mentioned previously, you won't have the same investment risk profile as everyone else, so it's important to find out what you're comfortable with before forming your investment strategy.

Below is a graph showing the risk–return trade-off. After completing the quiz, use this graph to help determine where you would like to be investing.

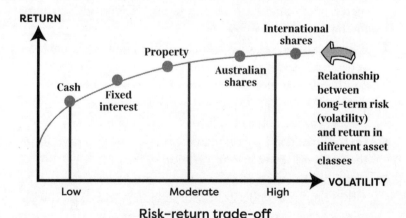

Risk–return trade-off

Please tick the appropriate options below:

1. How long would you expect to invest before you would need access to funds?

☐ A – Very short-term (the next six months)
☐ B – Short-term (the next 12–18 months)
☐ C – Short to medium-term (the next 18 months to three years)
☐ D – Medium-term (the next three–five years)
☐ E – Medium to long-term (the next five–ten years)
☐ F – Long-term (anything longer than ten years)

2. What type of investments have your previous (or current) investments been?

☐ A – I only have investment experience in basic banking products and term deposits (e.g. never invested in bonds, shares or property).
☐ B – I have had minimal exposure to basic banking products, as well as bonds and property.
☐ C – I have had some investment experience and some exposure to property and equities in the past.
☐ D – I have had some experience in all major asset classes, including Australian shares as well as some minimal experience with international shares.
☐ E – I have had a lot of experience in all asset classes, with particular focus on Australian and international shares.
☐ F – I have had a great deal of experience in all asset classes, including the overseas share markets and 'exotic' investment products such as artwork or luxury cars.

3. Which of the following best describes your investment objectives?

☐ A – To generate an income without reinvesting dividends.
☐ B – To generate an income and a small amount of growth.
☐ C – To generate an equal amount of income and growth.

☐ D – To generate a small amount of income and to have substantial growth.

☐ E – To generate growth with little to no income.

☐ F – To generate growth with no income. (This means you're constantly reinvesting your dividends to take full advantage of compound interest so you're left with the biggest possible income at retirement.)

4. If your investment strategy was for the long term (minimum seven years) how would you react if in six months' time your portfolio decreased in value by 20 per cent?

☐ A – I would not accept any declines in the value of my investment portfolio.

☐ B – I would transfer my investments to more stable investment markets.

☐ C – I would be somewhat concerned, but can accept very short-term volatility in the markets. However, if markets did continue to fall in the short term, I would discuss my investments with my adviser and ask for guidance.

☐ D – Primarily, I would adopt a 'wait and see' approach to see if the investments improve before making a decision.

☐ E – I know the risks and volatility levels are higher and so I would leave the original long-term strategy in place to let it run its course.

☐ F – As I expect long-term growth, I would intend on investing more money, given the current market conditions, to take advantage of the lower average investment prices.

5. In consideration of your investment objectives and the level of volatility you could tolerate, hypothetically, which of the below annual return scenarios (with a ten-year compound return) would you feel most comfortable with over the long term?

A	Year 1	Year 2	Year 3	Year 5	Year 7	Year 10
	2.4% pa	4.1% pa	3.5% pa	3.0% pa	2.5% pa	2.9% pa
B	Year 1	Year 2	Year 3	Year 5	Year 7	Year 10
	4.0% pa	4.5% pa	3.8% pa	4.0% pa	5.0% pa	4.1% pa
C	Year 1	Year 2	Year 3	Year 5	Year 7	Year 10
	5.0% pa	4.8% pa	5.2% pa	5.9% pa	6.1% pa	5.4% pa
D	Year 1	Year 2	Year 3	Year 5	Year 7	Year 10
	6.9% pa	2.0% pa	9.9% pa	5.2% pa	-2.9% pa	6.8% pa
E	Year 1	Year 2	Year 3	Year 5	Year 7	Year 10
	-2.8% pa	4.5% pa	11.5% pa	8.2% pa	-5.5% pa	7.9% pa
F	Year 1	Year 2	Year 3	Year 5	Year 7	Year 10
	9.4% pa	-3.7% pa	14.8% pa	-13.0% pa	10.5% pa	9.1% pa

Compound return options over a decade

Results: Add up your score by writing the number of times you ticked each letter.

A	B	C	D	E	F

If you mostly selected . . .

A – You're the newbie

Type A investors are novices when it comes to investing. With little to no knowledge of what each asset class has to offer, you associate the term 'risk' with high danger. When you make a financial decision, you may tend to focus on possible losses instead of possible long-term gains. Since you only seek basic returns and would like a low level of risk without growth, you might consider investing in fixed interest products for one to three years.

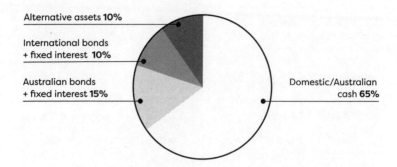

B – You're the conservative

Type B investors only have a basic understanding of investments. Your main goal is protecting your capital, which is why you seek moderate returns and do not wish to take on more than a low level of risk. You might consider an investment time frame of three to five years and structure your portfolio to have 70 per cent defensive assets and 30 per cent growth assets.

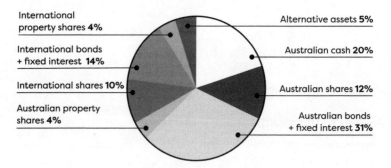

C – You're the moderate conservative

Type C investors have a general understanding of investments, but wish to have a broader understanding so they can explore more options. You are mostly focused on possible losses, but still optimistic of gains. Aware that some volatility is to be expected, you may consider an investment time frame of three to five years and structure your portfolio to have 50 per cent defensive assets and 50 per cent growth assets.

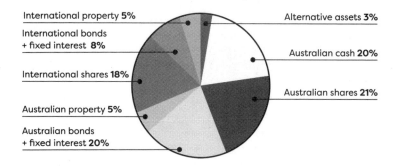

D – You're the moderate grower

Type D investors are all about diverse portfolios that protect them from inflation and tax. With a reasonable understanding of investments, you are more likely to focus on possible gains, but are still mindful of risk. You may consider an investment time frame of five to seven years and structure your portfolio to have 30 per cent defensive assets and 70 per cent growth assets.

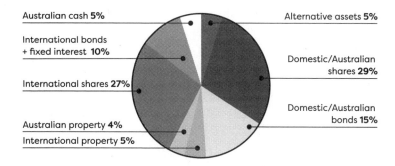

E – You're the growth investor

Type E investors are grow-getters! (See what I did there? Har har!) With a firm understanding of investments, you associate the word 'risk' with opportunity. Because your goal is to see your capital grow, you may consider an investment time frame of seven years or more and structure your portfolio to have 15 per cent defensive assets and 85 per cent growth assets.

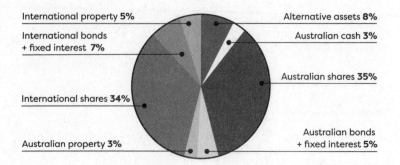

F – You're a high-growth investor!

Type F investors are in it for the long run. You are aggressive when it comes to reinvesting dividends because your aim is to grow a portfolio that delivers a substantial income at the time of retirement. Because you tend to focus on possible gains and equate risk with thrill, you may consider an investment time frame of seven or more years and structure your portfolio to have 100 per cent growth assets.

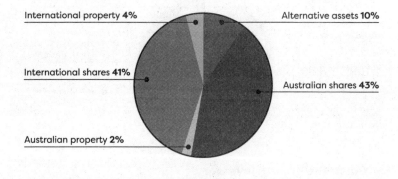

It's down to you

Deciding where and how you'd like to invest your money ultimately comes down to your values and personal financial situation. I always, always, always recommend speaking to a financial adviser because they're going to give you a customised strategy that puts you in the best position to achieve your personal goals. You also need to make sure that you have the correct lifestyle mindset to invest. This means maintaining good cash flow and saving habits so that you are able to contribute to your investment plan on a consistent basis.

● ● ● ● ● ●

KATRINA, 34 – VIC

I grew up raised by a single mum with minimal (and most often zero) child support or assistance. I have seen the financial struggles of living with an overdraft, living from pay to pay, lay-buys, buy now, pay later schemes and the juggling act this caused. There was never any conversation around money – it wasn't discussed. We rented. There was no mention of shares or investing. I started living a similar way, with history repeating itself (the money management part, not the single-mum part). I got a $30,000 car loan at 18, saving only for specific items, and then did 'nothing' in the middle with my finances.

Ten years ago something clicked when the company I worked for floated on the ASX and offered staff the opportunity to buy into shares. I had no idea what shares were but I participated anyway. It was at this point I realised that if I wanted my finances to improve I would need to do something different to the way I was raised. I chose to learn about finance and what on earth these shares I had just purchased were (and where were they?). I have spent time reading books, listening to podcasts and openly talking about finance to whoever I could to learn new information, which is a massive mindset change from my upbringing. I have changed my internal dialogue from 'I am broke' (I was always broke) to 'I have enough' (and now I always have enough). When I slip back to the previous mindset, my finances always slip off track.

I have gone from not knowing what shares are to having a small portfolio (I chose to sell down recently to enable me to take three months off and care for my mum in her final few months), sorting out my baseline by putting relevant insurances in place, and on my way to saving a house deposit and, for my future self, I'm opening a Vanguard ETF with a view to investing regularly as a non-negotiable. I've gone from it being a stretch to have $2000 in the bank to having $30,000 in the bank (allocated for specific purposes which require cash). All this despite coming from a family where money was never discussed.

EMMA, 28 – NSW

So, I'm 28 and working full time as a media consultant. I currently earn $56,000 a year (including a $10,000 car allowance). At 18, I received a $70,000 inheritance, as my dad died when I was five. I bought my first and second car with that money, a few horses (haha) and used $40,000 as a deposit on my property (which I feel is what that inheritance was meant for). I worked part time to keep myself and my horses afloat while doing uni. I did one degree in design and started a second in psychology before deciding I was sick of being broke and went back to full-time work at 26. I owe $590,000 on my property (currently worth $900,000, paid $650,000), have never had a credit card, never had Afterpay. I have only ever had two loans: one on my horse float (paid out early) and currently one on a car I got sucked into buying six months ago.

I do have a shares portfolio of about $56,000 – but that has been built up from a $10,000 initial investment by my grandma when I was born. She did this for all us grandkids, and I've kept mine reinvesting and will only be selling some shares to help wipe that car debt quicker (lesson learnt!). But for the most part, I pretend they're not there and I will continue to build that portfolio.

My biggest weakness is the horses – I have let my numbers get out of hand over the years and had to make some tough decisions. However, they have also been a tangible asset and I do usually make a profit when I sell them.

I have $10,000 in savings in the bank, and $12,000 joint savings with my partner. I think we're doing okay, and he has gone from zero savings to $10,000 in the past year, having taken on board some of the financial tips and tricks I've learnt!

My inheritance has been tough – a lot of people are under the impression my grandparents bought my property for me, when it was actually my dad's money used to buy it. I have worked hard and continue to pay it off and not squander the head start I got.

Although I obviously come from a financially cluey family, I really strive hard to earn things on my own and make my own way. I don't rely on handouts and I don't want to spend the money because 'it wasn't mine anyway'. I want to grow my wealth and retire comfortably with my own funds. Retiring at 40 like my mum would be the dream!

● ● ● ● ● ●

TAKE NOTE

Investing gives you the power to achieve and maintain your financial independence by making your money work for you.

....

The longer you leave the interest earned on top of the principal of the deposit or investment, the more exponential the growth becomes. #compoundinterest

....

If you're not comfortable with the share market and have a good amount of capital available, you can always explore investing in property!

....

Chapter 10

Home loans 101

It doesn't matter if you're a first-time homebuyer, seasoned investor or someone who chats confidently about offset accounts at dinner parties, this chapter is for you!

Buying a home or investment property can be incredibly exciting, and one of the proudest moments in your life. However, it can also be insanely stressful – especially the part about borrowing money. When it comes to saving for a deposit, choosing a mortgage broker and understanding loan structures, it's important to make sure you comprehend the true cost of purchasing your property, as well as what your lending options are. In an effort to help you either start off on the right foot or inspire you to explore the idea of refinancing, I've broken down the home-buying process.

One thing I'd like to remind you is that, unlike the experience of past generations, and home buying as depicted on episodes of *Home and Away*, it is becoming harder to enter the housing market due to the tighter lending practices that resulted from the 2017–2019 banking royal commission. While this frustrates many people, I actually think it's a great thing because it's putting the homebuyer first. By being held to higher standards, banks aren't allowed to give you access to a debt you can't service.

Basically, I want you to be realistic and patient. It might take someone ten years to save a deposit and get themselves in a position where they can purchase a property. That's not something you need to feel bad about – you're not 'behind'. It's also not something you have to do if you're not comfortable with it.

Timeline

When buying a house or block of land, there are two initial hurdles:

● Saving a deposit
● Determining your ability to service a loan

While your ability to save for a deposit is going to depend on your income, lifestyle expenses and saving habits, determining your capacity to service a loan is a little bit trickier. In an effort to protect themselves should the market go haywire, instead of vetting your ability to service a loan at 3.5 per cent, banks are going to look at your income, lifestyle expenses, rent repayments, whether you have a HECS or HELP debt, any credit card debt, personal loans, and your number of dependants and then ensure that you can still make your repayments even if interest rates climb to 9 or even 10 per cent.

Hot tip: Banks aren't going to just look at your credit card debt. They're going to look at the limits as well. Even if you have a $10,000 line of credit and the balance is zero, that's still $10,000 less you'll be able to borrow because you could potentially get into debt there.

It's important to have a good track record of saving and not spending all of your surplus cash. A bank will look at your transactions and say, 'It's all well and fine that you have the deposit, but you're spending all of your discretionary income.' You also need to be aware that if you're within a probationary period at a job, lenders most likely won't lend to you because you could have your employment terminated without any reason or real notice.

Self-employed? Listen up!

You may have heard that it's harder to get a loan if you're self-employed. This is especially true for those just starting out. Lenders will want to see two years' worth of earnings and conservative saving patterns. This is because self-employed people usually have a variable income. One month you could earn $1000 and the next month it could be $10,000. But lenders don't know what the future looks like, so they need as much evidence as possible that you'll be able to service the loan with a consistent income and positive trajectory.

Evidence you can provide lenders for reassurance includes:

- copies of your past two tax returns
- copies of your business schedule or workflow
- evidence of potential growth of your business
- evidence of a solid savings pattern.

If you're good at keeping records and your business is going well, this shouldn't be an issue.

If you've been asking yourself when you should start saving for a house deposit and practising the type of money habits you know a bank is going to want to see, the answer is – years ago! It's never too early to start establishing a solid credit rating and working towards your deposit goal PLUS costs. Realistically, you'll want to be able to show six to 12 months of bank statements when you apply for your loan.

Six–twelve months out

- Start living like you already have the loan.
- Clean up your accounts by reducing spending on unnecessary

items. Your accounts need to be in tip-top shape when sent to
the lender.
- Pay off and close as many debts as possible. These include
  credit cards, personal loans, car loans, and buy now, pay later
  programs.
- Find a mortgage broker you like working with. (We'll get to tips
  for how to choose one in a little bit!)

Four months out
Get pre-approval
A pre-approval, which is only valid for 90 days, is essentially an
approval in principle. The lender is saying that based on your
current situation and the information provided, they are happy
to approve a loan of X amount of dollars subject to you finding a
home. It's important to know this so you know what your budget
is when purchasing a house or block of land. Note: it can take your
broker up to a month to secure approval on a loan.

When speaking to your mortgage broker about pre-approval,
suggest being pre-approved for the maximum you would like to
borrow – you'd hate to miss out on a property for the sake of a
few thousand dollars. However, it's important for everyone to set
their limits and stick to them.

Issues with pre-approvals
Pre-approvals are not watertight. While for the most part you're
good to go, there are a few reasons why a lender may not formally
approve the loan after the purchase:

- they don't like the property for some reason
- they don't like the property postcode
- your circumstances have changed adversely.

When making an offer, particularly if you're purchasing a property
privately, I always suggest making offers subject to:

- finance
- pest and building inspection.

This gives you an 'exit' if the lender doesn't accept the property, or if the building turns out to be a lemon.

Warning: If you're buying at an auction, you need to be aware that the purchase is unconditional. That means that if you're the final bidder once the hammer hits the paper – you're the new owner. For that reason, it's critical you do the pest and building inspections PRIOR to the auction, and that your broker has checked the postcode of the property and mitigated any potential risk of your finance falling through.

What happens if finance falls through?

If for some reason the initial lender chosen doesn't accept the security of the property you're trying to purchase, you can go to another lender. This is yet another reason why it's important to see a mortgage broker.

Deposit

Notice how I said deposit goal PLUS costs earlier?

Most banks and lenders recommend that you should save a deposit of 20 per cent of the purchase price, aka LVR (loan to value ratio). This is because if they're only lending you 80 per cent of the asset cost versus, say, 95 per cent, their risk is slightly decreased. Once you start needing to borrow 85, 90 or even 95 per cent, they will want you to pay LMI (lender's mortgage insurance) and possibly even have someone go guarantor. We'll talk more about LMI below, but it is one of the ways banks protect themselves in case you become incapable of making your loan repayments. A guarantor is someone who would be fully responsible for the loan if you were to default. Depending on what state you live in and whether you're a first-time home-buyer, you may also have to pay stamp duty on top of the cost of the property. You also might need to factor in lender application fees, lender legal fees, conveyance fees, moving costs and the cost of furnishing the home.

Let's say you're a first-time homebuyer and you're looking for a house in Victoria for $500,000. Twenty per cent of the purchase price is: $100,000.

Additional costs could be:

- Conveyancing fees: $1200
- Moving costs: upwards of $1500
- Furnishings: $5000 (to get you started)
- LMI: Nil (because you have a 20 per cent deposit)
- Victorian stamp duty: because the property is under $600,000 and you're a first-time homebuyer, you don't have to pay stamp duty this time! Lucky you! (BUT if you did, it would be around $21,970.)

This means you would need to have saved at least $107,700 for a deposit.

Now let's say you are purchasing your second property (as an investment) in Victoria and only have a 15 per cent deposit. The price of the house is $500,000. Fifteen per cent of the purchase price is: $75,000.

Additional costs could be:

- Conveyancing fees: $1200
- LMI: $12,000
- Victorian stamp duty: $21,970
- Moving costs: nil – it's an investment
- Furnishings: nil – it's an investment

This means you would need to have saved at least $110,170 to cover the deposit required by the bank as well as the additional costs.

While these are just two of many different scenarios, it's a good way to see just how many more costs can be associated with buying a property. I also want you to remember that the bigger the deposit you have, the less you need to borrow, which means the less interest you're paying! I know it might sound all well and fine to just borrow the stamp duty or LMI, but now you're paying interest on that as well as the price of your home.

Stamp duty

Stamp duty is the tax that the Australian Government charges on the sale of property. Depending on the price of the property you're purchasing, whether you're eligible for an exemption and what state you live in, the amount of stamp duty will vary. What a joyful tax to have to pay! I hear you.

When saving for a deposit, be sure to speak to a mortgage broker to see if you will need to pay stamp duty, and how much. As previously mentioned, ideally it's best to pay this amount in cash – adding it to your mortgage will mean that you're paying more interest.

Stamp duty is considered by many economists as an archaic tax from the 19th century when governments didn't have comprehensive knowledge or control of their states. At that time, a range of documents, such as property transfers, required offical stamping to be legally binding, and this offered governments a way of ensuring taxes were paid. These days, however, Australia has a comprehensive property registry, making administering land tax easier. Despite this, and despite the fact that council rates are also charged to property owners, stamp duty still exists as the principle way state governments raise revenue from real estate. To find out what stamp duty you might be liable for on a property purchase in your state, access one of many stamp duty calculators online by googling 'stamp duty payable' and your state or territory.

LMI and guarantor loans

If you need to borrow more than 80 per cent of a property's value, you will be required to pay lender's mortgage insurance (LMI) unless you have someone go guarantor for you. Often people are able to ask their parents to guarantee the loan for them. This is an incredibly generous thing for someone to be able to do, but be mindful that this now means the following.

- That person is responsible for your loan if for some reason you become unable to service it. It's worth making sure you have insurance in place to prevent such a burden. (We'll talk more about this in Chapter 14.)
- That person is re-mortgaging their house to secure your purchase.
- That person may not be able to move forward with a loan of their own, even if yours is being paid on time.

First-time homebuyer grants and schemes

First Home Loan Deposit Scheme

The First Home Loan Deposit Scheme (FHLDS) was introduced in January 2020. The scheme allows the Australian Government to guarantee select low-deposit loans for a year. This means eligible low- and middle-income earners who have a deposit of at least 5 per cent of a property's value will not have to pay LMI or have someone go guarantor.

First Home Owner Grant (FHOG)

You have probably heard of the First Home Owner Grant (FHOG), which was introduced in 2000 to offset the effect of the GST on home ownership and ultimately encourage people to buy homes. Available Australia-wide, it varies by state and territory, but is essentially a one-off grant to an individual who has never previously purchased a property. In some instances, this grant has now been replaced by updated schemes as seen below.

ACT – Home Buyer Concession Scheme (HBCS)

The Australian Capital Territory phased out their FHOG in July 2019 and replaced it with the Home Buyer Concession Scheme, which allows people to purchase any type of house or block of land without having to pay stamp duty. To qualify, the purchaser must be over the age of 18, must not have purchased a property within the past two years and must pass an income test. Purchasers must also live in the home continuously for 12 months.

NSW – First Home Owner Grant and First Home Buyers Assistance Scheme (FHBAS)

New South Wales currently offers a First Home Owner Grant of $10,000 for the purchase of a new (or substantially renovated) home, as well as a First Home Buyers Assistance Scheme that provides an exemption or concession on stamp duty.

There are a few limitations:

- The new home must be valued at under $600,000.
- If purchasing land to build as well, the total value of the property must be under $750,000.
- To qualify for a stamp duty exemption, the new home must be valued at $650,000 or less. Concession rates are provided for new homes between $650,001 and $800,000.
- To qualify for a stamp duty exemption on a vacant block of land, it must be valued at $350,000 or less. Concession rates are provided for blocks between $350,001 and $450,000.

NT – First Home Owner Grant, Household Goods Grant Scheme, Home Renovation Grant and BuildBonus

As of 7 May 2019, the Northern Territory offers a FHOG of $10,000 to first-time homebuyers who are purchasing or building a new home. They also offer:

● First Home Owner Discount – This is a stamp duty discount of up to $23,928.60 on an established home.
● Household Goods Grant Scheme – This allows first-time homebuyers to apply for a grant of up to $2000 to buy household goods.
● Home Renovation Grant – This allows first-time homebuyers to apply for a grant of $10,000 to renovate their home.

Regardless of your past ownership status, they also have a BuildBonus you can apply for. This is a $20,000 grant that can be put towards the purchase of a new home. (This is limited to the first 600 applicants.)

QLD – First Home Owners' Grant

Queensland currently offers a FHOG of $15,000 for first-time homebuyers buying or building a new (or substantially renovated) home valued at $750,000 or less. They also have stamp duty concessions available if the home is valued at less than $550,000 or vacant land is less than $400,000.

SA – First Home Owner Grant

South Australia currently has a FHOG of up to $15,000 for first-time homebuyers purchasing or building a new home valued up to $575,000. Unfortunately, there are no stamp duty exemptions specific to first-time homebuyers, but you may be eligible for the state's off-the-plan stamp duty concession if you purchase a new (or substantially renovated) apartment valued at $500,000 or less.

TAS – First Home Owner Grant

Tasmania currently offers a FHOG of $20,000 to first-time homebuyers buying a new home, building a new home or buying an off-the-plan apartment. First-time homebuyers purchasing an established home can receive a 50 per cent discount on stamp duty if the property is valued at $400,000 or less. Note: From 1 July 2022, the FHOG amount will revert to $10,000.

VIC – First Home Owner Grant

In Victoria, there is currently a FHOG for first-time homebuyers buying or building a new home in metropolitan Melbourne valued at $750,000 or less. If purchasing in regional Victoria, the grant is $20,000 on properties valued at $750,000 or less. There is also a stamp duty exemption for first-time homebuyers buying a new or established home valued at $600,000 or less. For properties between $601,000 and $750,000, there are concession rates.

WA – First Home Owner Grant (FHOG) and First Home Owner Rate of Duty

In Western Australia, there is currently a FHOG of $10,000 for first-time homebuyers buying or building a new home. Depending on where in the state you live, you may be limited to a purchase price of either $750,000 or $1 million. There is also a first home owner rate of duty that provides an exemption or concession when purchasing a home valued at less than $530,000 or vacant land valued at $400,000 or less.

While you can visit state and territory websites to find out more about eligibility and how to apply, your bank, mortgage broker, buyer's advocate or solicitor should be in the know and able to guide you through this process!

Choosing a mortgage broker

As soon as you're thinking about buying a home, speak to a mortgage broker. Mortgage brokers are licensed professionals who research and find you home loan options based on your income and your ability to service the debt. I said this in Chapter 5, but I will say it again – you don't need to stay loyal to your bank, especially when it comes to choosing a home loan. Shop around!

Mortgage brokers are not one size fits all – it's important to find one who leaves you feeling educated and empowered. It's also a wise idea to make sure they're not only working for a select few banks. At the end of the day, you want the broker who can get you access to the best interest rates and loan structures available nationwide.

Tips and things to look out for when choosing and working with a mortgage broker:

- While yes, some mortgage brokers charge a fee, the majority are paid a commission by the bank. It's important that we break down the stigma around them receiving a commission, because realistically, this won't be coming from your pocket.
- That said, they are legally required to disclose what commission they're being paid.
- Referrals are golden. If you know someone that you respect and trust who raves about their mortgage broker – set up a meeting!
- If you leave your meeting feeling confused and unenthused, it's okay to walk away and try again.
- Be wary of brokers who work directly with select banks – that means they're not taking all of your options into consideration.
- Make sure your broker has a licence and has access to a large number of lenders – ideally around 45!
- If they're not offering you at least three different options, that's a red flag. Legally they only have to show you one option, but it's better to see a variety so you can make the best choice for you.

- A broker's role is to make sure you have a surplus at the end of the transaction. If they tell you to save a larger deposit, listen to them.
- Be upfront about undisclosed debt or access to lines of credit. I mentioned this before, but even if your credit card balance is at zero, your credit card limit is $10,000, so that's $10,000 less you can borrow. Pay it off and close it!

Types of home loans

While this isn't the most encouraging or inspiring graphic, it's incredibly important for you to see just how much of your money is going to go to interest when borrowing money from a bank.

Where your monthly mortgage repayment really goes. Example: $450,000 home loan at 3.5% pa

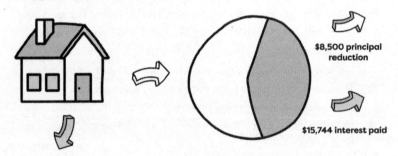

$8,500 principal reduction

$15,744 interest paid

Year 1 total repayments
$24,252

NB: Rates are at historical lows currently – the lowest home loan rate averages for the last 20 years had been 4.4%. At 4.4% in the above example interest payable would be $19,800 and principal reduction of $4,452.

Allocation of mortgage repayments

In Australia, there are multiple types of home loans to choose from.

- *Fixed rate loan* – This is a standard loan with an interest rate that doesn't change over the life of the loan.
- *Variable rate loan* – This is a standard loan with an interest rate that can fluctuate.
- *Interest-only loan* – This is a standard loan, but you delay the repayment of the borrowed amount and only repay the interest, not the principal, for the first three to five years.
- *Guarantor loan* – This is a standard loan, but you have someone guarantee your purchase by putting their own property on the line.
- *Low doc loan* – This is a standard loan that's popular among self-employed individuals who don't have access to the same documents (like a PAYG payslip) to provide a lender.
- *Line of credit loan* – This is when you borrow an amount of money based on the equity in your home.
- *Non-conforming loan* – This type of loan is also an option for self-employed individuals or those who have previously filed for bankruptcy or have poor credit.

Depending on where you get your loan, you can also add extra bells and whistles that help you pay the loan off quicker! These include:

- standard principal and interest (fixed or variable)
- offset account
- extra repayments facility
- standard home loan and standard redraw facility
- premium home loan.

Myth: You should go with the home loan that has the lowest interest rate.

Here's the thing about loans with super low interest rates – more often than not, they have no bells and whistles. This means you aren't offered the flexibility to make extra payments or redraw money. You're basically locked into the 30-year term. Don't fret: you may be able to refinance after two years. (More on refinancing soon!)

Standard principal and interest (fixed or variable)

This is the home loan that the majority of Australians have. It is cleverly designed to keep you in debt for as long as possible.

For starters, your income is going into a standard transaction account, which is probably earning 0.01 per cent interest. Second, you simply pay the minimum required repayment each month.

While some people will try or hope to make additional repayments to help fast track the debt reduction, the issue is that as humans we tend to spend what we have access to, leaving little to no surplus cash to make extra repayments.

If you do happen to make additional repayments, but your loan doesn't have a 'redraw' facility (which we will discuss in a second), then those additional funds will reduce the loan balance, but cannot be re-drawn back to you if you ever need to access money. Further to this, if the loan is on a fixed rate, you're capped (usually) to $10,000 pa in additional repayments.

Let's take a look at a standard loan graph over a 30-year period.

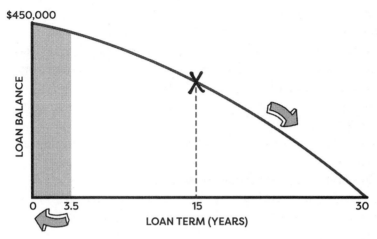

Standard home loan graph

- Approximately $300,000 in interest is payable on a $450,000 home loan across 30 years. (Where's the spew emoji when you need it?) This means that it will cost you $750,000 to pay off your $450,000 home loan.
- Interest is front-end loaded, which means you pay the majority of the interest in the first 15 years. You don't really start making progress on your principal repayments until then.
- Most people don't make it to the 15-year mark without making changes to the loan, which resets the clock back to zero for another 30 years.
- On average, every three or so years people become frustrated with their lack of progress and blame their home loan – usually their rate – and think that refinancing will solve their problems. Unless otherwise advised, the banks reset the loan term for another 30 years when you refinance, meaning you'll pay that higher interest component all over again.
- It's in the last 15 years that you're able to make good progress, because that's when the majority of the interest has been paid and most of your repayment starts going towards principal reduction.

People refinance their home loans for lots of reasons. Perhaps they want to consolidate debt, renovate a home or buy an investment property. Sometimes it makes sense to change the structure to add an offset account or a redraw facility. What doesn't make sense is to use the equity in your home to fund your lifestyle!

Offset accounts

The cash flow set-up for an offset account is almost exactly the same as the standard home loan. The only difference is that the funds you have in the offset account reduces the amount of interest on your home loan. For example: if you have a $450,000 loan and $45,000 in your offset account, you will only pay interest on $405,000.

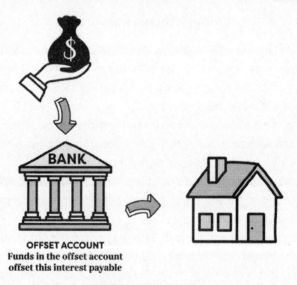

OFFSET ACCOUNT
Funds in the offset account
offset this interest payable

Offset account

Given that interest saved is mathematically the same as interest earned, the return on your cash is significantly better than cash in a standard bank account (home loan rate 3.5 per cent versus a 0.01 per cent in a standard transaction account). However, it doesn't pay off debt.

Let's go back to your $450,000 loan. Pretend you had $45,000 in the offset account from day one. (Also – let's be mindful that $45,000 is an extremely generous figure, as most people wouldn't have close to this in savings. But for the purpose of this exercise, let's pretend.)

- So you've got $45,000 in your offset from day one and you haven't touched it.
- That $45,000 offsets the interest, but it doesn't pay off your principal.
- It ultimately reduces the loan term from 30 years down to 27 years, saving $72,967 in interest (nice).
- There is only one way to pay off debt, and that is to pay down principal.

Offset accounts only really start to make an impact after ten years. This is the same as the basic home loan – but remember, no-one holds on long enough to realise this before refinancing and starting again.

Pros:

- Money in your offset account offsets the interest.
- It's useful if you're planning to convert your home into an investment property, or in any case where you don't want to pay off debt but would like your cash 'working' for you.
- You might pay your home off three to four years earlier if you're making standard repayments and have at least 10 per cent of the property value in the offset account.

Cons:

- It offsets interest but doesn't pay off principal.
- Money is too easy to spend, meaning less money to pay off debt.
- Offset accounts don't really start working until the 15-year mark.

Standard home loan and standard redraw account

The main differences between standard home loans, offset home loans and those with redraw accounts is that home loans with redraw accounts can have additional repayments made into the home loan to reduce the balance, as well as the ability to redraw those additional payments back out if you need them.

A redraw account is a useful place to park surplus cash, as interest on a home loan is calculated daily on the balance of the home loan. For every day your cash is in the redraw, pressuring down the debt, it reduces the interest payable at the end of the month – which means more of your repayment is actually paying off principal rather than interest.

Unfortunately, most lenders limit the use of redraw by adding fees or minimum redraw amounts. However, there are a few lenders who allow for a premium home loan set-up, so it's definitely worth speaking to your mortgage broker about them.

Premium home loans and redraw facility

Premium home loans reverse your cash flow and allow you to 'salary credit' your income directly into your home loan account. This immediately reduces the loan balance and keeps it as low as possible every day, meaning you pay less interest. You cannot pay more than your entire salary into your home loan, and the compound effect of you pressuring down the balance every day is enormous. There is also a psychological benefit, because you'll see the home loan balance drop and feel different about that money – unlike money in an offset or transactional account, which can feel more like spending money.

Of course, banks want you to deposit your income into an account where they pay you bugger all interest, only to then lend that money back to you. With a premium redraw facility, all your surplus cash is working as hard as possible each and every day without the need to manually transfer 'additional cash' into the home loan.

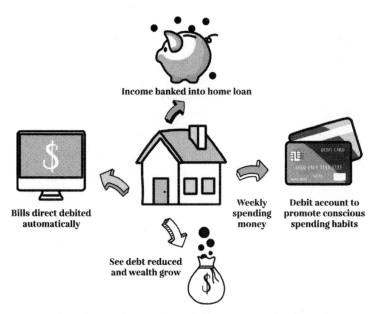

Premium home loan using fully transactional redraw

The power of time

Just as your investments need time to compound and grow, the longer you have a home loan, the more interest you will pay. With a home that you plan to live in long term, paying the debt off sooner will save you thousands!

In the graph below, the dark grey highlights the interest saved by paying the home loan off in approximately 17 years versus 30 years. Not only do you save interest, you save time! Once your home loan is paid off, you'll then have that surplus cash each month available to grow your wealth.

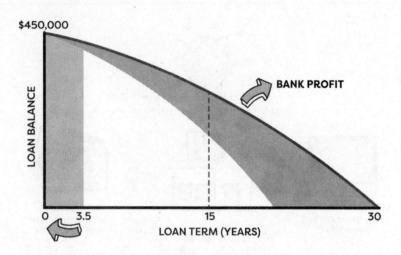

Accrual of interest – and bank profit – over time

Refinancing: when and why

As someone who encourages people to look at their finances holistically, I suggest doing a home-loan health check every year or so. With property markets, personal values, investment goals and incomes constantly changing, it's important that your home loan is adapting with you. For example, while you might have needed a guarantor loan for all or a portion of your loan five years ago, maybe it's time to get that deed released! Maybe you just inherited $100,000 and want to pay it off your mortgage, but your standard home loan only allows you to make $10,000 a year in extra repayments – in that case, it's probably time to explore a redraw facility with no repayment limitations.

Hot tip: When speaking to a broker about refinancing, you may want to ask that a bank doesn't reset the term of the loan. You might think lowering your monthly repayment makes sense, but if you have to pay a lower amount for a longer period of time, you might end up paying more in interest.

• • • • • •

MEERA, 25 – NSW

I finished high school in 2014 and started my business degree in 2015. In my first year of uni I was approached for a job by a bank representative. The job was full time, close to home – perfect if I hadn't just started a three-year degree. Nonetheless, I made it work. I took the job and continued my studies part time. Earning a full-time wage was a great feeling.

But I was raised by immigrants who arrived in a foreign country with nothing. Their hard work has led them to be very financially comfortable. So I knew I couldn't spend my entire pay like the rest of my friends. Instead, I started a budget to save. My first savings goal was to travel. The next year I was able to travel to Bali and across Europe.

My next financial goal was to buy an investment property. After three long years I saved 20 per cent for a house and land and built my first property. Today my rental income covers my mortgage repayments.

In the meantime, my boyfriend and I were very eager to move out. So we committed to a joint savings account and saved what we could. My financial goals never stopped me from millennial things. I went to festivals and concerts, I bought the clothes I wanted. But I would save on other things to compensate. I would rarely buy lunches when at work, and I would rarely purchase full-price items. These little things added up for me.

Six months after my investment property was complete, my boyfriend and I purchased our own home. At 25, yes, I am in $800,000 worth of debt, but I also have $1.2 million of property assets.

I am very proud of what I have achieved, but I believe there's always more to grow. I'd love for my boyfriend and I to start investing.

● ● ● ● ● ●

TAKE NOTE

Banks are going to look at your income, spending, debt and
potential to get into debt. Even if your credit card balance
is zero, they will count the limit on it against you!

....

Just because a loan has a low interest rate
doesn't mean it's the best option.

....

Make sure you're refinancing for the right reasons, and not
ultimately increasing the time or interest owed on the loan.

....

Chapter 11

Taxes are for winners

I know I just got you all excited about making money, but now I want you to get pumped about giving it away!

Hear me out: the more taxes you're paying, the more money you're making. I don't know about you, but I would be loud and proud if I had a huge tax bill, because this means that all my hard work is paying off. And remember, paying taxes means we reap the benefits of things like public education, libraries, healthcare, community events, the Australian Federal Police, the Australian Defence Force and, lest we forget, roads and public transport!

While you may only think about income tax at tax time, as a tax-paying citizen, it's important to factor it in to every financial decision you make. From buying and selling an investment property, to starting up a side hustle, to investing in the stock market, the tax implications require you to be both educated and savvy.

Taxes 101

Tax is the most important revenue stream for the Australian Government. It is collected and distributed by the Australian Taxation Office, aka the ATO. If you are an individual working and earning money in Australia, you must declare any and all income. While there are different rules for residents versus visa holders, for the purposes of this book I am going to focus on the taxable personal income of Australian residents.

All tax-paying residents are required to have a tax file number (TFN). You can apply for one from the ATO website, or look up your TFN if you've already got one and forgotten the number. This is an individual reference number used for tracking tax as well as superannuation. When you accept a job, your employer will ask for your TFN so that they can make tax payments and superannuation contributions on your behalf. You will also usually provide this number to your bank so they can declare the amount of interest paid on your accounts. In order to prevent identity theft and fraud, it's important protect this number fiercely.

In Australia, the financial year is counted from 1 July until 30 June. All money earned within this period must be declared to the ATO on your annual tax return, which must be lodged by 31 October unless you are using an accountant. Depending on your income and the amount of tax you've paid, you may owe money or you may receive a tax refund. This is determined by income tiers, as well as by how many deductions you were able to claim.

Income

Declarable personal income includes money coming in from:

- employment
- side hustle(s)
- investments
- capital gains

- rental income
- foreign income
- government payments
- pensions and annuities.

Income that is not subject to tax includes:

- lottery winnings and other prizes (however, interest earned on these things may be subject to tax)
- small gifts or birthday presents
- some government payments
- child support payments
- spouse or de facto maintenance
- the tax-free portion of a redundancy payment
- government super co-contributions.

Trust me, it's not worth trying to hide your income, especially if you're splashing your cash on bottles of Mumm and buying Louboutins while claiming you're only earning minimum wage. The ATO has a data-matching program for lifestyle assets. Their data-matching technology will send up red flags, and before you know it, your return will be reviewed. The ATO will then assess the assets you own and calculate the amount of income you would require to support that lifestyle. If they don't think you're being honest about your income, you may face paying extra taxes, penalties or interest.

Are you #blessed?

The ATO may access your public social media profiles and may look at your Instagram feed if they're feeling suspicious about what you're claiming. They can and will use any images they find of you 'living the dream' to support their assumption that you're not being honest about what you've earned. So remember, when in doubt, declare it! (Or speak to a certified tax accountant.)

Deductions

A deduction is an expense you incurred that was directly related to earning your income. For example, the running costs of a home office if you work from home, or a laundering service for your uniform. By deducting this amount, your taxable income is reduced, which means you end up paying less tax.

Tax deductions you may be eligible to claim:

- a work-related expense that you paid for yourself and were not reimbursed for. (If this is over $300, you must have written evidence other than a receipt to support your claim.)
- vehicle and travel expenses
- clothing, laundry and dry-cleaning expenses for your uniform
- home-office expenses
- tools, equipment and software
- investment property expenses, including loan interest
- ATO interest
- charitable gifts and donations
- cost of lodging your tax return
- interest, dividend and other investment income deductions
- personal superannuation contributions
- undeducted purchase price of a foreign pension or annuity
- union and/or membership fees.

Here are some other surprising things you may be able to claim:

- Your handbag – You might be able to claim your handbag to the extent that its use is as a work bag, to carry your laptop, notebooks and anything else you need for work. Sadly, this bag has to be practical and 'reasonable' in nature, so you'll have to save up your tax returns for that navy Chanel Boy bag with the silver hardware . . . sorry!
- Shoes – Work boots are an obvious deduction; however, flight attendants may be allowed to claim a second pair of shoes

if they're the same as those designated part of their uniform, but are more comfortable. And no, those Jimmy Choos don't count, even if you're wearing them to work.

- Make-up – As long as it contains high SPF and you work outdoors in the sun, you may be able to claim your make-up. If you work indoors and can prove that it's required in your job though, you might also be able to claim it.
- Mobile phone – If you're using your personal phone to make calls and check emails for work, you might be able to claim the cost of your work calls – but sadly, not the whole bill.
- Education – If you're studying subjects related to your current paid employer, those costs are tax deductible after the first $250. You might also be able to claim the cost of travelling to and from the place of your education.
- Sex toys – This only applies if you work in the adult entertainment industry. The ATO has a special guide about what can be claimed by adult industry workers. The list includes things like dance lessons, hair care, oils, tissues, lingerie and costumes.
- Dogs – People who use their dogs for work in security services or farming might be able to claim an associated tax deduction for things like vet bills, food and bedding.
- Income protection insurance – You're entitled to a tax deduction for insurance premiums paid against the loss of income. However, this isn't applicable for life insurance, or for total and permanent disability insurance.
- Your home internet – If you're working from home and the connection is in your name, you may likely be able to claim part of your internet expenses as a deduction.
- Subscriptions to work-related magazines and journals – If you work in media, this means yes, you might be able to claim your *Vogue* subscription!

If you're working from home, you can claim a number of different things:

- A portion of your heating, air conditioning and lighting bills for all the time you're using your home office.
- Depreciation of home office assets – You've decked your home office out with a nice desk and comfy chair, so you might be able to claim the write-off.
- Depreciation of your laptop or other office equipment – You may be able to claim a write-off for the decline in value.
- If you're renting, a portion of the rent.

If you're confused about what you can and can't claim, a good tax accountant will be able to tell you, minimising the chance of you being audited later.

Tax deductions you usually can't claim:

- an assistant to help you with your employment
- childcare.

Please be mindful that if you claim a deduction, you must maintain records to prove the claim. This includes receipts from the supplier of the goods and/or services that show the name of the supplier, the amount of the expense, the nature of the good/ service, the date the expense was paid as well as the date of the document. You must keep this proof for five years from when you lodged the tax return.

You'll also want to hold on to:

- income statements and payment summaries
- bank statements showing interest earned.

If you currently have money invested, you'll need:

- dividend statements (if you're earning from an investment)
- summaries from managed investment funds
- receipts for asset purchases and sales.

If you currently have investment property(ies), hang on to:

- sales contracts
- tenant and rental records
- receipts for repairs and maintenance
- evidence of depreciation.

While it's tempting to claim as much as possible to bump up your return, it's not smart to be blasé with your claims. There are some hefty fines if you get caught faking it, and with the technology the ATO now uses, it's highly likely that you will get caught. The ATO monitors people who lodge their own tax returns using the ATO's myTax software to make sure that they aren't over claiming. The software compares your claim to people who are similar to you in terms of income, employment, demographic and location, so if your claim is outside of the ordinary parameters, myTax will give you a flashy warning prompting you to reconsider it. If you ignore their advice, you could be in for a pretty serious audit.

If you're found to have claimed something you weren't entitled to, that doesn't just mean you have to repay what you claimed back – you'll also be paying interest of about 9 per cent pa. On top of that, if the ATO believes you have acted carelessly, you'll be slapped with a penalty of between 25 and 95 per cent of the tax avoided – it's not worth it!

In 2019, 84 per cent of Australian taxpayers anticipated getting an average refund of just over $2300. It's important to understand the ins and outs of what you are entitled to so you don't run into any trouble down the track. It's also important to be proactive about tax, instead of reactive. Once 30 June has come and gone, you need to wait another 12 months before you can claim an expense on tax.

Tax rates based on income

The 2020–2021 Australian Government tax rates for residents are listed below. They do change, so it's always wise to check the

ATO website to get the most current rate. Please note, this doesn't include a further 2 per cent Medicare levy (more on that below).

Taxable income	Tax on this income
0–$18,200	Nil
$18,201–$45,000	19 cents for each $1 over $18,200
$45,001–$120,000	$5,092 plus 32.5 cents for each $1 over $45,000
$120,001–$180,000	$29,467 plus 37 cents for each $1 over $120,000
$180,001 and over	$51,667 plus 45 cents for each $1 over $180,000
The above rates **do not** include the Medicare levy of 2%	

Australian resident tax rates 2020–21
(Source: ATO)

Tax-free threshold

The tax-free threshold is the amount of money you can earn tax-free. Currently, that figure is $18,200. When you are starting a new job, your employer should give you a tax file number declaration form. You will see the question: Do you want to claim the tax-free threshold from this payer? While most of the time you will want to tick 'YES', there are a few instances where you should tick 'NO'.

- Tick YES if this is your only job.
- Tick YES if this is the highest-paying job of all of your current employers.
- Tick NO if this is the lowest-paying job of all of your current employers.
- Tick NO if you've already ticked YES and earned this amount at a previous job in the same financial year.

Medicare levy and surcharges

On top of the tax you pay on your income, you are also required to pay 2 per cent towards Medicare. If applicable, you and/or your spouse may be eligible for a reduction or exemption.

You may also have to pay the income-tested Medicare levy surcharge, or MLS. This is applied if you earn over $90,000 (as an individual) or $180,000 (as a family). Please note, you do not have to pay the MLS if your family income exceeds the threshold but your own income was $22,398 or less.

Because of the MLS, a lot of financial advisers or tax accountants recommend that you take out private health insurance once you've reached the $90,000 income bracket. This is because, depending on your income, you could then be eligible for the private health insurance rebate (see below).

According to the ATO, an appropriate level of private health insurance cover for an individual must have an excess of $750 or less. Couples or families must have an excess of $1500 or less.

Private health insurance rebate

Depending on your income, you may be eligible for the government's private health insurance rebate. This is a government contribution to help offset the cost of your premium. The private health rebate is means tested, so your eligibility will depend on your income. If you've got a higher income, then your rebate entitlement might be reduced, or you might not be entitled to one at all. The private health insurance rebate can be claimed for the premiums you've paid for a private health insurance policy that provides you with private patient hospital cover, general cover (sometimes known as 'extras'), or combined hospital and general cover. But keep in mind that the government doesn't give this private health rebate on the lifetime health cover loading component of a policy. You're able to claim the private health insurance rebate as a reduction in the amount of private health insurance premiums you pay to your insurer each year. Alternatively, the ATO will calculate your private health insurance rebate when you lodge your tax return. This rebate is a refundable tax offset.

Capital gains tax

Capital gains tax (CGT) is tax paid on any profits made from the sale of items like an investment property, a block of land, shares, cryptocurrency, contractual rights and even collectables or personal use assets that are above a certain value.

If you sell an asset, like a share from your portfolio or a property you own, you will usually make either a capital gain, or a capital loss. That description sounds bland, but essentially is asking the question, 'Did you make a profit or a loss?' The difference between what you originally paid for the asset and what you made or lost in selling it is your capital gain or loss. You need to report your capital gains or losses as part of your tax return each year, and pay tax on any capital gains. This is because any capital gain is classified as income. When you make a capital gain, it is added to your assessable income and may significantly increase the tax you need to pay. As tax is not withheld for capital gains at the time these funds come to you, you may want to work out how much tax you will owe and set aside sufficient funds to cover the relevant amount. If you make a capital loss, you can't claim it against your other income but you can use it to reduce a capital gain.

Some exemptions are:

- your main residence
- a car or motorcycle
- personal use assets such as furniture
- depreciating assets such as business equipment or fittings in a rental property
- any asset acquired before 20 September 1985.

Please note that this isn't a separate tax. It is factored into your personal income tax.

Investments

As an Australian resident, you are taxed on your worldwide income. This means any profits from investments, capital gains from the sale of a property or income from work completed overseas is subject to Australian tax.

Good and services tax (GST)

The goods and services tax, commonly referred to as GST, is a broad-based tax of 10 per cent on most goods, services and other items sold or consumed in Australia.

If you are a contractor, sole trader or business owner who's turning over $75,000 per year, you are required to register for GST. This means you will need to add the 10 per cent GST to your invoices.

You will also need to register for GST if you have a non-profit organisation that turns over $150,000 per year or more or are a sole trader or business owner who provides a ride-sharing, taxi and/or limousine service for passengers, regardless of the amount you make. You'll also need to register for GST if you want to claim fuel tax credits for your business, regardless of business turnover.

The sharing economy

With more and more people selling services online, such as providing graphic or web design services, renting out rooms on digital platforms like Airbnb, or taking on a side hustle through apps like Uber, it's important to be mindful that you may be required to pay both income tax and GST. If you're unsure if the service you're offering online is subject to GST, check with the ATO.

Business activity statement (BAS)

A business activity statement is a document that you need to fill out as a business owner so that the ATO can estimate if you will receive a GST refund or bill. It can also be used to track business income tax if you're paying as you go throughout the year. Other uses for a BAS include estimating employee income tax, fringe benefits tax, luxury car tax, wine equalisation tax and fuel tax credits.

Why would I owe the ATO more tax?

If you're employed, your employer should be paying the correct amount of tax to the ATO on your behalf. If for some reason not enough tax was withheld from each of your pay cheques, you may need to pay more.

If you're a sole trader, you will need to make sure you're putting the correct amount of tax away each time you receive a payment. You can make tax payments throughout the year using a BAS, or pay a lump sum at the end of the financial year once you've factored in all of your deductions.

Lodging your return

There's a reason why more than 75 per cent of Australians use a tax agent, and that's because tax is not that simple. If you don't know exactly what you can claim, you might be missing out on some sweet returns, and if you get your return wrong, you could be in for some pretty hefty fines. When it comes to tax, it pays to talk to a professional!

The only way to get definitive tax return advice is from a registered professional. An experienced accountant will be able to highlight what you can claim, what you can't, and what you can do in the next financial year to maximise the amount you can claim back in the future. A good accountant is a worthwhile investment. They'll often highlight things you didn't know you could claim – and the best part? Seeing an accountant is a tax-deductible cost too!

Lodging the claim on your own?

When you log in to the ATO's myTax system, a good chunk of your personal and financial information may be pre-filled. Please ensure that you check all the information that the ATO has collected. Do not assume that, just because they are the ATO, the information they have is correct. Always make sure you're using your own group certificates, payment summaries and bank statements as the main source of information. Unfortunately, if you get questioned on your tax return, the legal responsibility lies with you, not with the ATO – even if the information was pre-filled by them.

Often, your refund gets held up due to making basic mistakes such as the following:

- If your name or address has changed, make sure that you update your ATO info before lodging your return. If you're lodging a return under different details, the ATO's data-matching technology won't be able to match it to your TFN.
- Make sure your bank details are correct – all tax refunds are now done via direct deposit. Gone are the days of receiving your return as a cheque in the mail.
- Didn't use spell check? If you've added an extra letter, or accidentally spelt something wrong in a key field, this will delay your return significantly, as the ATO will have to manually match your details. As you can imagine, this happens a lot, so the delays are substantial!
- Make sure you claim ALL your income – including those three Uber shifts you did last October, or that casual shift you do at a cafe on the weekends in addition to your full-time job. Not claiming income is something the ATO has been cracking down on, especially with the rise of the gig economy (Uber, Airbnb, social media influencers etc.).

● ● ● ● ● ●

ALEX, 24 – NZ

My money story starts with my younger years and never learning properly about saving or budgeting. I saw how my family would spend money and then deal with it later, and so when I started working in my gap year, I wasn't concerned with saving or savings goals at all. When I became a student, I found I couldn't spend as much as I wanted to, so I knew I had to have some sort of budget plan! I tried all sorts of things, but could never actually follow through with the plans (and my plans weren't that great anyway!). I had zero concept of saving for anything other than short-term big spending, and I couldn't curb my spending habits.

Eventually this led to a firm conversation with my partner (who was quite financially literate and frugal), who taught me just how much I could save if I put money away every week. He taught me what long-term savings means, as this wasn't on my radar at all! This prompted a big change in my finances, but soon enough, because I am self-employed and didn't put away any tax or student loan payments (eek!), I found myself in debt, and deep in an interest-free overdraft that would soon no longer be interest free.

I had to TOTALLY confront my spending and why I found it so hard to stick to budget plans, and then change my entire perspective on money and livelihood and habits. I am now on my journey to discovering the psychology behind my spending, and am working to change it – and ultimately change my money story!

● ● ● ● ● ●

TAKE NOTE

The more taxes you're paying, the more money you're making.

....

Don't try to fool the ATO by crying poor and then posting #blessed next to a pic of you and your LV tote.

....

Speak to a registered tax accountant or financial adviser to make sure you're maximising your deductions.

....

Chapter 12

Know your worth (and then add tax)

According to the Human Rights Commission, the average Australian woman has to work an extra 56 days a year to earn as much as a man doing the exact same job. While there are many contributing factors that are out of our control (for now), one of the reasons women still aren't earning as much as men is because we are less likely to ask for a pay rise. As strong and independent millennial women, we've got to change this statistic, and that starts with us knowing our worth (and then adding tax).

Negotiating promotions and pay rises

In her book *Lean In*, Facebook CEO Sheryl Sandberg talks about how men will apply for a job when they meet 60 per cent of the qualifications, while women only ever apply if they meet 100 per cent of the qualifications. What I see here is a huge lack of confidence, and an indicator that in order for us to achieve the same level of financial freedom as men, we need to start acknowledging what we are capable of before we apply for a job, as well as when we're doing it. I'm not saying you should apply for the role of a neurosurgeon when the only surgery you've performed is an ingrown hair removal. I'm saying that if you've been working in marketing for three years and a position opens up that asks for five years of experience, it's worth considering whether you've got what they're looking for. The worst they can say is no, but chances are they'll say yes and you'll knock their socks off!

Other shocking statistics I've stumbled on include:

- Just 7 per cent of women try to negotiate salary when taking a new job, compared to a whopping 57 per cent of men.
- Less than one in five women ask for a pay rise without being prompted by their manager, as opposed to one in three men.
- When women do ask for a pay rise, they're 25 per cent less likely to get it than men.

Twenty-five per cent less likely? Ouch. But you know what hurts more? Doing the same job as a man and earning less money. Of all the awkward conversations you'll need to have with your employer over your professional life, asking for a pay rise may be one of the most vomit-inducing, but trust me – it is 100 per cent necessary.

I think a lot of women fear asking for a raise simply because they're unprepared to make their case. Many make the mistake of thinking, 'Oh, I've been at my job for 12 months, that must mean I'm due for a raise.' Imagine walking into your boss's office and saying you want $5000 a year more and when they ask why, all you have to say is, 'Because I've showed up here every day for a year.' (Crickets.) Unless a pay increase timeline is laid out in your contract to adjust for inflation, asking for a raise shouldn't come down to how long you've worked somewhere.

You're also not entitled to a raise just because you feel like you're working outside of work hours. As a millennial, we don't work in the same way that our parents used to. Online task management platforms, global shared drives and access to emails on our phone mean we have the freedom to work wherever we want. The nine to five culture has shifted, and as a result we often feel we should always be online, in the loop and essentially on the job. Before accepting a job, you need to have open and honest conversations about what will be expected of you in and outside of the office, and make sure you negotiate a salary that reflects this. If you're told that your job should only be done within working hours, it's your manager's job to make sure your workload fits within the designated time frame. If you're working stupidly long hours outside of work, one of two things is happening.

1. They're giving you too much work.
2. You're fluffing around too much.

While I appreciate going above and beyond, I don't equate that to working out of your specified hours. It's about the value you're adding during work hours. Trying to show your boss that you deserve a pay rise because of the time you put in is not enough. Ultimately, it's not about your hours, it's about your value.

Determining if you deserve a raise comes down to knowing your value and how your time and actions are contributing to the success of the business. Once you sit down and list the ways that you've been directly responsible for hitting or surpassing sales and marketing goals or signing up new accounts, I guarantee you will feel way more relaxed about asking for compensation that directly reflects the value of your work.

Questions to ask in order to determine your worth:

● What are other people in similar roles in Australia earning? You can use websites like PayScale or visit the Australian

Government's Fair Work website to determine your industry's award wages.

- How have you directly impacted the profitability of your organisation? Can you list three examples?
- Are you meeting KPIs (key performance indicators)?

Tips when crafting your pay rise conversation:

- Don't use examples like, 'My goal was to earn $100,000 this year so I'd like a raise.'
- Use language like, 'I believe that I deserve a pay rise because I've done x, y and z and that directly impacted a, b and c.'
- Show the ways that you've been instrumental in the financial success of the company and team culture.
- Make sure all of your facts are indisputable.
- It takes confidence to articulate your worth, so strike those power yoga poses before walking in!

Something to think about . . .

Sadly, there's one major question you need to ask yourself: Is this pay rise even possible? When you're considering a job, you need to do your research, because some industries have enterprise bargaining agreements (EBAs) with unions that govern the minimum and maximum pay rates for employees.

Let's say you've climbed your way to the top and there's literally nowhere else for you to go, salary wise. You can still negotiate outside of salary. Try asking for things like:

- more flexible hours
- leave entitlements
- work from home hours
- a company car.

Being compensated adequately for your work is crucial for a whole lot of reasons. For starters, your mental health may suffer if you don't feel like you're being compensated fairly. You can become resentful and frustrated. The quality of your work may also decline because you start taking on lots of projects, or mentally just check out. Plus, your ability to achieve and maintain financial independence depends on it!

What happens if your boss says no?

- Let's say you wanted a $15,000 pay rise, but your boss only agrees to $5000 – challenge it. Say something like, 'It's not in line with my expectations' and then explain why you're worth more. If they still say no, ask if they will consider reviewing your request in another three months.
- Ask what you need to do in order to have your request reviewed again. Are there any KPIs for them to keep an eye on?
- Remember that your boss saying no to a pay rise request does not mean that you will never get one. It's simply a no this time around. However, if they do explicitly indicate that a pay rise is not possible, you will need to consider your options. I know that rejection sucks and you might feel deflated, but you should still be proud that you took that step. Learning how to negotiate is a skill, and one that will make you even more valuable.

The other thing you should do is go home and THINK. I want you to determine if staying in your job is going to allow you to reach your financial goals. If it's not, use your lunch break to start exploring other job options. But before you apply – be sure you know your worth from the start.

What's the deal with salary packaging?

The term 'salary packaging' refers to when employers package incentives that bring down your taxable income. Examples include salary sacrificing extra employer contributions to your superannuation fund, a company car, a company mobile phone, childcare, and cards that can be used to dine out. While salary packaging may sound great, it's not always as sparkly and shiny as it looks. Hear me out: even though you're saving money on tax, are you really in a better position? Money taken from your salary is now money that you're not making money on. Unless it's going to your super (where it is making money), it could actually be costing you money.

One issue I see a lot is healthcare workers getting $200 a week to dine out. This isn't money that can be used at a grocery store – it's restaurant specific. That means that instead of being able to budget and spend your money in a way that's in line with your values, you're forced to eat out. Same goes for a company car. Let's say the company car is worth $40,000 of your salary. If you had taken the money instead, you could have purchased a $15,000 car and had $25,000 to save or invest. When considering a salary package, I suggest doing a cost–benefit analysis. If it's going to save you from slipping into the next tax bracket or help create wealth for Future You, then YES. But if it's going to force you to spend $200 a week on chicken schnitzel, then you may just want to take the money!

● ● ● ● ● ●

STEPHANIE, 34 – NSW

I've recently been offered a consultancy role for an organisation that I've worked for before. Last time, they low-balled me in negotiations and I really lost out because they knew I needed the experience, so I didn't have much leverage. Last week they contacted me again for a new stint and I quoted them my daily rate, which is more than my previous one – and not by an insignificant amount. They questioned the difference in rate and reminded me what I was paid last time. I explained all that I had achieved in the time since, and how all that made me the right person for this current role, and I wouldn't budge on the rate. They came back to me with a contract for my full quoted rate! It feels good to know what I am worth and to have the confidence to negotiate for it. It's important that, as women, we develop more of this and get paid what we deserve!

COURTNEY, 24 – WA

I managed to negotiate three pay rises of $20,000 each in three years, doubling my income since I turned 22. This was as a non-technical person in the male-dominated IT industry. I achieved this just by asking for it and being confident about my worth compared to the market! Three years ago I started out at an associate level in an IT firm, which is a pretty intimidating place to be as a non-technical woman!

Anyway, after the first year I was quickly put into positions that were waaaay above my job description. Eventually I plucked up the guts to tell my boss that I didn't think I should be an associate anymore, as I was being used for solely non-associate tasks. Prior to the meeting, I did all the calculations to show how much revenue I was making for the company, minus any overheads etc., had a look online at jobs similar to what I was performing, and got a good idea of what I thought I was worth. Then I hit him with the data and he agreed! Initially they just promised to promote me, but wouldn't reveal details about the remuneration – so I forced them to sit down with me and talk numbers. I gave them my pre-determined figure and they accepted it! I ended up with a 20 per cent pay rise and a new job title.

BROOKE, 27 – VIC

When I moved to Melbourne I took an administration assistant position on $50,000 per year, because that is what I had come from – $50,000, same job title. I wanted something better, so I started applying for jobs that I wasn't technically qualified for or had experience doing. I trusted my capabilities, researched the roles and went for a few job interviews but didn't get them. I kept throwing my hat in the ring – then I landed one. It was a job I had never done, but I knew I could do the work. I almost doubled my wage in a day and am now on $90,000. I'm doing something completely different, but I love my job. I never thought I would be lucky enough to have a job I love, being 'just' an admin with no university degree, but I now run social media and events. I now know that when applying for jobs in the future, with a little research into what is required for the position and a bit of confidence, you can better yourself!

● ● ● ● ● ●

TAKE NOTE

Determining whether you deserve a raise comes down
to knowing your value and how your time and actions
are contributing to the success of a business.

....

Make sure all your facts are indisputable.

....

A pay rise doesn't always have to be monetary!
You could negotiate more flexible work hours
or the ability to work from home.

....

Chapter 13

The rise of the side hustle

It could be the rising cost of living in Australia and/or the fact that the internet (in particular, social networking sites) has made it incredibly easy to advertise goods and services, but the popularity of side hustles is growing faster than the NBN's complaint list. It seems like every third person I meet has a gig they do on top of their job, to either make extra money or fulfil a passion. As millennials, it's very on-brand for our generation to pursue multiple careers, and side hustles are a safe and fun way to test out a job we might like before going all in.

Side hustles are also becoming quite common among mums who've taken time off work to be a full-time parent. Even though they quite literally have their hands full 24/7, it's a way for them to earn extra money. We'll talk more about family planning in Chapter 16, but just be mindful that there might be some restrictions if you're collecting parental leave payments from the government.

I personally love side hustles. In fact, *She's on the Money* workshops started out as a passion project – something I did whenever I could fit them in. Like many side hustles, it evolved to become one of my main hustles! That's the thing about side hustles – they can be big or small, long or short, monetarily driven or purely done to feed our mind, body and soul.

Love real estate? Your side hustle could be:

- Airbnb host
- Airbnb cleaner
- Airbnb photographer.

Love animals? Your side hustle could be:

- pet sitter
- dog walker
- dog groomer
- obedience instructor
- cat whisperer (I don't know if that's a thing, but I definitely think it should be a thing).

Love writing? Your side hustle could be:

- blogger
- copywriter
- proofreader
- journalist
- product reviewer.

Highly organised? Your side hustle could be:

- virtual assistant who can:
  - transcribe
  - enter data
  - organise meetings and travel
  - create budgets
  - send invoices
  - make customer service phone calls.

Know how to find a diamond in the rough? Your side hustle could be:

- furniture restoration
- house flipping
- selling vintage goods.

Are you a hot-glue gun expert? Your side hustle could be:

- sewing and selling clothing
- making heirloom artwork for newborns
- framing artwork
- sourcing and selling cute costumes for cats and dogs.

Is marketing, branding and distribution your thing? Your side hustle could be:

- importing and selling custom T-shirts
- manufacturing 100 per cent non-toxic bamboo dinnerware
- consulting for local and international businesses.

Got mad design skills? Your side hustle could be:

- web designer
- graphic designer
- illustrator.

Love kids? Your side hustle could be:

- nanny
- babysitter
- hair braider or face painter at birthday parties.

'Victoria, should my side hustle be a multi-level marketer?'

Every time I get a private message from someone wanting to tell me about 'an exciting business opportunity I can do in my PJs' I immediately cringe – this is a hard no from me! Multi-level marketing, aka network marketing, is something you should be incredibly wary of. While it might be true that someone can indeed earn a very good living by recruiting team members and selling products through their social media channels, the odds of being successful are not in your favour.

Starting out

When starting a side hustle, I want you to ask yourself the following questions.

- What is your why? Is this side hustle a creative outlet or purely a way to make money? Determine where your drive is coming from so you can make the necessary decisions to either feed your passion or make the most money you can. And, as always, consider whether this hustle aligns with your values.
- Is this side hustle going to take over all of your free time? Is it going to prevent you from spending time with family and friends?
- Is it going to impact your capacity to perform 100 per cent at your full-time job?
- How much money are you prepared to invest in pursuit of this side hustle? Many side hustles require start-up costs like database registration, materials and advertising.

Many side hustles fall apart because of failure to structure. From not setting yourself up to scale your business, to trying to do too much on your own, there are some common mistakes that can easily be avoided.

Side hustle set-up tips

#1 Separate your finances

It will make your life much less muddy if you keep your personal and professional finances separate. This means having an account that is purely for business expenses like subscriptions, order-taking, expenses and saving money for tax. Yes, money earned from a side hustle is considered income, so make sure you're putting money aside for tax.

#2 Set yourself up to scale

- Register your business with the ATO.
- If you anticipate earning over $75,000 pa, you need to register for GST.
- Research how much money you need to be putting aside for tax.
- Pay yourself superannuation from the start (if you can!). While some people feel they need to reinvest every possible dollar back into their business to grow, it's important not to shoot yourself in the foot when it comes to your ability to retire. If you focus on paying yourself super, then you will price yourself correctly from the start. ALSO – making super contributions can be a smart way to save on paying higher tax rates by dropping your taxable income. Remember: super contributions as a sole trader/contractor/freelancer are also tax deductible!
- Invest in software like XERO or MYOB that makes accounting and customer communication easier.
- Research what insurance you may need. This is particularly important if you're doing a job that requires you to enter someone's home.
- Treat your job as if it makes a lot more than it does.
- Factor in fuel, wear on your car, cost of software etc. so you can price your work appropriately and also claim the necessary items at tax time.
- Make assets that legitimise your offering, e.g. a logo, website, booking forms, customer reviews and newsletters. When you're just starting out, there are plenty of affordable options to get you going.

- Need a website? You can buy and personalise themes yourself through companies like Squarespace, WordPress and Wix. Alternatively, a web designer can do it for you (and also help with branding, logo creation and copywriting).
- Need a logo? If you don't go the classic graphic designer route, you could try companies like Fiverr or Canva.
- Need help scheduling and planning content? I personally love Planoly! There are heaps of options out there.
- Need a digital newsletter? Companies like Mailchimp make it super easy to design and integrate on-brand email opt-ins, lists and campaigns to any website.

#3 Stockpile content

Chances are you're probably pretty busy working your main job as it is. One of the main reasons side hustles fail is the inability to keep up with content. Let's say you want to become a blogger and deliver weekly or bi-weekly content. I suggest writing 20 ready-to-go pieces so that if things ramp up at work, you don't have to stress about punching out a blog post. Same goes for advertising. If you want to do one social media post every three days for your hand-sewn baby-clothing business, plan and schedule that content! It's also a good way to test out if you actually have time for said side hustle.

#4 Outsource

Ever spent ten hours on something that you know someone else could have done in one? Don't be afraid to outsource work that will allow you to generate revenue in a different way.

#5 Stop undervaluing yourself!

Putting a value on your work is difficult, but incredibly important. This is particularly important for writers, designers and illustrators who have trouble understanding their worth. Believe it or not, I know many freelancers who've closed more deals when they raised their prices! Look at what your expenses are, from software to hardware to time. What amount per hour makes you feel comfortable? If your current customers aren't willing to pay it, market yourself to a new group.

Tips for renegotiating your fees with existing clients:

- Don't be apologetic.
- Be factual.
- Let them know they're a valued customer by offering them a preferential rate.
- Be prepared to walk away if they say no.

Hot tip: If you're feeling unsure about how best to approach your side hustle, find someone who's already doing it and ask them! This is as easy as a friendly call or email inviting them to coffee. On a behavioural psychology level, people love talking about themselves. If they're a good person, they won't see you as competition. If they say no, they could simply be too busy. Don't take it personally. It might also be a referral down the line!

Remember – you don't have to work for yourself to be successful. Your side hustle doesn't have to replace your employment. You can be passionate, enthusiastic, well-rounded and successful without being a business owner. Plus, when you're employed, you can take way more swings with your side hustle because you have a full-time job to pay bills.

Just a friendly *She's on the Money* PSA: If your friend has a side hustle and is breaking their back trying to supplement their income, do not ask them for a discount! Support them by using their services and buying their products.

● ● ● ● ● ●

BRYDIE, 24 – VIC

I'm 24 years old and currently working full time in allocations at a retail company. Growing up we only had Mum, so money wasn't always available. But she always worked so hard to give us what we needed, and instilled that work ethic in us from a young age. I've had jobs since I was 14! Currently I have $40,000 in the bank and am looking to enter the housing market in the near future. I'm lucky enough to still be at home, so when I get paid I have $300 go into an expenses account, $500 into short-term savings, $100 into long-term savings and $50 into a holiday fund. I also have a side hustle where I umpire and supervise my local netball during the week and get paid cash – this can vary from $100–$300 on a weekly basis depending on how much I pick up. I love to travel so I have money to go towards doing this usually yearly (or at least hopefully). I think I'm a really good saver; that's something I've always wanted to be. I saw Mum struggle when we were younger so I like working hard now to have that safety blanket.

CHRISTIE, 27 – VIC

When I was 24, I moved out of home with zero savings and a $4000 debt to my parents (from a big European holiday the year before, when I blew my budget!). When I moved out I was still at uni studying a master's. I had limited hours to work during the week, but luckily I was paying below-market rent at my friend's house. To reach my financial goals and make some more money on the side, I started a side hustle alongside my casual job. I used the money from my side hustle to pay back my mum and dad and fund my travel over the last few years.

I worked really hard at uni to secure a great (and financially secure) government job when I finished studying. I'm now 27 and I've been working full time for two years. I earn about $96,000 before tax per year. I have $20,000 in savings for a house deposit, $1000 in my rainy day fund, a couple of hundred bucks in my travel/holiday account, $1000 in my share portfolio and about $25,000 in super. I have about $80,000 in HECS debt and although I do have a credit card for emergencies, I keep the balance at zero. Otherwise, I have no debt.

I plan on investing another $5000 into shares. I put this cash aside for my investment portfolio, but lent it to my partner last year *when he was travelling and ran out of money!*

My money goal is to buy an old-ish two-bedroon apartment in inner-city Melbourne, do it up and sell it for a bit of a profit. This will be my project alone – not with my partner, as I like the idea of having a little slice of financial freedom apart from him. Then I'll use some of that money (or the equity, if I decide not to sell) to buy a small house to renovate with my partner. Hopefully we can add heaps of value to that property and make enough money by then to buy a family home. For me, my physical environment is the most important thing for my wellbeing. So, I want to make sure I live in a beautiful space knowing that I have worked hard to create it!

As I grow older, I'm hoping that smart investments in my share portfolio will enable: (1) my kids to go to good schools, (2) regular travel, and (3) some plastic surgery here and there – lol, I know that last one seems a bit vapid but tbh, I place value on feeling and looking good.

● ● ● ● ● ●

TAKE NOTE

Side hustles can be big or small, long or short, monetarily driven or purely done to feed our mind, body and soul.

....

Set yourself up to scale!

....

Ask someone who is already doing what you want to do for guidance.

....

Chapter 14

Insurance

Home, car, travel, health, Gigi Hadid's legs – if you can name it, you can insure it.

While not all insurances are created equal, they essentially do the same thing: provide a guarantee of some sort of financial compensation due to loss, damage, illness, injury or death.

Did you know that Australia is one of the most underinsured countries in the world? Given that we're a First World nation, it's shocking that this is an area we're lacking education in. In South Africa, 80 per cent of the workforce has income protection. Not even 50 per cent of Australians have that. And if an Australian does have income protection, it's probably by default from their superannuation, which can have a whole lot of issues associated with it. (But more on that soon!)

Having the right insurance policies in place at the right time is incredibly important, and something I want you to be constantly reassessing. While at 18 you may only need to worry about travel insurance for your trip to Bali, as you get older, you will need to factor in protecting your income, your assets and your life.

- Did you just welcome a baby into the world? Never has it been more important to protect your loved ones from potentially inheriting your debt. It's time to look into life insurance.
- Spend your weekends rock climbing? Perhaps you want to consider taking out a total and permanent disability policy.
- Want to protect your income, aka the money you put your blood, sweat and tears into? Of course you do! You'll want to shop for an income protection policy.

Of all the things you can and should insure, I first want to talk about personal insurance.

Personal insurance

Personal insurance is a type of cover that provides financial security to you and your family in the event of serious injury or illness, the loss of the ability to earn money or your total and permanent disability or death. People often get personal insurance to make sure they are able to maintain their lifestyle, achieve their bigger savings goals, cover living expenses and pay outstanding debts if they were to lose their ability to work. Personal insurance policies can be held inside or out of your superannuation fund, and come with both pros and cons.

Acquiring personal insurance

In Australia, there are three ways you can acquire personal insurance.

1. Through a financial adviser

The type of cover you can get through a financial adviser is known as retail cover. A financial adviser will review your personal situation, your values and goals and compare multiple products from a variety of insurers to determine the best type of cover for you.

The advantage of going through a financial adviser is that you get expert advice on what levels of cover you need. An adviser also has access to a wider variety of insurance products than you will have access to. Going through a financial adviser often costs a bit more than getting insurance via the methods discussed below, as you will have to pay for this advice.

2. Directly from the insurer

As an individual, you can compare policies online and apply for one directly from the insurer. (I've listed important things to consider and questions to ask later in this chapter.) This gives you the advantage of being able to pick out almost any kind of cover. However, doing it yourself means you will have access to less products. While this route is often cheaper than going through a financial adviser, it does carry some risk if you don't read the product disclosure statement (PDS) completely or you don't understand all the terms and conditions. Finding the right cover can also be time consuming, complicated and difficult. That said, it's not impossible!

3. Automatically through superannuation

Life insurance is often included as a default through your superannuation. If this is the case, you pay for your premiums with the money you contribute to your super. The main advantage here is that the cover can be cheap, but you generally have limited options, and the lump sum paid out is often not enough insurance for most people.

Types of personal insurance

There are four types of personal insurance:

- income protection
- life insurance
- total and permanent disability (TPD)
- trauma.

Income protection

Income protection protects your income. Wild, I know. Given the importance of your income, it's alarming that so few people make it a priority to insure it. We place so much value on insuring our cars, houses, jewellery and smart watches, but few people insure their income, which is the very thing that helps us sustain our lifestyles.

Imagine if you were diagnosed with breast cancer and had to endure six months of chemotherapy that made you so sick you couldn't do your job. While your medical bills may be covered by Medicare or private health insurance, you will probably still need help to ensure you can afford the essentials like groceries, electricity, rates and rego! This is where income protection comes in.

Regardless of your income, the earlier you can get income protection, the better. This is because as you get older, it becomes more expensive to be insured. It's worth it, trust me – you'll want the ability to achieve all your financial goals whether or not you have the capacity to work. While you can claim this cost as a deduction on tax, be mindful that if you do end up receiving income protection payments, you'll need to pay income tax on that money. Be sure to set money aside, because you'll end up with a tax bill at the end of the year.

If you told me I could only keep one form of insurance, this is the one I would keep. Why? Because cash flow is QUEEN, and if you've got money coming in you'll find a way to be okay. Income protection covers you until you're able to re-enter the workforce, or until you reach retirement (in cases where you're permanently disabled and unable to work again).

Hot tip: It's important to ensure your policy is until age 65. Not a two- or five-year policy. This will ensure you're properly protected.

There used to be two options for income protection policies: indemnity value and agreed value. Since 1 April 2020, the latter has been phased out. Anyone who currently has this type of policy can keep it, but moving forward you are only able to apply for indemnity value.

An indemnity value policy means that even though you're paying to cover your income, the insurer will want to verify that you did in fact earn the amount you're claiming. Once satisfied, they pay you roughly 75 per cent of your income. While verifying your income isn't an issue for a salaried employee, it can become a bit tricky for a freelancer or sole trader whose income is variable. In this instance, an insurer will look at your last two to three tax returns and take the best 12 months.

You might be thinking – only 75 per cent! But here's the thing: insurers need there to be an incentive for you to return to work. It is in their best interest to get you fit, healthy and back in the workforce.

Even though this is not-so-secretly my favourite type of personal insurance, it's probably not the only one you'll need.

Life insurance

Life insurance is set up to extinguish your debts so that whoever is left behind isn't burdened. This becomes particularly important if you've taken out a mortgage. That's a huge amount of debt that could be passed on to your parents or next of kin. While the amount of cover you choose will vary depending on your lifestyle and debt, as you get older and take on more debt (such as an investment property or business venture), or have a spouse or kids who are dependent on your income, you'll want to look at increasing your policy amount.

Total and permanent disability (TPD) insurance

TPD insurance is designed to provide financial security if you become totally and permanently disabled. It covers immediate medical needs, your mortgage and any personal debt, as well as the potential expense of altering your house to cater to your disability. This could involve anything from adding a ramp and handrails to hiring a full-time nurse. This insurance is sometimes confused with income protection. They are not the same, but they do often work together to ensure you're financially secure. TPD will only pay out if you're permanently disabled, unlike income protection, which wants you to recover. The truth is, TPD is expensive, but you don't want to be on the back foot when it comes to this. As you become more financially secure and have fewer dependants, you may become more self-sustainable and might not need TPD anymore.

Hot tip: You may already have a TPD policy included as part of your superannuation. Check and make sure. If established early on, it may mean that you don't have any exclusions associated with this policy. A financial adviser can help explain why you might keep these insurances and top them up with a different policy.

Trauma insurance

Trauma insurance is a stand-alone insurance policy that you usually hold outside of your super. Sometimes called critical illness insurance, it provides a tax-free lump sum payout to cover medical expenses or other financial needs when a critical illness or injury occurs. This insurance will cover you from the time you are diagnosed until the time you've recovered. While not every single type of illness is covered (you'll need to read the PDS of the product you're considering to understand what's included and what isn't), most policies cover the most common terminal illnesses like cancer, organ failure, organ transplants and multiple sclerosis. Trauma insurance is important because it helps to ensure financial security at a time when you're experiencing emotional and financial hardship.

In regard to all four of these insurances, the biggest thing an insurer bases its prices on is risk. Your policy will be priced according to your job, age, health and habits. For instance, a 25-year-old with an office job will probably pay less for cover than a 68-year-old construction worker. If the latter also already has a pre-existing back condition, you can bet your bottom dollar they'll be paying much higher premiums.

Interesting fact: Some insurance companies won't cover air traffic controllers because of the risks associated with the job. In this case, you would need to self-insure.

What does it mean when your policy is held inside superannuation?

When a personal insurance policy is held inside of superannuation, it means that the fund owns it and pays for it. This could be an external policy that a financial adviser or insurance broker sets up in your fund on your behalf or a standard superannuation insurance that came with the fund at the time you established it.

While you can have income protection, life insurance and TPD inside your superannuation, super will not usually provide trauma insurance.

What does it mean when your policy is outside of superannuation?

When a personal insurance policy is held outside of superannuation, this means you personally own the policy and pay for it with your after-tax income.

Pros of having your personal insurance held inside super:

● There are fewer health checks, because most health funds accept you at a default level even if you have a high-risk job. However, always read the PDS to make sure the exclusions don't apply to a pre-existing condition that you have, because if that's the case, you're paying for something you can never claim on.

● It's often cheaper to have life insurance through super because the fund will buy policies in bulk.

- You have the choice to easily increase your cover. However, this may prompt a more thorough health check if your cover is increasing by a significant amount.
- It's easier to pay. You don't get a monthly or yearly bill – it just automatically comes out of your superannuation.
- It's tax-effective because your salary sacrifices and contributions are taxed at the lower 15 per cent, so you're paying for your policy with less expensive money.

Cons of having a personal insurance policy held inside super:

- The PDS can change at any time, which means you may have once been covered for something and now you're not. For example, they might cover lung cancer one year and then drop it off. When you have a policy outside of super and in your own name, the insurer isn't legally allowed to change the policy if it negatively impacts you. (They can add benefits, however.)
- Inside super policies can have time limits. For example, income protection payouts can be limited to two years, versus getting a personal policy which will pay out until you're 65.
- TPD and life insurance held within super usually end at 65. When held outside of super, they usually continue beyond that age. While you can't go and establish a new policy at 70, they can't take an existing one off you.
- The amount of cover is usually lower.
- If you change super funds and don't make sure your insurance is going to continue and roll over, you're at risk of not being eligible for coverage again. If you're going to change or renew your super, review your options before you leave, because the existing insurance policy usually won't have any exclusions.

It often makes a lot of sense to hold some policies within super and some without. For example, I hold my TPD and life insurance through my superannuation, but I have my trauma and income protection in my personal name. (Remember, you cannot hold trauma cover in super.) I am also able to write off my income protection at tax time.

The best way to look at your personal insurance policies is to see how they can work together to cover all your bases. Let's say there's a history of breast cancer in your family. Upon reviewing your automatic superannuation policies, you notice that your life insurance and TPD policies aren't as big as you'd like, but that they don't have any exclusions. These are likely worth keeping because if you go to apply for a new policy, there's a high probability that they will want to exclude breast cancer because they deem the risk of having to pay out too high. However, you may want to make sure you get income protection and trauma insurance to supplement where the superannuation policies fall short.

What's the difference between group insurance and individual insurance?

Group life insurance is a single life insurance policy that covers a group of people. These are most commonly used by superannuation funds to cover members, and businesses looking to cover employees. While these usually come with cheaper premiums and more lenient health checks, they don't usually have very high payouts, and won't continue to cover you if you leave your job or super fund.

Individual insurance is where the policy is held in your own name. It doesn't matter what job you have or if your fund pays for it or not, the policy will cover you as long as you pass their health checks and don't have any exclusions due to pre-existing conditions.

Things to know

As of 1 April 2020, personal insurance is no longer provided to new super fund members under the age of 25. If you want it, you have to write and request it. You MAY get it if you work in a dangerous job, but that's highly discretionary. Super funds are also going to cancel insurance on inactive accounts that haven't received contributions for 16 months. It's really important to check on your super accounts to see if they have any associated insurance policies you want to keep so they don't get cancelled if that's not what you want. Often, insurance issued on the establishment of a super account doesn't have any exclusions, which can be very beneficial!

They're also planning to cancel insurance on super accounts with less than $6000. Don't worry, they will contact you before cancelling, but if you want to keep your insurance, you need to tell them or start contributing money to the fund.

Disclosing your medical history

When applying for any type of personal insurance, you will need to disclose your medical history. I cannot stress how important it is to be honest and upfront from the get-go. Imagine paying for a policy for 15 years only to be denied a claim because you weren't truthful about your slightly elevated blood pressure? It's best to make sure your insurance company understands your history so there are no surprises. Insurance should make your life easier, not give you more hurdles to jump over.

How to compare and choose personal insurance policies

When reviewing policies, you're going to come across a few things you might not have heard of before. Ignoring them may cause you to choose the wrong policy for you and your family. To make sure you pick the right policy with the right premium structure for you, you need to first know what type of insurance premium you want, so read on, my friend.

Insurance premiums

Stepped premiums

These are calculated based on the policy holder's age. The younger the policy holder, the cheaper the premium. The catch is that as your age increases, so do your premiums.

Level premiums

These premiums are the opposite of stepped premiums. Here, you tend to pay a higher amount at the beginning, but end up paying less as you grow older. While this sounds BRILLIANT in theory, you do need to consider whether paying more now is the right thing to do for your cash flow and life stage. You should also consider the TOTAL premiums paid over the life of the policy.

Hybrid premiums

This is a mix of both level and stepped premiums. Hybrid premiums increase until a predetermined age and then they level off. Not all insurers offer this option.

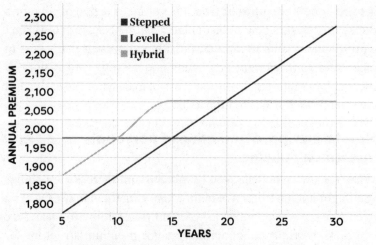

Stepped, levelled and hybrid premiums

Additional questions to ask when shopping for a personal income protection policy:

● What is the waiting period to claim? This is usually between 30 and 90 days from the time of the illness or injury. Note: the longer the waiting period, the lower your premium will be. If you're 30, single and have no savings, I probably wouldn't recommend a 90-day waiting period because you can't afford that. You don't have an emergency fund or a partner with an income. If something happened to you, how quickly would you need access to cash? When you get more financially secure, you could look at reducing these premiums.

● What evidence is needed to verify your salary?

● Is the insurance going to be inside of your superannuation or outside?

● What do they class as 'total and permanent' disability?

● Do they have a pre-existing conditions list?

How much cover do I need?

Calculating life insurance

This is an incredibly important question, and one that many of us struggle to answer. After all, how do you put a value on a life? It's important to look at this in detail, though, to ensure you are able to protect your family's financial future. The reality is that the ideal amount of life insurance varies greatly depending on your personal circumstances, life stage and the state of your finances.

To work out the level of cover you might need, you need to calculate how much money your family would need in order to maintain their current lifestyle if you weren't around to financially contribute anymore. An easy way to do this is:

● Calculate your outstanding debts – this includes your mortgage, credit cards, and any other money you owe. Sadly, the only debt that dies with you is HECS/HELP – if you pass away, all other debts will be passed on to your family. This might not be applicable for your current life stage, but it's important to know that if your financial situation changes (i.e. you buy your first home or an investment property, or take on a car loan) you need to update your insurance to take that into consideration.

- Tally the income you currently bring in and what needs to be covered. Think about any expenses your family will still need to pay for if you're not around. This could be a range of things from living costs, investments or even replacing homemaker duties. It's a common misconception that stay-at-home parents don't need life insurance because they don't have an income – it's expensive to replace the duties carried out by this person! How much would home maintenance, housekeeping, child transportation and child-minding cost? This figure will astound you, and it's absolutely worth making sure you're covered for it.

- Price your funeral expenses – this is an estimate of your funeral and legal costs when you pass away.

- To avoid over-insuring, work out what assets you have that your family could turn into cash. This will be personal, though, as you might want your family to keep those assets, not sell them.

Calculating trauma (or critical illness) insurance

Have a think about the rough amount you'd need to live comfortably if you experienced a traumatic event, and the rough costs associated with living with a major illness such as cancer.

Calculating total permanent disability (TPD) insurance

When working out how much TPD cover you need, you should take into consideration how much money you'll lose from not working (factor in your income protection cover if you have it), your ongoing expenses, your debts and mortgage, and any costs associated with a change in lifestyle – for example, having to renovate your bathroom to accommodate a wheelchair, putting a ramp or lift in your home, or hiring a carer.

'This all sounds great. I'd like to take out $300 million in insurance please, Victoria!'

Hold up right there. There are actually limits to how much insurance you can apply for.

Maximum sum insured

The maximum sum insured is the maximum amount of life insurance you can take out depending on your personal situation and the policy you choose. Many life insurance policies will offer the maximum sum insured, which can change depending on your age, occupation and other personal details.

Maximum cover for additional benefits

Sometimes additional benefits will also have a maximum additional benefit that is applied. For example, a particular plan might provide your family with funeral expenses up to a maximum of $15,000.

Maximum sum insured for TPD

Life insurance underwriters will look closely at the amount of cover you apply for in a TPD policy to make sure it doesn't go beyond what you would be entitled to if you had continued working. Life insurance companies do not want policies that will provide you with more money than you'd have if you had continued to work.

Maximum sum for trauma insurance

Similar to TPD insurance, you will need to clearly explain your reasoning if taking out a large trauma insurance policy. Being able to afford the premiums isn't enough. You must be able to articulate why you require such a large payout. Most policies only offer up to $2 million in cover.

Other factors that affect the amount of cover you're allowed to take out include your age, your occupation, pre-existing medical issues, some hereditary medical conditions in your immediate family (biological parents and siblings) and any dangerous pastimes or hobbies you're involved in, such as BASE-jumping, flying planes or even playing a professional sport.

If you don't want to do this alone, a good financial adviser will be able to make recommendations on all of the mentioned insurances based on your personal situation, your wants and your needs. A financial adviser can also provide you with insurance-only advice if you don't want advice on investment or superannuation at this stage of your life.

• •

PERSONAL INSURANCE AUDIT

Income protection

☐ Yes ☐ No

Inside or outside of super .... How much cover ....

TPD

☐ Yes ☐ No

Inside or outside of super .... How much cover ....

Life insurance

☐ Yes ☐ No

Inside or outside of super .... How much cover ....

Trauma

☐ Yes ☐ No

How much cover ....

• •

Private health insurance

When it comes to public health care, Australia is known as a very lucky country. Whether you're insured or not, if you need to see a doctor or have a life-threatening injury or illness, you can and will receive care regardless of your income.

While having private health insurance is financially beneficial to those who earn over a certain amount every year, it's also appealing to people who value the option of having elective treatments done sooner, access to private hospitals and/or extras such as optical, dental and physio.

A common misconception is that by having private health insurance you won't have to pay out of pocket for anything. This is definitely not the case. While yes, you will be able to have an operation in a private hospital with the doctor of your choice, you may still be stung for having a special anaesthetist or a private room. Also, private health insurance usually only covers certain medical bills and little else, which is why you'll still need to consider personal insurances. Higher levels of coverage can be amazing, but unfortunately there are still gaps. For instance, your private health policy is never going to cover you for loss of income if you can't work due to a medical condition.

Depending on your values, the four types of personal insurance can work well in collaboration with private health insurance.

Hot tip: A lot of people just assume that if you're paying for private health insurance you get to be treated as a private patient in a private hospital. This is not always the case! It may just mean that you can be treated as a private patient in a public hospital. If this is a concern, make sure you select 'private hospital' and not just private extras. This will guarantee that you're able to access treatment in a private hospital. Another thing to note here while we're talking about public versus private hospitals is that if an emergency eventuates you're more than likely to end up in a public hospital instead of private regardless of your health insurance – the public system here in Australia is far better equipped to deal with emergency situations than a private hospital is, and patients are often transferred to public hospitals in emergency situations.

Where to find and compare policies

To be completely frank, I'm not a fan of online comparison websites because they get paid by the insurers to advertise their products. This can mean the recommendations are not objective. I really like privatehealth.gov.au. You can use their comparison tool as well as read about any private health insurance changes and incentives.

Questions to ask when shopping for a private health insurance policy:

● Are there any waiting periods?
● Are there any exclusions?
● Does the policy cover private hospital stays?

Other insurances

As a financial adviser, I only work with clients on personal insurances. That said, it's still important for you to factor in other insurances into your budget because they will help protect your assets and wealth. Be sure to re-evaluate your deal every year to make sure you're getting the best bang for your buck!

Other insurances you may like to consider include:

● home and contents insurance
● building only insurance
● contents only insurance
● landlord insurance
● car insurance
● travel insurance
● pet insurance

- professional insurances
  - public liability
  - professional indemnity
  - tool insurance.

I feel really passionately about ensuring you understand the importance of insurance. If you've been reading along thinking 'I'm young, I'll worry about this part later down the track', think again, my friend. Insurance from a young age is so valuable, because you're unlikely to have experienced a serious health issue or trauma; establishing insurance now will ensure you have the least amount of exclusions, or even ensure that you can be insured! Once you've experienced a significant health event, many insurers won't cover you at all – so put Future You first here, and please, please review your insurance policies and ensure you're appropriately covered. Seek professional advice if you need it.

• • • • • •

RENEE, 26 – NSW

I was diagnosed with a rare cancer at 25. I was raced into surgery with a one-year recovery. I had to quit my job unexpectedly and Centrelink couldn't offer me much. I applied for income protection and it took well over a year to come through. In that year, I had no personal income but, thankfully, I had my parents. It was a year of living off $200 a week (which barely covers bills), and medical costs were building. I fell so far behind everyone else. My friends were buying houses, going on holidays and I was just stuck. She's on the Money *got me through that tough situation and made me financially aware. I now have savings and an emergency fund ready to go, because I learnt the hard way how important that is.*

• • • • • •

TAKE NOTE

You don't need to be a wealthy homeowner
to warrant having life insurance.

....

Some insurances make sense to have inside
your super, while others don't.

....

Your insurance needs will change as your lifestyle changes.

....

Chapter 15

Relationships

It doesn't matter if you're six days, six months or six years into a relationship, having conversations about money can often feel about as comfortable as an echidna cuddle. But unlike roaming the bush to find and hug a little spiky friend, talking about money with your partner is 100 per cent necessary.

Cited as the number one thing couples argue about, money can quite literally make or break a relationship, which is why it's important that you get on the same page as your partner as quickly as possible. While personal finance is personal, achieving and maintaining financial independence doesn't mean you're not allowed to share your money. Combining incomes, assets and savings can enable you to set and achieve large goals that give your life meaning. That said, being in a relationship does not mean you have to put all your money into one account and give your partner complete control. It's simply about making shared decisions that put both parties in the best possible position.

The best way to get and stay on the same page as your partner is to make sure that you have a clear understanding of each other's money stories. It's crucial that you both know how you were raised and how money was spoken about. In my opinion, it's never too early to talk about money with someone. I'm not saying you should ask them how much they earn, how much they have in super and what their investment portfolio looks like on your first Bumble date. Having money conversations needs to start with non-confrontational topics like how we FEEL about spending and saving, rather than what we personally do.

Potential questions to ask:

- When you were growing up, did your mum or dad manage the money? Or was it more of a joint effort?
- Was money scarce or in abundance? (Offer up what your experience was like.)
- Did you work during high school?
- Were you a good saver?
- Do you have goals for any overseas travel?
- What's your ideal retirement age?
- Have you ever been in debt?

That last question can be a tricky one, particularly if that person is currently in debt. For many, admitting that you have debt can feel shameful and embarrassing. When you're in the early days of dating someone, you hardly want to advertise the fact that, oh hey, you've got a $14,000 personal loan. But the thing is, that debt is going to affect your relationship. The sooner you can both be transparent about your financial situation and define what you want it to look like, the sooner you'll find out if you share enough beliefs and values to make things work.

When entering a relationship, ask yourself the following questions:

1. Are you at risk of an STD? (I'm talking about sexually transmitted debt!)
2. Are you ready to support your partner's goals even if they're different to yours?

3. Are you ready to feel like a united force?
4. Do you want the accountability that comes with shared finances?

It's common to see conflict in couples when one person has grown up in a family where money was scarce, while the other had it in abundance. People who grew up in a household where money was tight may be quite hesitant to spend or invest. They might quite literally hoard their savings. Those who grew up with money never being an issue might be excited to invest, or might not be fussed about saving. In order for you to correctly identify (and then rectify) your friction points, you need to figure out what your money stories look like, share them with each other and then talk about what you want your new money story to look like as a couple.

The best way to start having constructive conversations with your partner about money is to remember that you're on the same team. It's you and your partner against the problem, not you and your partner against each other. If you're currently in a relationship and eager for your partner to change their money habits, it's important to remember that you can't just magically change the qualities you don't like about someone. You need to have open and honest conversations that empower them (and/or you) to start forming positive money behaviours and habits. If you can create solid goals together that you're both passionate about, it will be a lot easier to change behaviours, because you'll both know WHY you're changing them. This is far more constructive than 'You're not very good at money and I want you to be.' People need to see the carrot on the stick. Change is uncomfortable, and the average person is not going to make themselves uncomfortable unless they can see a really big reward.

The same sort of conversations need to be had around investing. I've had clients come to me where one person wants to purchase an investment property and the other wants to enter the share market. I have had to remind them that it all comes back to values. If you can't articulate the reasons why you value investing in a particular asset class, go back and do more research. The excuse that you want to buy stocks because your parents buy stocks will not cut it. Show your partner WHY this is where you think your money should go.

Thinking about combining finances?

Determining if and when it's right to combine finances with your partner is a completely personal decision. It may seem daunting to share your life savings, but remember, you can still maintain financial independence in a relationship where you have shared money goals. Each person's set-up and cash-flow system can look different. I've seen couples pool all, some or none of their personal incomes. It's okay to say that you don't want to put your personal savings into a shared goal. Just because you enter a relationship doesn't mean that person gets your savings or assets. You have to do what both parties feel comfortable with. Equality in a relationship is up to us. One of the biggest hurdles I see couples run into is disproportionate amounts of savings or income. While it may look like one person is better at saving than the other, it's important to acknowledge that this discrepancy is often circumstantial.

Let's say you have $80,000 in your savings account and your partner only has $1000. Before you make assumptions about your partner's ability to save, ask yourself: Why am I in this position and why are they in theirs? Perhaps you were able to live rent-free at home until the age of 30. Perhaps your partner had to leave home at 17. Same goes for income. Some people may have a high-paying trade that they've been doing since the age of 15, while others might be investing heavily in their education at the moment. At the end of the day, if you know that you are ready to have shared goals with this person, maybe it's your savings or their income that will get you both there.

I always encourage couples to ensure that both parties know how to pay bills, invest and create wealth. It's fine if you want your partner to do the actual mechanics of it, or vice versa, but being in the know about which bill is being paid from which account is vital. You both need to be aware of where money is coming from and where it's going. Relationships and circumstances can change in an instant, which is why having financial literacy as well as open and honest communication is key.

In every relationship, people tend to gravitate towards different roles. One person may love doing laundry, while the other prefers yard work. I personally love cooking, but have friends who would rather pressure-wash their bins than whip up a pasta dinner for two. Managing money is just another one of these roles, and whoever is doing it probably feels like it's their way of contributing to the relationship. It can be hard for someone to hear that their partner wants to be more across the finances, because this can make them feel like they're not doing a good enough job. Try dialogue like, 'Hey, I don't understand how this works. Can you show me in case I need to do it?' or 'I'd really like to help with structuring our cash flow. Can you talk me through how you're currently doing it?'

I also think it's imperative for individuals to maintain one private savings account. Having access to money puts you in the position where you're able to make financial decisions independent of your partner. This is important, because it may help get you out of a situation you don't want to be in, such as your relationship or job. That money could save you. When it comes to making decisions that protect your safety and mental health, you don't want to be completely dependent on your partner. I don't want anyone to feel like they can't make a change because of money. We'll discuss financial abuse later in this chapter, but being proactive about protecting yourself financially is absolutely imperative.

While there are multiple degrees to which you can combine finances, a common way to start is by figuring out a cash-flow system. In Chapter 2, we discussed mapping out your money. You and your partner can do this as a team and set up a cash hub, automatic bill payments and joint savings accounts that will help you reach your shared financial goals.

Aside from the initial sit-down sessions of budgeting, goal setting and organising your cash flow, I don't feel like you need to have special date nights or breakfast meetings to talk about money. You should be talking about it all the time. It shouldn't be something that creates anxiety – both parties should feel inspired, empowered and in control. If money is the thing that you and your partner yell about when the kids are in bed at night, you need to go back to your money stories and get on the same page. Just remember, talking about money can trigger an emotional response like no other. It's important to take a step back to keep the conversation unemotional and, in many cases, less accusatory. If you're finding that you or your partner completely shuts down, try speaking to a therapist or financial counsellor. Having a third party present can make things more civilised and help you to gain a new perspective.

Creating a shared budget, setting goals and structuring a no-fail cash-flow strategy will make it much easier for you to communicate why you can or cannot support your partner's future purchases. Having this visually laid out in a spreadsheet means you'll be able to say, 'It's not in the budget for us to do this activity, and here's why' or 'Does taking on that extra payment delay us from reaching our goals?'

Speaking of goals . . .

● ●

YOUR MUTUAL GOALS WISH LIST

You've already identified your personal goals in Chapter 4 – now it's time to work on your shared goals. Depending on your relationship, some of these might be the same as those you've listed in the personal section. Take this time to talk about them with your partner. Make sure you both feel the same way about them. Find out what goals your partner has. Tap into their desires and find out what they want to do in the future. Dream all the dreams. Write down every goal that can be achieved with money. These could include a holiday, retirement by age 55, a shared side hustle, a home, an investment property or a savings goal that can be invested.

....

....

....

Now choose the goals that you both want to accomplish (like, yesterday). ....

....

How many are there? ....

Do they seem achievable with the budget you currently have?

....

....

Remember, your values, beliefs, goals, income, mental health and energy levels are always changing. Your budget is allowed to change with you, and can be constantly adjusted to reflect new goals. Every month, make sure your budget is set up to help you and your partner achieve your goals.

● ●

YOUR FIRST FIVE GOALS

Choose five goals to focus on together. One long-term, two medium-term and two short-term.

Goal 1 – Long-term

Our specific goal is: ....

We will measure this goal by: ....

....

Our milestones for this goal are: ....

....

We will know we have achieved our goal when: ....

....

When we achieve our goal we are going to: ....

....

Think: ....

Feel: ....

Do: ....

Goal 2 – Medium-term

Our specific goal is: ....

We will measure this goal by: ....

....

Our milestones for this goal are: ....

....

We will know we have achieved our goal when: ....

....

When we achieve our goal we are going to: ....

....

Think: ....

Feel: ....

Do: ....

Goal 3 – Medium-term

Our specific goal is: ....

We will measure this goal by: ....

....

Our milestones for this goal are: ....

....

We will know we have achieved our goal when: ....

....

When we achieve our goal we are going to: ....

....

Think: ....

Feel: ....

Do: ....

Goal 4 – Short-term

Our specific goal is: ....

We will measure this goal by: ....

....

Our milestones for this goal are: ....

....

We will know we have achieved our goal when: ....

....

When we achieve our goal we are going to: ....

....

Think: ....

Feel: ....

Do: ....

Goal 5 – Short-term

Our specific goal is: ....

We will measure this goal by: ....

....

Our milestones for this goal are: ....

....

We will know we have achieved our goal when: ....

....

When we achieve our goal we are going to: ....

....

Think: ....

Feel: ....

Do: ....

● ●

When things don't work out

Unlike a Disney movie, real-life relationships don't always work out. I think it's incredibly healthy and brave to recognise when a relationship is no longer serving you or your partner. Unfortunately, many relationships continue longer than they should due to the anxiety about losing a dual income and the fear of splitting money and assets. When you factor kids into the mix, you're even more likely to hang on.

If you're in a de facto relationship or are married, it's important to know what you and your partner would be entitled to financially if you were to separate. When it comes to finances, de facto relationships in Australia are treated the same as marriages, especially when children are involved. A de facto relationship is defined as two people living domestically together for two years or more. However, if you share children you may be held to this same standard after only a few months.

In a perfect world, couples who are separating should be able to pragmatically decide how to divide assets. But let's be honest, emotions usually get in the way. More often than not, feelings get hurt, the urge to seek revenge may rise and then you need someone to mediate. Needing a mediator isn't a bad thing. In fact, it's important to seek independent legal advice about your situation because so many factors contribute to the outcome of a separation. Are there kids? Does one partner require child support payments? Do both partners work? Who earns more? Is one financially dependent on the other? Does superannuation need to be split and paid to one partner? Is someone entitled to spouse or de facto maintenance payments? Since we're all about saving money here, it's in everyone's best interest to avoid going to court because that's when lawyer fees can become quite hefty! A great place to start is the Family Relationship Advice Line (FRAL) 1800 050 321.

Hot tip: In Western Australia, if you are in a de facto relationship and separate from your partner, superannuation is not considered an asset for the purpose of property division. That means if you were a de facto homemaker for 20 years and then separated from your partner, you wouldn't be able to access half of the money you and your partner had saved for your retirement. It's an antiquated practice that is leaving many de facto partners disadvantaged. Thankfully, there is legislation in place to change this, but it has yet to come into effect.

Financial abuse

Financial abuse is any situation where the actions or behaviours of someone you trust make you feel like you're not in control of financial decisions that directly impact you. It's important to know that financial abuse doesn't discriminate. It can happen to anyone, and it's not limited to romantic relationships.

Red flags and signs of financial abuse

- A partner forces you to stop working or earning money. This often arises when a couple decides to have kids. While this is 100 per cent an okay decision for you to make yourself, it's never okay for someone to tell you that you can't return to work after having a baby.
- You've been isolated from friends and family, so when you do need to reach out for support, you don't feel safe to do so.
- Someone is making you feel like you're not competent enough to handle money.

- There is lack of transparency around your financial life and the feeling that information is being withheld.
- You are being asked to sign documents without fully understanding what you're signing.
- A family member is forcing you to claim benefits you're not entitled to.
- A family member is forcing you to take out a loan in your name.
- A family member is forcing you to go guarantor on a mortgage.
- Someone is racking up debt in your name.
- Someone is selling possessions of yours without your permission.
- A family member forces you to change your will or sign over ownership of accounts and assets.

While this insidious type of abuse can come in many different shapes and forms, it does most commonly occur inside a romantic relationship.

Sadly, 98 per cent of women who report domestic violence to police also suffer from financial abuse. For some, this means actively being prevented from going to work and earning money. For others it means being provided with limited amounts of money and denied access to their own bank accounts. For many, it's a slow grinding down of their independence and confidence until they barely feel able to look after themselves.

According to Core Data, three in five Australian women in relationships are leaving themselves open to financial abuse, because they don't have savings or assets of their own. Nine out of ten domestic violence victims don't have the necessary money to leave an abusive relationship. This is why I'm such an advocate for having a personal emergency fund that enables choice, as well as a financial escape plan.

While some relationships can be so violent it's important to leave the moment you can, others should be exited with a financial strategy in place. This puts you in the best position to find some sort of independence.

Things to consider when exiting a financially abusive relationship:

- If you don't have your own emergency savings fund set up, try to open a bank account in your own name.
- While you may not have access to your own money, try to take small additional amounts out while doing the grocery shopping. Use this money to build a nest egg that will support you when you finally leave.
- When considering where to open this account, be mindful that some banks like the Commonwealth Bank and NAB have savings accounts that may make you eligible for a domestic abuse grant.
- Determine what assets are on the table. When you leave you'll want to be able to tell your lawyer if you own a home, have money invested in shares, own an investment property, etc. Take photos or copies of every document that can prove this. These can include, but are not limited to, bank statements, bills and mortgage statements. If you don't feel safe keeping these in your home, try giving them to a friend, family member, financial adviser or lawyer.
- You should also take copies of your (and your children's) identification documents. These include a passport, driver's licence, Medicare card, citizenship certificate and/or visa information. Again, if you do not feel safe having these copies in your home or on your computer, send them to a trusted source.
- Is your name attached to any lease? Once you do leave, you'll need to notify the landlord that you've left an abusive relationship and are no longer liable. The same goes for utility bills.
- Contact Australia Post and notify them of your change of address. CAUTION: They will usually mail a card saying that your mail has now been redirected. While they won't list the

new address, it's important to be aware of this in case you're trying to act discreetly.

- Make a budget. If you're able to safely leave with money in a bank account, determine what is the lowest amount of money you can survive on.

Resources to get help:

- DVConnect Womensline 1800 811 811
- Kids Helpline 1800 55 1800
- Relationships Australia 1300 364 277
- 1800RESPECT 1800 737 732

● ● ● ● ● ●

JESSE, 26 – NSW

I came from a single-income family. I had both parents, but my mum stayed at home while raising us. My dad was also a low-income earner and while we had everything we needed, we rarely had surplus or blow money. The consensus growing up was that money is always tight. I think this left me always wanting to have some money and not wanting to struggle.

When I started working full time I bought a car for $10,000 in cash and also saved another $10,000 in under two years. I was also renting, so I wasn't doing this while living at home. I loved the idea of saving money and budgeting, and would actually have friends come over and I'd help them with their budgets. Then I got married. Goodbye to my $10,000 savings. We got married within six months of engagement and saved $25,000 for the wedding, but also used the $10,000 I'd saved. We ended up with $14,000 on my dad's credit card afterwards. I thought, 'We'll get rid of that in six months'. But paying off debt is much harder than saving. After we got married I changed careers and started full-time study alongside work, so I went down to four days instead of five. Within three months of marriage my husband got a rugby injury and couldn't work for three months because he had a physical labour job and no income insurance. We were earning $600 a week and our rent was $480. I was stealing toilet paper from my parents. I will never ever be in that position again. We paid off half of the credit card and then I sold my car to pay off the other half because it felt like the debt was not moving and the car had a lot of expenses.

Flash forward: After a year I had fully transitioned into my new career. I had a new job as a skin therapist earning great commission. We moved in with my dad, as I really wanted to move overseas. We saved $15,000 in a year and then moved to the UK to travel. We moved without jobs and without anywhere to live. I found a job in two weeks, thankfully, and we've been here for a year and a half. We have a £1000 emergency fund and £800 in savings. We still put away £300 a month for travel, because that's what we moved here for, but now we don't have to worry about buying a loaf of bread or some toilet paper. My husband has income insurance because he still plays rugby and has new injuries all the time. I've just added a regular voluntary contribution to my pension fund here. I'm watching our super in Australia to make sure it is doing okay even though we aren't contributing, and I have a goal to come home in September with £5000 so we don't have to build from scratch.

JESSICA, 22 – SA

I started working at ten years old to support my family. All my money has always gone to the family because my mum was ill and my dad was on the disability pension, despite being fit enough to work. When my parents separated, I purchased my mum's half of our house because my dad told me if I didn't my brother and sister would be homeless and it would be all my fault. I was being charged half the mortgage, plus a quarter of the bills and $200 a week to live at home. Soon after, we sold that house so the family could relocate to the city and the same thing happened – I purchased part of the property due to emotional manipulation. I chose to stay in my home town and never lived in that property, but I still had to pay a third of EVERYTHING. I was also renting my own place. I was in a really bad mental space because every time I had money, I would get a phone call from them begging me to give them some. I reconnected with my therapist who told me I had a very toxic parent and I needed to sever ties. I approached a lawyer to help me tell my dad I wanted to sell (I had previously *mentioned this and it triggered a huge fight), and the house was put on the market pretty quickly. Smooth sailing to sell – I got confirmation today (6/2/20) that we have officially sold the house. I've never cried so much. Knowing I'll be free both financially and emotionally is the best way to start a new year!*

BRONTE, 24 – VIC

I started working doing a paper run at age 13. I've worked consistently since then. I've always had a job and worked lots of hours. But somehow I always thought having savings was an elusive thing that would 'come with time', something that just happens to you once you reach a certain age. Eighteen turned to 19 turned to 21 turned to 23. I moved from regional Victoria to Melbourne with nothing to my name. Not a dollar. No real assets to speak of other than my car, a bike and a couple of good holidays. I moved with my boyfriend, who was in an incredibly financially healthy position, but leeched my money instead, so by the time we broke up, I was dead broke, depressed and emotionally scarred. But it was also a good kick in the butt. Almost 12 months later I have developed a ridiculously automated spreadsheet that tracks EVERYTHING, putting my expenditure right there in front of me – there's no escaping it. I finally have almost $3000 in my Raiz account and over $5000 in my savings. I've continued to work through my studies and have gone from a mid-level insurance claims role to being a communications adviser for the state government. If you'd told me a year ago I'd be where I am now, I wouldn't have believed you for a second. It took a nasty break-up and some self-realisation for me to realise the importance of financial independence, but gosh, once you work it out, it sticks with you.

● ● ● ● ● ●

TAKE NOTE

Achieving and maintaining financial independence
doesn't mean you can't share your money.

....

Change is uncomfortable, and the average person
is not going to make themselves uncomfortable
unless they can see a really big reward.

....

Creating a shared budget, setting goals and structuring a no-fail
cash-flow strategy will make it much easier for you to communicate
why you can or cannot support your partner's future purchases.

....

Chapter 16

Family planning

Whether you've been thinking about having a family since playing mums and dads in kindy or, unlike me, you've only just started to ponder the topic, you'll probably want to pay close attention to this chapter.

While babies are all sorts of adorable, and kids can bring a new sense of purpose and meaning to your life, the truth is – they're expensive. (Totally worth it, but expensive.) Whether you're embarking on this journey alone or with a partner, it's easy to under-estimate the potential expenses associated with starting a family.

According to the Australian Institute of Family Studies, the average essential cost of raising one kid is $297,700. This covers things like food, clothing, school and utilities till the age of 18. If you factor in you or your partner taking extended unpaid parental leave for the first one to four years, you could also miss out on a substantial amount of income. For example, let's say you were earning $90,000 a year. After your paid maternity leave ends, you want to stay home for another three years. That means you're potentially missing out on $270,000, bringing the true cost of having your child closer to $567,700.

For a lot of people, having kids is a major life goal. You know I love goal setting, so let's look at how you can save and budget to have kids without compromising on your financial freedom. While you can't anticipate what your experience will be, there are numerous costs you should be mindful of, so let's start by researching different scenarios.

Below are three hypothetical case studies on the cost of becoming pregnant, delivering a baby and raising kids in Australia.

Getting pregnant

Although it may seem like everyone is getting pregnant left, right and centre, the truth is, it can be extremely difficult to fall pregnant. Some women need to shell out $50 for an ovulation test, while others will choose to drop thousands and thousands of dollars on IVF treatments.

While Medicare does offer some rebates for reproductive procedures and costs, many of these need to be paid for out of pocket. The same goes for privately insured patients. When it comes to fertility issues, if your doctor and specialist think you need IVF, about half of the costs will usually be covered by Medicare.

Meet: Fertile Myrtle, Clucky Lucky and Resilient Rhonda

The cost of pregnancy can differ depending on your situation. Fertile Myrtle, Clucky Lucky and Resilient Rhonda present three cases in point:

Fertile Myrtle
- One month of prenatal vitamins – $35
- Peed on one pregnancy test – $15
- Visit to the doctor to confirm – $80
- Total: $130

Clucky Lucky
- Six months of prenatal vitamins – $210
- Six months of ovulation tracking tests – $300
- Six pregnancy tests – $90
- Visit to the doctor to confirm – $80
- Pregnancy loss and associated care – $1000
- Three more months of ovulation tracking tests – $150
- Three more pregnancy tests – $45
- Visit to the doctor to confirm – $80
- Total: $1955

Resilient Rhonda
- Twenty-four months of prenatal vitamins – $840
- Twelve months of ovulation tracking tests – $600
- Eighteen pregnancy tests – $270
- Fertility specialist appointment – $450
- Pregnancy loss and associated care – $1000
- Laparoscopic surgery to flush tubes – $3000
- Three rounds of IVF – $42,000
- Medication: $3000
- Total: $51,160

Being pregnant

Now that Myrtle, Lucky and Rhonda are pregnant, let's look at the potential costs that they could incur throughout their pregnancies.

Fertile Myrtle
- Nine months of prenatal vitamins – $315
- Gets hand-me-down maternity clothing from older sister – $0
- Visits to the doctor and scans – $400
- Husband takes a very gram-worthy selfie of her cute bump – $0
- Total: $715

Clucky Lucky
- Nine months of prenatal vitamins – $315
- Mylanta for heartburn – $300
- Visits to the doctor and scans – $800
- Maternity clothing (just needs some jeans and maxi dresses) – $300
- Nine months of prenatal yoga classes – $1000
- Calm birth class – $790
- Maternity photo shoot (one hour) – $450
- In-depth 'what's happening to my baby?' app – $19
- Total: $3974

Resilient Rhonda
- Nine months of special prenatal vitamins that don't make her sick – $440
- Doctor visit and prescription for anti-nausea tablets – $160
- Visits to the doctor and scans – $800
- Office-appropriate maternity clothing – $700
- Physio and massage appointments for back pain – $800
- Maternity photo shoot (three hours) – $860
- Total: $3760

Giving birth

Depending on where you live and your level of health cover, the cost of giving birth can range from zero to $14,000.

Fertile Myrtle – public patient
- Vaginal delivery in public hospital – $0
- Hospital bag contents – $50
- Total: $50

Clucky Lucky – private patient
- Vaginal delivery in private hospital – $9000
- Doula – $2000
- Hospital bag contents – $100
- Total: $11,100

Resilient Rhonda – private patient
- C-section – $14,000
- Hospital bag contents – $100
- Total: $14,100

From conception to birth, here's what our girls spent.

Myrtle: $931
Lucky: $17,029
Rhonda: $69,020

Remember, this was the cost of just getting to hold their babies in their arms. See how wildly different it can be? I know it's frustrating not to be able to predict what your road to motherhood will look like, but if becoming a parent is your number one goal then you may want to adjust your savings goal. If you don't end up needing the money, then lucky you – more money to throw in your superannuation, an investment or to kick start a savings account for your new family member!

After the birth

While I'm not going to go into as much detail about what you may want or need after your baby has been born, let's have quick look at the list of potential costs:

Infancy

- Nursery items: bassinet, crib, port-a-cot, car seat, pram, lounger, carrier, playmat, baby monitor, nappy bucket, baby carrier, linen, towels, burp cloths
- Nappies and wipes
- Creams, balms, and other baby-safe toiletries
- Formula, bottles and a steriliser
- Dummies, teethers, toys, stroller and car seat accessories
- Newborn photoshoot
- Nikes that they only wear for four months
- Oh and DAY CARE (more on this in a second)

Toddlerhood

- Kids love to get sick at this age, so factor in:
  - antibiotics
  - cough syrup
  - allergy medicine
  - worm medicine
- Airfares from the age of two
- Babysitters
- DAY CARE still . . . plus pre-school costs
- Your gym membership, because it's the only place that makes you feel sane, and you're also probably drinking wine again

Little kids

- School fees (yes, even with a public education you'll still need to pay some fees!)
- Uniform fees
- Extracurricular activities
  - Birthday parties (hosting is expensive, plus you attend one nearly every week)
- Streaming services
- Holidays are also more expensive now because you have to travel during school holidays

Big kids

- Increase in school fees
- Uniform fees
- Extracurricular activities
- Travel costs for sport
- Tutoring
- Social life
- Potentially a phone and computer
- OMG groceries – how do they eat so much?

Really big kids

- Uni fees
- Mum and Dad bail-out fund
- Weddings
- Gifts for the grandkids!

I think you get the point – the cost of having kids can be exponential. Don't freak out though, there is a pragmatic way to look at this. The best place to start is by figuring out your parental leave options.

Planning your parental leave

As an employee

If you are employed, parental leave can be taken:

- when you give birth
- when your spouse or de facto partner gives birth
- when you adopt a child under the age of 16.

In Australia, full-time employees are legally entitled to 12 months of **unpaid** parental leave. You may also request an additional 12 months. To be clear, this means that you are entitled to take one to two years off without the risk of losing your position.

Many companies offer **paid** parental leave. The amount of leave offered depends on your employment contract and company's policy. You may not know how much leave you want to take until after you have a baby, but it's never too early to find out what your employer offers and consider your options. For example, your company may offer 12 weeks at full pay. It might be worth asking if they'd consider 24 weeks at half pay to help with budgeting, as well as potentially spreading your payments across financial years for tax purposes.

Regardless of what your work contributes financially, the Australian Government will pay you for 18 weeks at minimum wage through the Paid Parental Leave scheme. To qualify, you must have averaged two days of work per week for the 40 weeks before you had your baby.

Eligible working spouses or de facto partners can also receive two weeks paid leave at minimum wage. While this is a fantastic initiative, some couples find it difficult to have to drop down to a minimum wage level. If your partner would like to take spouse or de facto leave, have them speak to their employer to see if they have a paid parental leave policy. Alternatively, they could make this a personal savings goal as well.

As a freelancer or sole trader

While it's a bit harder to walk away from your own business or side hustle, it's important to have a financial cushion for the first 12 to 24 weeks after having a baby.

If you meet the government's eligibility requirements, then you should be able to receive 18 weeks of paid parental leave at minimum wage.

Before applying, ensure you can prove that:

- you're an Australian resident
- you're the primary carer of the newborn or adopted child under the age of 16
- in the financial year before the date of birth or date of adoption, you had an adjusted taxable income of $150,000 or less
- you worked approximately ten months out of the 13 before your child was born/adopted
- you worked at least 330 hours (just over one day a week) in that ten-month period
- you didn't take more than eight weeks off between days worked during that ten-month period (after 1 January 2020 this was extended to 12 weeks)
- you will actually NOT BE WORKING while on leave.

If you don't qualify for government assistance, or if you don't think you can cover your costs on minimum wage, prioritise setting up your own parental leave account. The figure you'll be able to contribute will depend on your personal situation, but the goal is to supplement your income with this money.

Child care

When you're ready to go back to work (or not ready, but have to) OR simply want to put your child into child care so they can socialise and you can have a moment to #breathe, child care can be a fantastic option! As the country with the third-highest cost of child care worldwide, Australian parents are at the mercy of the government for help to cover these costs. As of 2018, the Australian Government offers a Child Care Subsidy that gives eligible families access to either 36, 72 or 100 hours of subsidised child care per fortnight. Entitlement is calculated according to how many hours of work, training or study a parent does. To be eligible for the subsidy, both parents must work or study at least eight hours a fortnight, you must send your child to an approved child care provider and your child must be immunised. This is also an income-tested scheme.

Unfortunately, despite the exorbitant cost of child care, it's one of the few options available to those wishing to sustain their careers. For example, when my friend Sally was 26 years old she was earning $50,000 a year. Fast forward three years and two babies, and Sally decided to put both kids in child care full time so she could go back to work and keep moving forward in her role. Full-time child care in her suburb for one child cost $105 a day, which means she was paying $210 a day for both kids to be in child care. Let's do the maths:

- $210 × 5 days a week = $1050
- $1050 × 52 weeks in a year = $54,600

Sally's Child Care Subsidy was $7500 per child due to her husband's income. So:

- $54,600 – $15,000 = $39,600
- Sally's income ($50,000) – day care fees ($39,600) = $10,400

So Sally was working full-time hours and taking home just $10,400 a year. A lot of people would argue that it's not worth it, but think about how Sally's career looks now, versus how it would if she'd tried to re-enter the workforce five to seven years down the track. Let's also consider her mental health. While some people are 100 per cent fulfilled staying home with their children, Sally still wanted to feel connected to her career, contribute financially and set an example for her kids.

Before you start sweating at the idea of spending $39,600 on child care, remember that the costs can vary drastically depending on the state you live in and, in particular, the suburb. Daily rates range between $75 to $130 a day per child. This includes both child care centres and family day care.

State	Median cost in major cities	Median cost in regional areas	Median cost in all areas
NSW	$494	$391	$490
Vic	$490	$440	$490
Qld	$419	$404	$417
WA	$473	$505	$475
SA	$460	$445	$458
Tas	$435	$389	$429
ACT	$560	N/A	$560
NT	N/A	$450	$450
National	**$465**	**$417**	**$460**

Median weekly cost of 50 hours long day care
(Source: ATO)

Families earning $189,390 or less per year will not have their Child Care Subsidy capped. Families earning over $189,390 and under $353,680 will have an annual cap of $10,560 per year per child.

What is your combined family income? This determines what percentage of the hourly fee you'll be subsidised.

CCS family income thresholds^	Subsidy per cent
Up to $69,390	85%
More than $69,390 to below $174,390	Decreasing to 50%
$174,390 to below $253,680	50%
$253,680 to below $343,680	Decreasing to 20%
$343,680 to below $353,680	20%
$353,680 or more	0%

This table shows the percentage of child care fees or the hourly rate cap (whichever is lower) the Australian Government will contribute based on a family's combined income.

^ These amounts are correct for 2020–21 and may be adjusted through indexation in subsequent years

*Subsidy gradually decreases by 1 per cent for each $3000 of family income.

Subsidisation of childcare based on income
(Source: ATO)

Child-minding alternatives
Au pair – $$$
Having an au pair can make a lot of sense if you require help outside of day care hours, have kids who may require rides to after-school activities, and/or need someone to go grocery shopping, make dinner and keep you cool, calm and collected!

Mum-sharing – $
I think I just invented the term 'mum-sharing', but the idea is: if you need to work one to two days a week and have a trusted parent friend who does as well, you could agree to watch all the kids for two days while they work and then they watch them the other two while you work. The ideal set-up for this would be if you had the same number of kids, around the same age.

Education

In Australia, there are three popular options when it comes to providing an education for your child: government schools (aka public schools), Catholic schools and private schools.

Government schools
Government schools are free for children who are Australian residents. However, they do ask for a voluntary contribution. This can be anywhere from $60 to $1000 pa. While this contribution is not mandatory, and a government school does consider everyone's financial circumstances, it makes providing things like instruments and/or sporting gear just that bit easier! Government schools also usually require your child to wear a uniform, which you will need to purchase. Government schools will also host activities which are usually optional for students like school camps, or off-campus activities that do require you to cough up some additional cash. Some also sell lunches and goodies at the canteen. Some of these costs are subsidised for families based on their income.

Catholic schools

According to the National Catholic Education Commission (2019), the majority of Catholic schools keep fees below $6000 per student per year, with 73 per cent charging less than $3000 per year. While this is higher than government school fees, it is significantly lower than the average fee ($22,450) charged by private schools. You don't actually need to have a religious affiliation to be able to attend a Catholic school (I can confirm this personally, as an individual who attended a Catholic high school without being Catholic! No communion for me!).

Private schools

Thinking about sending your child to private school? Depending on where you live, tuition fees could be up to $41,000 per child per year. While the cost is slightly less for infants and primary students, it's still a hefty price tag. Want them to board? Go ahead and tack on another $25,000 per year. And let's not forget the other costs. From application fees ($100–$500) to enrolment fees (one-off payments that can be north of $8000) to compulsory technology like a tablet or computer ($1000 +), the true cost of a private school education is actually much higher than just the tuition price tag. As with government and Catholic schools, you'll also need to factor in uniforms, paid lunches and costs that come with playing an instrument or sport.

Trying to figure out the best way to save for your child's school fees? You could try purchasing a bond like the ChildBuilder from Generation Life. I love that you don't have to report them on your tax return if you're the parent.

Deciding where to send your child very much depends on your values, your child's ability to learn in a particular setting, your financial capabilities and often where you live. If you want the option of a private-school education for your child, then you should consider a savings or investment plan to help cover these costs.

● ● ● ● ● ●

ROBYN, 35 – QLD

We had been following a very strict budget with a clear savings goal for 18 months, which allowed us to buy a house. We then found out that my partner has serious fertility issues that can only be treated by the most expensive form of IVF (ICSI). Because we had rainy days funds saved, had saved more than we needed for the house and also bought something more affordable, we had the money in the bank to be able to start treatment. I know other couples who never consider that this might happen and have neither the insurance coverage nor the cash – resulting in hardship and heartbreak.

● ● ● ● ● ●

TAKE NOTE

Children are always more expensive than
you anticipate them to be!

....

Everyone's fertility journey is different and can
vary significantly when it comes to cost.

....

Even if you're not planning on having a child in the near future,
it's helpful to know what kinds of expenses they might incur.

....

Chapter 17

Estate planning

If you've been wondering if you need a will, the answer is yes. But even more importantly, you need to organise a power of attorney and enduring guardian. These three things will work in unison to ensure that financial and medical decisions can be made on your behalf if you become incapacitated. They'll also ensure that your assets are distributed in the way you would like after your death.

I know these discussions can fill people with anxiety. Try looking at them as actions you can take to make things easier for your family and friends if something were to happen to you.

I find a lot of young people don't think they need a will until they buy a house, get married and/or have kids. But here's the thing: if you've been paying into a superannuation fund, you have an asset that will need to go to someone when you die. Chances are, it also has a life insurance policy attached to it. While I'm not saying it's the first thing you should go out and do on your 18th birthday, it is definitely something that should be added to your life admin to-do list.

The thing I DO want you to explore immediately is who you would want to have as your power of attorney and enduring guardian. This is because the chance of illness or injury is greater than death.

Power of attorney

Power of attorney is a document that appoints someone to deal with your finances if you're alive, but incapacitated. This piece of paper allows them to sign financial documents on your behalf and gain access to your bank accounts. If you're in a relationship, it's quite common for your partner to be your power of attorney. However, it's recommended that you have an alternative, just in case you and your partner were to be ill or injured at the same time.

For example, let's say you are in a terrible accident that requires you to move into assisted living. You're also a home owner. In order to help cover the costs of your new living situation, your family wants to sell your house. If you're unable to sign the contract of sale or access your bank accounts, this transaction cannot happen.

Another example: Let's say you're married with two kids and your husband or wife is placed into a medically induced coma. Unfortunately, they didn't have you sign a power of attorney form, which means you're prevented from making financial decisions that require their signature. This is particularly inconvenient if you have separate bank accounts or a shared home loan. It can leave you feeling helpless and strapped for cash.

When you have not designated a power of attorney, your partner or a family member has to apply to become your financial manager through the Guardianship Tribunal. Since the person applying was not recommended by you, the tribunal will set up a meeting to decide if your partner/family member is suitable. And then, even if their request is granted, they're heavily monitored and required to report back to the tribunal. This can be a lengthy process and one that's particularly not fun when you're also coping with the stress of a loved one being ill or hurt.

Abuse of power of attorney

Being a partner, friend or family member's power of attorney essentially means that you could walk into their solicitor's office tomorrow, action the form and then take all their money out of their bank accounts and sign their assets over into your name. Terrifying, I know. Most of these horror stories usually involve adult kids who aren't acting in the best interests of their parents.

To prevent this, there is a box you can tick on the form that states that a letter from your doctor is needed every time the power of attorney form is actioned. While this may seem like a no-brainer when it comes to protecting your assets, it ultimately ends up creating roadblocks for your partner or family member who is trying to help you. Many times older parents are worried about their children taking advantage of them and stealing money. In those cases, they may feel more comfortable ticking the box. But for most people, it makes the process simpler if they choose someone who they fully trust. It's also important to ensure that you've spoken to your designated power of attorney about the responsibility you're asking them to take on.

Hot tip: While you still have capacity, you can revoke power of attorney and assign it to someone else.

Most solicitors are conscious of assessing your capacity to make these types of decisions and are also mindful of family members with ill intentions. For instance, a solicitor may not see a client if their adult child demands to be present to influence how a will is drafted or power of attorney is chosen. Nine times out of ten, the adult child is just trying to help their parent get necessary paperwork done in order to go into an aged care facility. However, some are there to simply gain access to their parent's money.

Enduring guardianship

An enduring guardianship is a legal document that gives someone the power to make health and medical decisions on your behalf if you are alive, but incapacitated. When it comes to choosing an enduring guardian, you need to make sure you've chosen someone you trust and who understands your wishes, because they will be giving consent to things like surgery and/or palliative care. While this conversation can be general, you can make it much more thorough by including an advance care directive. This is more common for someone who is terminally ill. You've probably heard of a 'Do Not Resuscitate' order, but these are usually given through a hospital or doctor.

Similar to the power of attorney, if you have not designated an enduring guardian, then your spouse or family member will need to go to the Guardianship Tribunal and apply. Again, their actions will be heavily monitored, making an already difficult situation more difficult.

Will

A will is a legal document that states who you'd like to receive your assets after your death. When you're single, you typically choose a parent or sibling to be the beneficiary of your estate. When you're in a relationship, it's usually your partner. When you have kids, it's usually your partner and then your kids equally.

Where it becomes complicated is when you have a blended family, or a will that doesn't mirror your partner's will. For example, let's say your will states that you'd like all of your money to go to your mother, while your partner's will states that they want all of their money to go to their child. If you were both to die and you had joint assets, you would most likely have to divide the money between the two people.

While assets are the main thing covered in your will, if you have children, you can also express who you'd like to gain guardianship of them if you and your partner were to die at the same time. It can be a good idea to list more than one option, if possible – and of course, make sure you also have these discussions with the person(s) you've chosen.

On average, people update their wills every five to ten years. This could be because they bought a house, got divorced, had babies, their executor died, they've changed their mind about who they want to be the guardian of their children and so on. Just like your utilities, budget and home loan, I want you check in regularly to make sure the systems you've put in place are still in line with your values. I suggest at least every two years.

Tips for creating and maintaining an up-to-date will:

- First things first, revisit your superannuation fund and make sure you've selected a beneficiary.
- Obtain copies of all of your insurance policies and make sure your solicitor has copies on file.
- Ensure that all names are spelt in full and correctly on all documentation.
- If your name has changed, make sure you have a certificate to verify the change.
- With every major life event, such as marriage, divorce and having children, check your will to make sure it still reflects your values.
- Decide just how specific you want to be. Some people detail that they'd like their car collection to go to their brother, while their daughter gets their engagement ring. A solicitor can include a page (or pages) of specific requests, but be mindful that people can spend a lot of money changing their will all the time because (hypothetically speaking) the car collection is gone now, or they decide they want to give a particular asset to a particular family member.

'Hey, Victoria! Can I just write my own will?'

You can pick up a will kit from Australia Post if you want. However, I wouldn't recommend this if your situation may be complicated. A good will, even a simple one, is well worth the few hundred-dollar investment.

Inheritance

While a solicitor may write your will, it's best to speak to a financial adviser or accountant about how you are going to distribute your assets. These instructions will need to be provided to the executor of the will. If young children are involved, it's quite common for a parent to state that their inheritance is to go into a trust account that they will have access to at the age of 18, 21 or 25. There can also be terms outlined by the executor of the will that will allow the guardian of the children to use the money for the children's education, advancement and maintenance. Essentially, an executor simply has to carry your wishes out. If you say in your will you want your money invested, then that's what they have to do. If you say you want cash distributed equally to your children, that's what they do.

Contesting a will

Depending on which state or territory you live in, only certain people can contest a will. This is usually a partner or children. It can sometimes be a grandchild, but only under certain circumstances, such as if the child had been raised by the grandparent. Legally, you have 12 months from the date of death to contest a will.

At the moment, the law sees it as a moral obligation to leave something to your partner and children, so the odds of winning if you're a partner or child are pretty good. However, they also look at eligibility, health and need. They want to know what your current financial situation is, whether you have dependants and why you were left out of the will to start with.

Contesting a will is a long and painful process. It can also be expensive. It's better for everyone if you can settle quickly. This is another reason why speaking to a solicitor about your will instead of making one on your own is a good idea. They can flag any issues about potentially leaving someone out of your will.

What happens if you don't have a will?

Dying without a will is called dying intestate. A lot of people think your money goes to the government when this happens, but that's not true. Generally, your partner will inherit and then your children. Again, this becomes complicated if it's a blended family, but ultimately the law tries to find eligible immediate family members and work their way down. In most cases, a partner, parent or child will go to a solicitor and explain that you've died without a will. The solicitor will then make an application to put an action plan in place.

● ● ● ● ● ●

JIORDY, 24 - WA

After a massive tragedy, I find myself having to take on an estate administrator role for my dad's estate, and being the sole beneficiary of his estate and life insurance after he and my brother passed away. I'm kind of finding my way through the dark and struggling, being 24 years old and having no idea how any of it is supposed to work! He had cars, houses, super, life insurance, SO MANY THINGS to sort out and there's no-one really to help me. It's taken 16 months and I'm almost at the tail end of it now after inquests and applications, but now I've done all this work I can see that there will be a never-ending financial journey coming up that I'm just not sure how to deal with!

I grew up in a family where my mother was heavily affected by mental health issues and I had a FIFO dad who she hid the truth from. I was very independent at a very young age and understood the value of money, as I started working at 14 to pay for anything over and above basic food on the table. We were poor. After high school I went straight into full-time work and was overwhelmed by the fact that all this money was mine! I gave a lot of it to my mum to pay bills and board and then the rest was for me. I saved every penny and then splurged it all on a laptop and clothes and things I'd never had before. I was so good at saving, but only for something specific, like a trip to New Zealand and then a six-week European adventure (in the same year!). Since working, I've always felt that I'll always get more money, so have never been too stressed about it. I'm living in my own place now, but often let my guilt get the better of me and I financially assist others because 'I can always get more money', but that's starting to affect my savings goals. I'm trying to change, but my bleeding heart is getting in my way.

● ● ● ● ● ●

TAKE NOTE

Power of attorney is a document that appoints someone to deal with your finances if you're alive, but incapacitated.

....

An enduring guardianship is a legal document that gives someone the power to make health and medical decisions on your behalf if you are alive, but incapacitated.

....

A will is a legal document that states who you'd like to receive your assets after your death.

....

Chapter 18

Financial freedom is the new retirement

If the Great Australian Dream was a movie, the final few scenes would show a couple reaching the age of 67, saying goodbye to the offices they worked at for 40 years, downsizing to a unit and then packing up a campervan to road trip around the coast of Australia. Their beachside lattes and campsite fees are proudly paid for by their hard-earned super pensions. While this does sound like a beautiful way to wrap up a life story, I like to think about retirement slightly differently.

Personally, I don't want to wait until my late 60s (and let's be honest – by government standards, my generation will probably have to be in their 70s) to be able to retire. I want the option a lot sooner than that, which is why I think of retirement as achieving financial freedom. We've talked a lot about financial freedom, but let's break down what you realistically need to have in place before you're able to choose whether to work or not.

According to research done in 2018 by the Association of Superannuation Funds of Australia (ASFA), a debt-free single retiree who would like to maintain a modest lifestyle needs roughly $524 per week, or $27,248 per year. For a debt-free retired couple also looking to live modestly, they need $754 per week, or $39,208 per year. For a debt-free single retiree looking to live a more comfortable lifestyle – that includes things like owning a car, having private health insurance and the ability to go on holiday – they need closer to $820 per week, or $42,640 per year. A debt-free couple would need $1154 per week – $60,008 per year. While these examples are great, do keep in mind that this isn't what I suggested earlier on – I recommend you aim closer to $100,000 per year as a base to ensure you're more comfortable.

Knowing how much money you'll need comes down to what type of lifestyle you want to maintain and how much debt you have at the time of retirement. To help you get on and stay on the path to financial freedom, I've listed some helpful steps for you to take. Depending on your age, health and goals, you may need to revisit these steps and adjust them as your values change.

Steps to financial freedom

Step 1 – Identify your values

Of course, we are going to start by talking about your values. While you may be saving for a trip, house or education now, you also need to think about what Future You will want to spend money on. Will you need money to take the grandkids on holiday? Do you want to be able to donate to causes close to your heart? Is it a trip around the world? Is it daily yoga classes? Bi-weekly golf trips? By figuring out what you might want retirement to look like, you'll be much closer to accurately estimating just how much money you'll need to live that lifestyle.

Step 2 – Account audit and budget

I hate to break it to you, but budgeting is something you'll need to do throughout your life – especially when it comes to managing the wealth you've created for yourself at the time of retirement. As you grow closer to scaling back work, have another look at where your money is going. Break down what you earn, spend, owe and own. This is the best way to calculate how much money you'll need to maintain your lifestyle.

Some potential costs include:

- car costs
- insurance costs
- utilities and bills
- food fund
- holiday fund
- leisure activities
- gifts for the family.

Step 3 – Say goodbye to debt

This will probably come as no surprise, but in order to be in the best possible financial position at retirement, you're going to want to be debt free. This means your mortgage is paid off, and you don't have any credit card debt or personal loans. For some, this means delaying retirement by three to five years. While you may have one or more investment properties, make sure they are well and truly positively geared.

Step 4 – Minimise risk

As you begin to near the age you'd like to retire, it's important to adjust your risk profiles across your investment portfolio and superannuation. This could mean scaling back to a low-risk fund, moving money to government bonds, and adjusting the risk profile of your superannuation fund. You used to have time to mitigate any risk and correct markets, but now you need to focus on preservation and stability.

Step 5 – Identify your income streams

When planning your financial freedom, it's important to know where your income will be coming from. It could be your superannuation, a government pension, interest earned from an investment or cash you have in a high-interest bank account. While ideally you will have put assets in place from a young age to create wealth, there are government pensions and incentives to supplement your income. I also want to point out that many people think retirement means you never work again – this is not always the case. Many people who 'retire' continue to work part time or begin a side hustle.

Step 6 – Explore what government entitlements you qualify for

The government currently offers concession cards that provide seniors, retirees and pensioners with discounts on banking, health care, transport, some goods/services and utilities. These incentives vary by state and territory, and are usually income and asset tested. It's best to visit your local Centrelink office to see if you qualify for a:

- pensioner concession card
- senior card
- Commonwealth Seniors Health Card.

Another thing worth looking into is your eligibility for tax offsets, which can be done through the ATO.

Step 7 – Do an insurance check

Things change all the time, so you're going to check in on your insurances and ensure that you're covered for everything we've spoken about. One of the best ways is to write all your insurances down and what you're covered for on one page, and then work out how much income you'd need in the event of illness or injury. This will vary depending on your current life stage.

Step 8 – Revisit your estate plan

Check that your will is up to date and that you're still happy with your chosen power of attorney and enduring guardian. It's also good to double-check who the beneficiary is on your superannuation fund.

Accessing superannuation

While most people wait until the age of retirement to access their superannuation, you may be able to qualify for payments when you reach your preservation age.

Your date of birth	Age you can access your super (preservation age)
Before 1 July 1960	55
1 July 1960 – 30 June 1961	56
1 July 1961 – 30 June 1962	57
1 July 1962 – 30 June 1963	58
1 July 1963 – 30 June 1964	59
After 1 July 1964	60

Accessing your super by age
(Source: ATO)

Super benefits can be paid in a variety of ways:

Option 1: Transition to retirement pension (TTR)

A TTR pension can be beneficial for those wanting to access a portion of their superannuation while continuing to work in some capacity. The thing I like about this option is that because you're still working, you'll continue to receive superannuation contributions. You'll also pay less tax, because your TTR payments are tax-free if you're over 60. If you're 55 to 59, then you're taxed at the marginal rate, but will get a 15 per cent tax offset. The only downside of TTR is that it does reduce your super balance, which means less money when you actually fully retire.

Option 2: Collect a retirement income

This option involves changing your superannuation to retirement phase. Superannuation has two broad phases, the accumulation and retirement phases, but it's important to note that they aren't distinct. Someone can have some of their super in accumulation and some in retirement. The accumulation phase of super is what you're probably in now – it's where we all start when we are contributing to super. All of these contributions are locked away (or 'preserved', in superannuation terminology) until you reach retirement. The retirement phase of super (which is also referred to as the pension phase) is when you begin taking an income from your super (sometimes referred to as a pension).

Hot tip: Some super funds require you to take the money out or transfer it to another fund when you reach 65. Be sure to check your fund's PDS.

Option 3: Take a lump sum

The majority of superannuation funds will allow you to take out lump-sum payments. However, the government has set minimum amounts that must be withdrawn from your income stream each year. While lump-sum payments are beneficial for those looking to clear debts, do a house project or fund a trip, those looking to invest the money need to be mindful of the tax implications.

The amount of tax payable on superannuation income depends on a number of things, including your age, amount of payment and other income streams. It is best to speak to a financial adviser or registered tax accountant when choosing how you'd like to receive your super pension.

Collecting a government age pension

In Australia, the age pension is money that will let you 'retire', i.e. cease work. The amount you are eligible to receive depends on your age, relationship status, income and assets.

Date of birth	Age pension eligibility age
Before 1 July 1952	65 years
1 July 1952 – 31 December 1953	65 years and 6 months
1 January 1954 – 30 June 1955	66 years
1 July 1955 – 31 December 1956	66 years and 6 months
From 1 January 1957	67 years

Pension eligibility
(Source: ATO)

As of 2020, the maximum age pension per fortnight is:

- $860.60 for singles
- $1279.40 for couples.

When determining how much money you can receive, the government measures your income and the value of your assets. If your income and assets are above certain limits, your pension payment may be lowered. Some people may not be eligible at all.

The age pension income and asset tests

When looking at your income, the government will examine income coming from employment, superannuation pensions, investments (both domestic and international), and salary packaging. When looking at your assets, they will factor in investment properties, cars, caravans, boats, and business assets.

It's important to note that they do not consider your primary place of residence an asset. They also factor in debts. For example, let's say you have a $600,000 investment property with a $230,000 mortgage. They will only value that asset at $370,000.

To see if you are eligible for an age pension, visit your local Centrelink office.

Do I need to downsize?

Unless downsizing was part of your wealth-generating strategy or you're simply tired of maintaining a large home, I hate the idea of someone having to sell their home because they need the income. For most people, their family home is the one they went to work for every day. It's where memories are held and rooms have been set up to keep grandchildren safe and warm. In my perfect world, you would have other assets in place so that you don't need to sacrifice your optimal primary place of residence. This doesn't mean you won't choose to move, though; we just don't want you to be in a position where your hand is forced.

In 2016, Investment Trends' Retirement Income Report listed 18 things retirees wish they had done:

1. Make extra (or earlier) super contributions (44 per cent of respondents)
2. Start investing earlier in life (25 per cent of respondents)
3. Save more outside super (24 per cent of respondents)
4. Learn more about my finances

5. Retire later
6. Buy an investment property sooner
7. Learn more about how much I need in retirement
8. Get financial advice from a financial adviser
9. Buy a home sooner
10. Leave more money in super when I retire
11. Invest in safer assets
12. Learn more about how much I could receive in retirement
13. Consolidate my super funds earlier
14. Change investment options within super
15. Buy insurance sooner
16. Get financial advice from my super fund
17. Change super funds
18. Invest in riskier assets.

Let's benefit from the wisdom of our elders so that we won't have any of the same regrets when we reach later life!

● ● ● ● ● ●

TAKE NOTE

Planning for your retirement isn't a job for Future You, it's a priority for you right now, regardless of how old or young you might be. There's no such thing as beginning too early.

....

For younger Australians, financial freedom is the new retirement – so as soon as you have enough passive income streams to support your lifestyle, you can choose whether or not to continue working. And that could be much earlier than age 67!

....

Chapter 19

Choosing a financial adviser

While I've often mentioned during the course of this book that you should consider speaking to a financial adviser, I haven't formally explained just what one does! Typically, a financial adviser is a licensed professional who provides financial advice and management across an individual's or family's investments, insurances, taxes, and/or estate planning. From advising which funds, businesses or properties to invest in to finding the best personal insurance policies for your particular situation, to helping set up a trust for your children, they can essentially be your guiding light to financial freedom.

Having a financial adviser is a bit like having a general doctor. If you're not comfortable with them then they're not the right adviser for you – and that's actually okay. We can't be everything to everybody, so don't get disheartened. Your perfect adviser is out there, I promise! When searching for yours, remember that your relationship with your financial adviser is a really special one.

They're not just an accountant who looks at your finances and prepares your tax return. They're the person you will share your goals, dreams and aspirations with. They'll become that person you call when you've got a big money decision to make. They'll know how you feel about your goals, and even about your partner. This person will also get a pretty good sense of you medically, too, as you discuss insurances.

Like most professionals, financial advisers are not one size fits all. Some offer only budgeting and cash-flow advice, while others will cover all the bases. Some won't speak to you unless you have $500,000 to play with, while others just want to see that you have $500. Some charge fixed fees, while others charge percentage-based fees or commissions. Some are elderly and narrow-minded men managing family wealth that goes back generations, while others are laid-back millennials who have no trouble relating to our need for Sunday brunch.

You need to choose someone who clearly understands your values, goals and money story so that they can help you to the best of their ability.

When should I get a financial adviser?

This is a question I get asked all the time! While you probably think I'm going to say, 'When you have $25,000 in savings,' the answer is actually not a numerical figure – it's a mindset.

You should get a financial adviser when you're ready to invest in advice and have proven to yourself that you can save and stick to a budget. Depending on your goals, this could also be when you're ready to commit to investing a consistent amount monthly. Basically, you need to feel like you're ready to supercharge your wealth creation and build a team of players who will help you succeed.

It's true that many financial advisers won't take on a client unless they have a minimum amount of wealth to manage, but this shouldn't stop you from looking for one who does not have a minimum starting amount. I always say that it's important to 'date' a couple of financial advisers to see if they're the right fit for you, and to make sure you're making the right decision for yourself in the long term. Most financial advisers will offer a complimentary initial consult – use these to your advantage. Make sure the adviser actually cares about you, not about how much you earn or how much you have in super. Make sure they're asking about your goals, and talking to you about how they can help you achieve these things over the long term.

What do I need to know about financial advisers?

In order for a financial adviser to work professionally, they must have a Series 65 licence. Depending on the range of services they offer, they may require even more licences. A good financial adviser should be transparent about which licences they hold. From the moment you book your initial consult, the financial adviser should send you a copy of their FSG (Financial Services Guide) and adviser profile. This will detail what they get paid, how they get paid and when. It will also outline what areas they can give you advice on and their history. If your adviser hasn't given you those – it's not okay.

Another thing to consider is which industry body they're adhered to. In Australia, they would usually belong to the AFA (Association of Financial Advisers), FPA (Financial Planning Association) or both. These are important because they dictate a code of ethics advisers must follow, as well as mandate fee disclosures. I'd also always look up a potential adviser on the ASIC website to ensure they're registered to give advice, and check to see if there are any complaints made against them and which areas they're legally allowed to advise on. Remember, some advisers can only do tax or property. Ideally, you want someone who can give you holistic financial advice.

How much does a financial adviser cost?

In relation to what financial advice costs, this is SO hard to explain because it's very dependent upon what you're working with. For example, someone wanting to invest $50,000 will be charged much more than someone who just needs to find the right super account. Most financial adviser–client relationships begin by the adviser providing a Statement of Advice, which usually requires an up-front fee. From there, a client pays monthly fees to cover the cost of advice and execution of investments, tax documents, transactions and insurance products. Some advisers take performance-based fees or commissions on the investment products that they write – that's not okay in my opinion.

The Financial Planning Association conducted the CoreData FPA Member Research in 2018 that found that, on average, FPA members charge $2435 to prepare a Statement of Advice for new clients, and $3354 per year for ongoing advice for clients.

FPA's research also investigated how their members calculated the fees they charged clients. Sixty-one per cent charged a fixed price, 38 per cent charged based on assets, and just 16 per cent charged an asset-based fee.

At the end of the day, these fees will depend on how much you're investing, where you live and who you decide to work with. While it may seem like a lot of money to come up with, you are actually able to pay for financial advice by using funds in your superannuation account. Speak to your financial adviser about how to best facilitate this, as sometimes it's better not to make this decision.

Where can I find a financial adviser?

- Referrals are golden – ask a friend, family member or online finance community group.
- If your ideal financial adviser doesn't have space for you, ask for a trusted referral.
- I also really like the Your Best Interests website, which has a list of authorised financial advisers.

As a financial adviser myself, I like to shape my services around my clients. I believe that the pursuit of your purpose, goals, dreams and aspirations can and should be supported by easy to understand, straightforward financial advice at any age or stage, and I definitely believe that it is never too early or too late to reach out to an adviser to get your finances working for you.

How do I engage a financial adviser?

Once you've narrowed your search down and are ready to meet with a potential financial adviser (or two), you can give them a call or shoot them an email – but first, make sure you know exactly what you want from them. So many times someone will call and say, 'I want to work with you' and I have to ask, 'On what?' Be ready to tell the adviser whether you want help with budgeting and strategy, investments, insurance, super, or all of those things. This will change how they charge for advice and allow them to be more prepared.

The most important thing for me personally when looking for a financial adviser is feeling like you're on the same page as them. If you're going to engage in this relationship, it'll be one you're in for the long term so it's essential that you're comfortable with the adviser you pick and like engaging with them. An adviser is much like a doctor: if you don't feel comfortable telling them your concerns or you're not okay being really open about your life plans and goals, they're not going to be able to help as much as possible. And Future You deserves to be put first, always.

● ● ● ● ● ●

TAKE NOTE

Financial advisers can do much more for you than just taking care of your accounting – this is a special relationship that can work wonders in guiding the life decisions that will get you to financial freedom.

....

Take your time to find the right adviser who understands your story, values and goals and who you feel comfortable with.

....

Chapter 20

Accountability partners

Now you have the tools, it's time to take action. Just like going to the gym, quitting drinking or learning to live without gluten, changing money habits and behaviours can be easy for some and extremely painful for others. But here's the thing: I'm not expecting you to do it alone. I want you to find a friend or partner who will join you on your journey as your accountability partner, celebrate your wins, encourage you to get back on the horse if you fall off and remind you of just how capable you are!

Accountability partners are a thing because they work! On an emotional level, people need to feel supported, but they also don't want to let someone down. (Interesting how we're willing to let ourselves down, though.) Sharing a specific goal with someone, and your exact plan of how to achieve it, makes you more likely to achieve it.

If you don't feel like you're ready to share your financial goals with someone you know personally, I promise that the *She's on the Money* community will welcome you with open arms. We are all about applauding money wins, helping you knock the dirt off your knees if you fail and continuing to educate ourselves so we can be financially literate people.

● ● ● ● ● ●

TAKE NOTE

Having an accountability partner is an amazing hack that will help you to see your financial goals through to completion.

....

Share your goals, questions and achievements in the *She's on the Money* community whenever you feel you need some extra support.

....

12-month action plan

I don't want to sound too sappy, but can I just say how excited, proud and happy I am that you took the time to read my book in an effort to take control of your finances? Nothing brings me more joy than someone who's ready to take ownership of their life, and I feel honoured that I get to be part of your journey.

Because I know how easy it is to stay motivated in the short term and how common it is to lose steam along the way, I have created a 12-month action plan to help you create habits and behaviours that will set you up for long-term financial success.

● ● ● ● ● ●

MONTH 1

Money story and budgeting

This is the month you are going to find your starting point!

- Using the tools and resources in Chapter 1, take a moment to write out your money story.
- Refer to Chapter 2 to conduct a bank account audit and determine your Earn, Spend, Owe and Own figures.
- Use the *She's on the Money* budget template (available from shesonthemoney.com.au) to create your budget and determine if you have a surplus or deficit of income.
- Find an accountability partner.

MONTH 2

Goal setting and money mapping

This month is all about creating a foundation and cash-flow system that gives every single dollar a job and puts the necessary hurdles in place for you to either pay off debt, meet a savings goal or execute an investment strategy!

- Using the tools and resources in Chapters 2 and 3, map out your money and create your cash-flow structure.
- Use the *She's on the Money* goal-setting activity in Chapter 4 to set five goals.
- Keep a money diary this month to really solidify your budget and make sure you haven't missed anything or underestimated your expenses. Those additional coffees add up!

MONTH 3

Find your experts

Depending on your goals and values, you may be ready to have an expert (or experts) on your side!

- Get tax ready: An accountant is only going to be able to help you get your tax affairs in order BEFORE the end of the financial year (for example, self-employed people making sure they buy work-related things before the end of the year, or making additional super contributions for tax).
- Create an investment strategy: Meet with a financial adviser to discuss an investment strategy or review your existing one to make sure you're meeting your money goals.
- If you don't want to meet with an adviser, this month is about researching your investment options and creating a strategy for your own wealth creation using the tools and resources from Chapter 9.
- Thinking about finding personal insurance policies or buying a house? Start researching mortgage and insurance brokers. Remember, your financial adviser may be able to provide these services!

MONTH 4

Superannuation

This is the month you sort out your super!

- If you don't know where your super is or how many super funds you have, you can start with my.gov.au. You can also search for and reclaim any lost super via the ATO.
- If you have more than one super fund, now's the time to evaluate them and consolidate your super into your preferred fund to save yourself management and administration fees. Revisit Chapter 8

for tips on protecting your existing insurances held within super, as well as how to review your investment risk profile.

MONTH 5

Protection

Now that you've made a budget and set your goals, it's time to protect those goals with the right types of insurances by revisiting Chapter 14.

- Review all personal insurances outside of super and make sure they complement the ones inside super. This could be a great month to speak to a financial adviser or insurance broker.
- Take a look and decide if you need/are getting the best rate for the following insurances:
  - private health
  - home and contents
  - car
  - pet.

MONTH 6

Halfway checkpoint

Now that you've been on your journey for six months, it's time to take a moment to reflect on how everything is going. This is something you should be doing annually for the rest of your life. If you started in June you're now at the end of the year and about to begin a new calendar year – which is a great time to review, renew, change or cancel services.

Services to review:

- mobile plan
- internet plan
- streaming services

- electricity bills
- home and contents insurance
- car insurance
- festive season gift budget.

MONTH 7

Self care

This month's goal is to promote positive money conversations.

- Take a moment to journal about how you're feeling about your current financial situation.
- Write down wins.
- Write down fails.
- What do you want to do more of?
- What do you want to do less of?
- Review your spending on a personal level – while you're saving money, are you feeling good about it? Are you allocating enough of your budget to making sure you're enjoying the journey, not just saving it all for the destination?
- Have a big check-in with your accountability buddy.
- Have a conversation with your partner about money and your money goals.

MONTH 8

Estate planning

On the off-chance you become incapacitated or die, having your affairs in order will make the entire experience easier on your loved ones.

- After reviewing Chapter 17, nominate (or review your nomination for) a power of attorney and enduring guardian. Be sure to speak to them about your choice and your wishes.

- Create or update your will, either by using a will kit or seeing a solicitor. (I recommend the latter!)
- Check that you have nominated a beneficiary on all of your life insurance policies.

MONTH 9

Double down on debt/ramp up your savings

It's important to review your spending and how you're tracking with your money goals. If you're not meeting your goals, now is the time to consider changes to your plans so you can still achieve them.

- Do you need to set up a direct debit into savings?
- Do you need to change the time frame of one of your goals?
- Do you need to save a little more each month to achieve a goal?
- Review your debts – are you paying off the lowest balance debt first?
- Are you able to consolidate your debt into a lower interest rate option?
- Is it time you gave up your credit card?
- Speak to a mortgage broker about paying your loan off faster (e.g. getting a lower interest rate but making the same monthly contribution will mean you pay it off years ahead!)

MONTH 10

Continuing education

Use this month to learn more about a money topic that you've always wanted to know about.

- Take the *She's on the Money* online course.
- Start having conversations with friends and family about the topic so you can hear their points of view.
- Listen to a podcast on the topic.

MONTH 11

Spending detox

This month, focus on limiting any and all discretionary spending. This one-month challenge will help prove to yourself that you're in control of your spending and your life.

MONTH 12

Celebrate!

Celebrate your successes and look back to see how far you've come.

- Share the highs and lows of this year with your partner or accountability buddy.
- What have you learnt this year?
- What do you want to do more of, and what do you want to do less of?
- What are you planning to do for the next 12 months and how are you going to keep yourself accountable?

A final word

I'm so proud of you and how far you're going to go. Congratulations on prioritising your financial health, and putting in the hard work to restructure your finances for a brighter, more prosperous future. From little things, big things really do grow – so it's important to remember that when it comes to your finances, it never pays to be complacent. Take time out periodically to reassess your cash flow, spending and saving strategy. That way, you'll always be on the money!

Glossary

ABN An Australian Business Number (ABN) is a unique 11-digit number issued by the Australian Business Register (ABR), which is run by the Australian Taxation Office (ATO). So many acronyms, so much fun.

Accumulation fund A type of superannuation fund in which the benefit a member receives reflects total contributions as well as whatever they have earned, minus expenses and tax, so the benefit reflects the performance of the fund's investments.

ASIC The Australian Securities and Investments Commission. ASIC's role is to regulate companies and financial services and enforce laws to protect Australian consumers, investors and creditors.

ATM fee A fee that you pay to use an ATM machine to withdraw or deposit cash (arguably you shouldn't have to – if you're still paying ATM fees maybe look at moving to another bank).

Australian Taxation Office (ATO) The Australian Government's principal revenue collection agency.

Bad debt Debt that does not contribute to future wealth creation or furthering your education. Bad debt is most often any type of debt that you won't be able to claim on tax, and you haven't used to purchase an asset that increases in value. Personally, I categorise personal loans, credit cards and car loans as bad debt.

Bank fee Charges your bank may pass on to you for utilising their facilities.

Behavioural finance What really drives investment markets. It can be thought of as a marriage between psychology and finance which attempts to explain how humans make financial decisions in real life and why their decisions might not appear to be rational every time. For example, many people will sell shares in a falling market when that is a time of opportunity, and logic would suggest that during a falling market is when you should be purchasing. Smart investors keep their feelings in check. As the great Warren Buffet says, be fearful when others are greedy, and greedy when others are fearful.

Bond A bond is a fixed income asset that represents a loan made by an investor to a borrower. Bonds are issued by governments and corporations when they want to raise money. When you invest in a bond, you're lending money to a company or the government and the bond pays interest at regular intervals.

Budget A budget is an epic tool for you to use to create a plan for your money. When you create a budget it's not like a diet – it's a tool to ensure that every dollar that comes into your bank account has a job and is put to work. A budget isn't a guesstimate, it's what you're really spending. When you create a budget you need to be honest with yourself about your spending habits.

Capital The cost of your investment, or the initial starting funds.

Capital gains tax (CGT) Tax due and payable when an investment is sold if it is sold for more than what you initially purchased it for. The gain is added to your taxable income on your tax return.

Cash A highly secure asset class that is usually great where liquidity is key.

Compound interest Compound interest is the eighth wonder of the modern world. It is the interest earned on money that was previously earned as interest. It causes your money to compound over time. It's brilliant for savings and investments, but can work against you if you're paying interest on a loan. Frequency, time, the interest rate, and your starting amount all make compound interest powerful.

If you understand it properly, you'll earn it. If you don't, you might end up paying it.

Concessional contribution A concessional superannuation contribution is a payment made into your super fund from your before-tax income. This includes your SG (super guarantee) contributions. Concessional contributions are taxed at 15 per cent when they are received by your super fund. The concessional contributions cap each year is $25,000; however, your cap might be higher if you didn't use the full amount of your cap in previous years.

Credit card A card issued by a bank, building society, etc., allowing the holder to purchase goods or services on credit. Usually purchases made using this card will incur interest.

Credit score A credit score is a number between 300–850 that depicts a consumer's creditworthiness. The higher the score, the better a borrower looks to potential lenders.

Cryptocurrency A form of digital currency.

Debt consolidation Combining various debts, whether they are credit card bills or loan payments, into one monthly payment.

Deposit A sum of money paid into a bank or building society account.

Diversification of investments Diversification is the practice of spreading your investments around so that your exposure to any one type of asset is limited. This practice is designed to help reduce the volatility of your portfolio over time.

Dividend The income you receive from shares, just like receiving rent on a property or interest from a bank. It is a sum of money paid regularly (typically annually) by a company to its share-holders out of its profits (or reserves).

Dollar-cost averaging When you regularly contribute the same amount of money to an investment at the same time each month regardless of the price of that investment. Dollar-cost averaging can be a very effective way to manage risk when investing in assets like shares as it can in some cases take away the 'timing risk' of trying to pick the bottom of the market (which is impossible because we aren't able to accurately predict the future!)

EFT Electronic fund transfer. Moving money from one account to another.

Estate planning An estate plan is a comprehensive plan that includes documents that are effective during your lifetime as well as other documents that aren't in effect until your death.

ETF An exchange traded fund. A basket of different investments that are selected to create diversification, and provide exposure to a variety of assets, including stocks, bonds and commodities.

Family trust Family trusts are a common type of trust used to hold assets or run a family business.

FIFO (fly in, fly out) A type of work in which employees fly to their workplace (usually for a week or two at a time), then fly back home.

Financial abuse Financial abuse involves a person using or misusing money which limits and controls their partner's current and future actions and their freedom of choice.

Financial adviser A person whose job is to provide financial advice to clients.

Financial freedom Financial freedom is the point at which you no longer have to go to work to create an income and have created investments that pay you a passive income so you've got the freedom of choice without the worry of needing to financially sustain your lifestyle.

First Home Owner Grant The First Home Owner Grant is a government scheme introduced in 2000 to offset the effect of the Goods and Services Tax on home ownership.

Fixed interest A secure asset class which usually refers to bonds. It's relatively secure if you lend to financially stable companies or the Australian Government.

Good debt Debt which contributes to wealth creation or furthering your education. Good debt can be a home loan, or an investment loan.

Guarantor A guarantor is someone who agrees to pay your money owing on a debt if you don't pay it, for example, a parent or close relative.

Health insurance Insurance taken out to cover the cost of medical care.

HECS-HELP debt HECS-HELP is a scheme that assists eligible Commonwealth supported students to pay their student contribution amount with a loan. HECS-HELP loans are available at all public universities and at a handful of private higher education providers.

Home loan A home loan or mortgage is a loan advanced to you by a financial institution in return for security over the property you are using the loan to buy.

Income protection insurance An insurance designed to pay you a benefit if you are unable to work for a period of time because of illness or injury. Income protection allows you to protect your largest asset – your ability to work and produce an income! An income protection policy can pay up to 75 per cent of your pre-tax income for a set period of time.

Income statement A document formerly known as a group certificate issued to employees at the end of each financial year. It outlines the income you have received over the last financial year and the amount withheld for tax purposes.

Index fund An index fund is a portfolio of stocks or bonds designed to mimic the composition and performance of a financial market index.

Indexation Indexation means adjusting a price, wage, or other value based on the changes in another price or composite indicator of prices. Indexation can be done to adjust for the effects of inflation, cost of living, or input prices over time, or to adjust for different prices and costs in different geographic areas.

Inheritance Inheritance refers to the assets that an individual leaves to his or her loved ones after he or she passes away. An inheritance may contain cash, investments such as stocks or bonds, and other assets such as jewellery, cars and real estate.

Interest Money paid regularly at a particular rate for the use of money lent, or for delaying the repayment of a debt.

Lenders Mortgage Insurance LMI is a one-off, non-refundable premium that can be paid upfront or added to your home loan when you don't have a whole 20 per cent deposit or a guarantor. The purpose of LMI is to protect the lender in the event that you default on your home loan, by reducing the risk to the lender – not to protect you as a lender.

Life insurance Typically, life insurance is an agreement that if you die, or are diagnosed with a terminal illness, a sum of money will be paid out to (typically) your spouse or children. You can also have this death benefit paid to other members in your family.

Lifestyle creep Something that happens to the best of us! Lifestyle creep occurs when your income increases and former luxuries become new necessities. For example, when I was at uni I would buy make-up at the supermarket, and now that I've got a full-time job I purchase all my cosmetics from Adore Beauty.

Liquidity How easy it is to convert your investment back into cash by selling it. For example, the liquidity of a share is approximately three days to sell and be back in your bank account, but when you sell a house that asset could take more than three months to land cash in your pocket.

Maternity and parental leave Leave from work granted to a parent before and after the birth of their child. In Australia we have Parental Leave Pay, which is a payment for up to 18 weeks while you care for your new child and is based on the weekly rate of the national minimum wage.

moneysmart.gov.au A government website with plenty of fantastic resources to further your financial education, which I absolutely adore because it's a destination that carries no bias.

Money story Your money story is a very personal narrative about money that started to form in childhood. Your money story makes up your thoughts, feeling and beliefs about money and deeply affects your ability to make financial decisions. You can't choose the money story you're born with, but you can choose to change your course now.

Mortgage broker A legendary human that brokers the best possible loan outcome for you when it comes to all things property. A mortgage broker is a go-between who deals with the banks and other lenders so you don't have to.

Negative gearing Where the rental income you receive on a property you own is less than the interest payments and expenses you incur each year, meaning the property costs you money each year to own.

Neutral gearing Where the rental income you receive on a property you own is equal to the interest payments and expenses you incur each year, meaning the property breaks even each year.

Non-concessional contributions (NCCs) Money you put into your super using your 'after-tax' dollars or your personal savings. These are personal contributions that you make into your own super account that are not claimed as a tax deduction.

From 1 July 2017 the non-concessional contributions cap (the most amount of money you can put into your super) is $100,000, meaning if you put more into your super you'll have to pay additional tax.

Offset account An offset account is a transaction account that is directly linked to your home loan. You're able to make deposits or withdrawals from it as you would any other regular bank account. Holding money in an offset account over a period of time can reduce the amount of interest charged on your home loan. The higher the balance of your offset account and the longer you hold that money in the account, the less interest you'll end up paying. Say you've got a $500,000 home loan with $20,000 in your offset account. This means you'll only be charged interest on $480,000 instead of the full $500,000. This will keep happening for as long as you've got the $20,000 cash in your offset account.

Okay debt Okay debt is debt that isn't as bad as 'bad debt', and debt we don't want to have for the long term, but it's debt you've used to either purchase assets that increase in value, or debts that you can claim on tax. An example of okay debt is your HELP loan, where you don't accrue interest and you've used it to further educate yourself so you can increase your income in the future.

Payday loan Payday loans are short-term high-interest cash loans based on the borrower's personal check held for future deposit or on electronic access to the borrower's bank account. We want to avoid these at all costs.

PAYG Simply stands for 'pay as you go'. It is an acronym used for two different processes systemised by the Australian Tax Office (ATO) for businesses in Australia: PAYG instalments and PAYG withholding.

Performance fee A performance fee is a payment made to an investment manager for generating positive returns. Performance fees don't exist on all investments but are definitely something to understand.

Personal loan A loan which allows you to borrow a specific amount of money, usually from a financial institution, and then repay the debt with interest in equal payments over an agreed term.

Positive gearing Where the rental income you receive on a property you own is more than the interest payments and expenses you incur each year, meaning the property makes you money each year.

Redraw facility A redraw facility lets you access extra principal payments you've made on your home loan, which can come in handy when you need some extra cash down the track. Say you make the minimum monthly repayments on your home loan

($2000) and you're currently paying an extra $200 a month into your loan – which is equal to $2400 per a year. This additional $2400 could be available to you to withdraw at a later date.

Salary packaging Salary packaging is when you arrange to receive less income after tax in return for your employer paying for benefits out of your pre-tax salary. For example, you might salary package a car or phone which will be paid for with your pre-tax income.

Salary sacrificing An arrangement between an employer and an employee, where the employee agrees to forgo part of their future entitlement to salary or wages. This is in return for the employer providing them with benefits of a similar value.

Savings account A savings account is an interest-bearing deposit account held at a bank or other financial institution. Your savings accounts shouldn't have fees and if they do you need to change that, pronto!

Self-managed super fund A self-managed super fund (SMSF) is a private super fund that you manage yourself. Typically I would only ever suggest a SMSF if someone is very interested in managing their super more actively and has a minimum of $600,000 in their account.

Share Sometimes referred to as a stock or security, a share is a unit of ownership in a company. If you buy a share in a company you own a part or a 'share' of that company. This part ownership is sometimes referred to as holding equity. As a shareholder you generally have certain entitlements, like receiving a portion of the profits that company generates and to be able to sell that share at a profit if the company increases in value.

Share market The share market (some fancy pants people like to call it the stock exchange) is a transparent and regulated marketplace in which shares in public companies are bought and sold. Here in Australia we have a national share market – the ASX, or the Australian Securities Exchange.

Side hustle A business, job or exercise that you're able to work on top of your 'normal' or 'regular' employment. It's a flexible second job that brings in additional money, and often is something one is passionate about. People take up side hustles for many reasons, not just money.

Stock See the definition for share – it's the same thing.

Superannuation The first thing to remember about super is that it is NOT an investment. Superannuation is a tax structure. Your own hard-earned money is invested on your behalf by your superannuation fund to provide for Future You. Also known as 'super', it is a way of investing money while you are working and earning an income, so that you will have an income when you retire. Generally speaking, the moment you start earning more than $450, you'll be putting money aside for your super. Take superannuation seriously now, as one day it is very likely going to be your largest asset class.

Superannuation guarantee (SG) This is a percentage set by the government that your employer pays to your superannuation fund. If you're an employee, you might see SG on your pay slip. The current rate for SG payments by an employer is 9.5 per cent of your salary at the time of publishing this book but will increase to 10 per cent after 1 July 2021 till 30 June 2022. The SG will then increase to 10.5 per cent on 1 July 2022 till 30 June 2023.

Term deposit A term deposit is a cash investment held at a financial institution. Your money is invested for an agreed rate of interest over a fixed amount of time, or term.

Transaction fee A transaction fee is a charge that a business has to pay every time it processes a customer's electronic payment. The cost of the transaction fee will vary depending on the service used.

VET Student Loan (VSL) A Commonwealth assistance loan that helps eligible students studying for a diploma qualification or higher to pay their tuition fees. There is a limit to how much you can borrow, called the 'loan cap'. The loan cap amount is different depending on the course you study.

Volatility This is how much the price of an asset fluctuates over time.

Will A will is a legal document that exists to direct what happens to your assets when you pass away. A will gives you the ability to express exactly how you would like your assets distributed and what happens to any children (or pets!) instead of letting the law decide for you. According to ASIC, approximately half of all Australians die without a will.

Acknowledgements

Everything I've been able to achieve and create in life (including this book!) was not accomplished by me alone. Writing this book was one of the most challenging – yet rewarding – things I've ever done, and without the support of my friends, family and the *She's on the Money* community this book could never have come to fruition.

It's been a long, windy path, but everything I've been through has brought me to here: writing acknowledgements for a book that I hope will touch and change the lives of so many women across the country. I am eternally grateful for the support every single person in the *She's on the Money* community has shown me, but there are a few special people I'd like to single out.

To the people I've met along the *She's on the Money* journey who have inspired me to keep going even when the seas were rough: thank you. I've seen your strength, resilience and passion echoed time and time again in our community members who are taking charge of their financial lives. It makes me insanely proud.

To my parents, Eric and Judi Devine, you're the reason I get to do everything I love and I am forever grateful to you for being both kind and strict in raising me. Dad, your passion for life, building, spreadsheets and finance has obviously rubbed off on me, and I'm so grateful you taught me from a young age the value and power of both money and education (regardless of whether I listened, or sat at the dining table crying over times tables). Mum, you are my hero. You are the strongest and kindest person I know, and everyone you meet is better off for having met you. Thank you for showing me (and deeply believing) that I am capable of achieving anything, and gifting me absolutely every opportunity you could. I will forever be in awe of you, and one day I hope to become half the mother you are to me.

To my partner, Stephen. When I am with you, I am home. You've never treated me as anything other than your equal, you're my greatest supporter and you are truly the best person I know. You challenge me to be a better person every day, and remind me to always bring the best version of myself to the table. Thank you for hearing me and for encouraging me even when I'm not on the right track. You are constantly striving to understand me in all my forms, and for that, you deserve the applause of thousands. I love doing life with you.

To my sister, Alex, who has always put up with having an older, nerdier sister, and who introduced me to her younger, cooler friend – Georgia King. I'm so proud of the woman you've become, and that I get to be your sister. While you're the absolute opposite of me in nearly every way, I'm so glad we have each other.

To my publishers for bringing this book to life, making me cry with the cover and keeping me on track throughout the process. Izzy Yates, what would I do without you? Thank you for seeing the value in this book before I'd even finished pitching it. To not only know you and have you as my publisher, but to also know you came from the *She's on the Money* community, makes my heart incredibly full and makes me feel I couldn't be in safer hands.

To Summer Land for helping me shape and bring out the best in this book. You've spent endless hours with me on Zoom over the past year making sure I get every statistic right, every paragraph completed and every money story documented. This book has become everything I ever imagined, and a lot of that is attributed to your loving support and guidance.

Stefanie Booker, you've got the sweetest smile and kindest heart. You've been there for it all, from writing our theses together, to helping me pick the name 'She's on the Money' – you've always believed in me and my passion. You're one of the best friends I could ever have asked for and without you and your support over the past few years I wouldn't have been able to achieve what I have.

Rose Bernard, you're one of my biggest cheerleaders, and that friend who turned up to my events with bells on, even though you'd heard my presentation 17 times and you knew only five people were attending. You're one of my favourite people and I'm so grateful I get to call you a friend. Thank you for always supporting me (even from the other side of the world!) and being part of my life.

Harriet Stevens, you've known me since before I was born, and despite often living in different states I could say you're my loudest cheerleader. Watching you grow, and being part of your journey, has been an absolute privilege. When I grow up, I want to be more like you.

To Zara McDonald and Michelle Andrews, thank you. You believed in my vision of creating a podcast from a Facebook group about money and helped me to bring to life the first season of *She's on the Money*. You've both taught me so much, and I'm genuinely so grateful for everything you've done.

Ryan Jon, wow. You've championed both myself and *She's on the Money* since we met, and I'm so grateful that you've so quickly become an integral part of the community. You help to harness the potential I have within myself, while consistently pushing me to strive further.

To Jessica Ricci, you stepped into my life at exactly the right time and I now struggle to understand how I functioned without you. Your hard work and dedication to the *She's on the Money* community does not go unnoticed, and I feel genuinely blessed that you choose to work with me every day. To me, you're more than just a team member – in you, I believe I've found one of my greatest friends.

And of course to the aforementioned Georgia King, sometimes I'm convinced you know me better than I know myself. You bring light and heart to the world, and I know the community adores you. You're the sassiest human I know, and I admire every single thing about you. Thank you for always being the voice I need to hear.

And to you, the reader of this book. I'm so eternally grateful that you chose to pick up my book and put Future You first. I'm so proud of you and your journey, and even prouder that I get to call you a member of the *She's on the Money* community. Thank you.

Discover a
new favourite

Visit **penguin.com.au/readmore**